D1420434

DOMITIAN

DOMITIAN

Tragic Tyrant

Pat Southern

London and New York

For
CMD
Causa amicitiae
and
'*Trajan*'
'*Optimus Felis*'

First published 1997
by Routledge
11 New Fetter Lane, London EC4P 4EE

© 1997 Pat Southern

Designed and typeset by David Seabourne

Printed and bound in Great Britain by
Butler & Tanner, Frome, Somerset

British Library Cataloguing in Publication Data
A catalogue record for this book is available from the British Library

Library of Congress Cataloguing in Publication Data
A catalogue record for this book has been requested

ISBN 0-415-16525-3

CONTENTS

LIST OF
ILLUSTRATIONS

LIST OF PLATES

(BETWEEN PAGES 120 AND 121)

1. Head of Vespasian
2. Frieze B from the Palazzo della Cancelleria reliefs
3. Head of Domitian from Palazzo della Cancelleria reliefs
4. Head of Domitian from Palazzo della Cancelleria reliefs
5. Statue of Titus
6. Bust of Domitian as a young man
7. Cuirassed statue of Domitian
8. Undated bronze coin: Domitia and *Divus Caesar*
9. Bronze bust of Domitian
10. Head of Domitia Longina as a young woman
11. Marble bust of Domitian
12. Aureus of 82: Minerva wearing helmet
13. Aureus of 85: seated figure of Minerva
14. Frieze A from the Palazzo della Cancelleria reliefs
15. Bronze coin: *Germania capta*
16. Julia, daughter of Titus
17. Head of Domitia Longina as a mature woman
18. The Piazza Navona, Rome, site of Domitian's stadium
19. View of the Forum Transitorium
20. South perimeter wall of the Forum Transitorium
21. The Domus Augustana from the Circus Maximus
22. Facade of the Domus Augustana
23. Sunken peristyle of the Domus Augustana
24. So-called stadium of the Domus Augustana

PREFACE AND ACKNOWLEDGEMENTS

Domitian has been portrayed by some authors as a monstrous tyrant, an inflexible pedant with no imagination, an incompetent general; by others as an able administrator and defender of the Empire. He rarely emerges as a living, breathing, person, subject to happiness and satisfaction, trauma and disappointments, like anyone else. The portrayal of the tyrant has been amended, the administrator debated and his character analysed, and anyone embarking upon a new biography owes a great deal to B. W. Jones, who missed nothing in the way of evidence, and to K. H. Waters, who attempted to understand Domitian. The contribution that this book hopes to make is to add a psychological dimension to the study of this complex man.

The author owes a massive debt to Karen Dixon for suggesting that it was possible to write books in the first place, and to Charles Daniels for all the past encouragement and listening. Much gratitude is due to Professor Anthony Birley for continual benign assistance, and for saving me from errors. Charles Daniels and Ian Stephenson also read drafts and entered into discussions; Dr Julian Bennett conversed at length on points of detail, and allowed me to read his work on Trajan before it was published; Dr Jon Coulston advised on architectural and sculptural matters, and allowed me access to his enviably extensive collection of slides; Graeme Stobbs produced maps with minimum fuss and maximum speed and efficiency. The above-named do not agree with everything stated in this book, and faults remaining are to be laid at the author's door, preferably by politely worded letter.

I should also like to thank Peter Kemmis-Betty and Charlotte Vickerstaffe for their encouragement and advice, and their quick response to queries. Similarly the staff of Newcastle University Library have always been unfailingly helpful and patient, and in particular the Inter-Library Loans staff consistently perform above the call of duty.

The following museums kindly provided photographs: The British Museum. London; Ny Carlsberg Glyptotek, Copenhagen; Vatican Museums, Vatican City; Capitoline Museum, Rome; Toledo Museum of Art, Ohio; Museum of Fine Arts, Boston; Hermitage Museum, St Petersburg.

I
EARLY YEARS

The eighteen years between Domitian's birth on 24 October AD 51 and 18 December AD 69 when he first properly entered history, are singularly lacking in documentation. Suetonius records that Domitian was born on the ninth day before the Kalends of November in the year that his father was consul elect, in a house on Pomegranate Street (*ad Malum Punicum*, probably corresponding to the modern via delle Quattro Fontane) on the Quirinal Hill in the sixth region of the city of Rome. Apart from the date and place of his birth, there are scarcely any recorded facts about the early life of the third and last of the Flavian Emperors which can be truthfully described as wholly unsullied by retrospective bias. This charge applies equally to the favourable as to the hostile sources. The few statements of Josephus relative to Domitian do not touch on his early life, and in any case Josephus carries the flag of Flavian propaganda so blatantly that his statements have to be weighed just as carefully, if not more carefully, than those of Tacitus, Pliny, or Suetonius.[1]

The authors and poets who worked during Domitian's reign, such as Silius Italicus, Statius and Martial, are hardly less partisan than Josephus, however different their writings, their backgrounds, or their motives. Tacitus, Pliny, Suetonius and Juvenal, who had all lived through the reign of the 'monster', published their works after Domitian's murder, when expression of opinion about the deceased Emperor no longer incurred mortal danger. Despite the creditable efforts of Tacitus and Suetonius to search out and reproduce the truth, these authors cannot help repeating what was by then the accepted version of Domitian's dreadful character, all traceable, by implication if not actual affirmation, to his earliest years. Suetonius' account is a collection of facts, some of them credible, some of them shading off into anecdotes of dubious authenticity, but whilst it is not exactly favourable, neither is it wholly derogatory. Tacitus was intent on correcting the official Flavian party line, in order to reveal it for the propaganda that it was. In the late first century this propaganda was no doubt all-pervasive and much more extensive than the remnants that have survived. Josephus and the Flavian poets suffice for modern scholars to detect a consciously favourable representation of Flavian history that was both selective and economical with the unpalatable truths. In Tacitus' own day, after a quarter of a century of Flavian rule, there would be reminders in all aspects of life, in virtually every building in Rome, in art and literature, on the coinage, in the laws and in living memory. It would be a monumental task to set the record straight in mere words. *Damnatio memoriae* and Tacitus have not succeeded in eradicating Domitian, only in obscuring him.[2]

Had there been a fully documented and authenticated version of the first eighteen years of Domitian's existence, compiled not in retrospect but contemporaneously and therefore imprinted in living memory, Suetonius, for instance, would not have needed recourse to hearsay. As it is, he covers himself by using non-committal phrases such as 'it is said', or 'there are those who affirm', which is a neat way of circumventing the problem of including all the rumours while avoiding the obligation of vouching for their accuracy. As reported in the hostile sources, Domitian displayed from an early age the characteristics of a depraved tyrant. The undoubted terror that marred the last years of his reign required explanation in the form of readily believable antecedents, whereby Domitian could be seen to possess all along a latent inclination towards tyranny, at first cunningly and successfully repressed, but later given free rein. If he displayed any creditworthy attributes, then he must have been simply pretending: *simulavit et ipse mire modestiam*, says Suetonius, dismissing as deliberate shamming Domitian's early modesty during the turmoil of AD 69. The accusations against him as a youth are that he spent his early years in poverty and infamous conduct, selling himself to one Claudius Pollio, who kept the letter of assignation to prove it. More interesting is the charge of having been debauched by Nerva, the Senate's choice of Emperor after Domitian was murdered in 96. In connection with this story, Nerva has been described as 'the future paragon', and it is difficult to comprehend how this scandalous affair confirms Domitian's moral turpitude without staining Nerva's reputation.[3]

Suetonius leaps from Domitian's birth to the events of 69 in a breathless three sentences, none of them complimentary, and one is left with the impression that they were included merely to provide packing for the void of uncertainty between the few facts that are ascertainable. It is unfortunate that Domitian enters history before he had embarked on his career. Had he been a few years older, he would probably have taken the first steps on the *cursus honorum*, thereby affording modern researchers some clues as to his past education and future ambitions. In the absence of this information, speculation based on knowledge of Roman custom is the only tool available to reconstruct a possible life history for Domitian up to the Civil War of 68–9.[4]

When Domitian was born in 51, his father Titus Flavius Vespasianus (Vespasian; pl. 1) was forty-two years old, and had just attained the suffect consulship for the months of November and December of that year. His brother, Domitian's uncle Flavius Sabinus, was governor of Moesia, and would not return to Rome for about another five years. The two brothers were the first generation of their family to achieve senatorial status. Their grandfather Titus Flavius Petro of Reate (modern Rieti, 77 km (48 miles) north-east of Rome) had served in the army of Pompey and had fled from the battlefield of Pharsalus in 48 BC after Caesar's victory. He returned home, obtained pardon and *honesta missio*, and launched himself on a financial career. His son, also Titus Flavius Sabinus, followed him in tax-collecting and banking, in which he was eminently successful. He may have achieved equestrian status for himself, and definitely acquired sufficient wealth to provide both his sons with the minimum fortune necessary for a senatorial career.[5]

This rise from plebeian to senatorial status in only three generations demands explanation. In the Republic it would not have been possible; in the first century of the Empire it was not unusual. The civil wars between Caesar and Pompey, followed by those between Octavian and Antony, had eased the path of promotion and democratized it – a trend which was not reversed in the Augustan and post-Augustan ages. Opportunity allied to unusual circumstances provided the initial spur, but in isolation did not lead directly to advancement. Wealth, conspicuous ability and connections with the right people in the right places at the right times, were all equally important.[6]

Despite the Flavian family's satisfactory financial position and upwardly mobile careers, a persistent theme in Vespasianic iconography was their poverty and obscurity. It is quite true that the Flavii were newly arrived on the political scene. They were not of the old nobility and consequently were unable to display ancestral *imagines* or portraits of illustrious forebears who had held curule magistracies. Yet obscurity was no obstruction to advancement. Real poverty, on the other hand, would have been a very serious disadvantage. It is difficult to accept it as genuine, however, and Brian Jones describes it as a myth, pointing out that since the property qualification for entry into the Senate was 1,000,000 sesterces, and since both Sabinus and Vespasian, Domitian's uncle and father, became senators, it can hardly be said that they were poor. Flavius Petro, their grandfather, had engaged in a profitable money-lending business and had also married the wealthy Tertulla, who owned land around Cosa. The next generation built on this foundation and it was Sabinus, Vespasian's father, who was the true provider of the family's wealth, by a combination of hard work, shrewd business sense and a useful marriage to Vespasia Polla, whose brother was a senator and whose lineage was modest but impeccable. As a tax-collector in Asia, Sabinus seems to have been not only successful but also honest: Suetonius reports that statues were erected to him in several Asian cities, inscribed in Greek 'to an honest tax farmer'. He died in Switzerland, *apud Helvetios*, where he had established his banking business, survived by his wife and two sons, who were presumably far from destitute.[7]

Behind this carefully fostered myth of Flavian poverty there may be several motives. One interpretation could possibly be the nuance that Dio puts upon it, that though Vespasian was prepared to indulge the population with expensive festivals and everything for their welfare, his own style of living was deliberately and ostentatiously simple, so that it could be clearly seen that he did not spend money on his own pleasures and did not amass wealth for selfish reasons. Thus far the propaganda is probably truthful and undertaken for virtuous and honourable purposes. There may be alternatives, however, not quite so honourable. It may perhaps have been best, for example, to keep silent about the wealth and position acquired by the Flavii during the supremacy of the notorious Sejanus and during the reigns of Caligula and Nero.[8]

In addition to wealth, a rising aspirant to higher office required ability and ambition. Suetonius and Tacitus both imply that Vespasian was a little indolent and irresolute, lagging behind his elder brother Sabinus in enthusiasm and ambition. The story goes that he displayed a marked reluctance to enter the Senate, and did so only because his mother kept reminding him that he seemed content to remain almost as a sort of client of Sabinus. It is true that Vespasian's career was certainly not one of rapid promotion. He served as military tribune in Thrace at an unknown date, then as quaestor in Crete-Cyrene, in about 34 or 35. His first attempt in the elections for aedile failed, and he finally reached that post in 37 or 38. He became praetor in 39. In 41 or 42 he was sent to Strasbourg as legate of *II Augusta*, which he led to Britain in 43 when Claudius ordered the invasion of the island under the command of Aulus Plautius. The date of his return from Britain is not established – he may have been back in Rome by 45, or he may have remained in Britain until 47. He was awarded *ornamenta triumphalia* on his return, and a few years later at the age of forty-two he reached the consulship. Thus far, his career was neither distinguished nor extraordinarily inadequate; Vespasian at forty-two could almost be described as 'middle of the road', a consular courtier with the all-round administrative and military experience required of Roman higher officials.[9]

Money, capability and ambition were not sufficient, even in combination, to guarantee success in Roman political life. It was essential either to be admitted to the court circle or at least to form alliances with men and women who had the Emperor's ear. Patronage and clientship were engrained in the Roman way of life from earliest times, and never more so than in the Empire. Without someone of influence to intercede on one's behalf at court, the attainment of any appointment would have been impossible. Such connections with the court could be made in several ways, by marriage alliances, for example, or by entering into client relationships with influential families.[10]

In the matrimonial sphere, the previous generations of the Flavii had married shrewdly, for wealth or for influence. Vespasian looked elsewhere for assistance. He married Flavia Domitilla, whose father was a quaestor's clerk and whose freeborn status had to be established in a court of law. In Vespasian's case it was not his wife but his mistress, Caenis, who interceded for him at court. Caenis was a freedwoman of Antonia, the daughter of Mark Antony, the mother of Claudius and the grandmother of Caligula. There could scarcely have been a more direct means of ensuring that the name of Vespasian came to the Emperor's notice. Reinforcement came from the Imperial freedman Narcissus, the wealthy and influential secretary *ab epistulis* of Claudius. It was reported to be Narcissus who obtained for Vespasian the post of legionary legate of *II Augusta* – an appointment important for two reasons. In the first instance it demonstrates that Vespasian had survived the transition between the court of the Emperor Caligula and that of Claudius. It was not always easy for adherents of one regime to be accepted in the next, especially when the previous regime had ended in disaster and assassination. Secondly the appointment cannot have been as casual as it may seem at first sight: Claudius could not afford to leave an incompetent man in command of *II Augusta* once it had been chosen as part of the invasion forces of Britain, nor could Narcissus risk his reputation by recommending someone unsuited to the post.[11]

Apart from connections with men and women resident at court, the support of influential families was still necessary for a *novus homo* such as Vespasian. The Petronii, Plautii, Pomponii and Vitellii were the most powerful families in Rome when Vespasian embarked on his career. One of Claudius' advisers was L. Vitellius, while the general chosen to lead the invasion of Britain was Aulus Plautius. Under Claudius these families, and Vespasian himself, prospered and advanced their careers. Life must have seemed entirely satisfactory to Vespasian at the end of 51 – he was consul for the last two months of the year, his second son Domitian had just been born and his first son Titus, eleven years old, was being educated at court alongside the Emperor's son Britannicus. He could look forward to further appointments after his consulship and the eventual promotion of his two sons in their careers. Unfortunately the rise to power of Agrippina, fourth wife of Claudius and mother of Nero, left neither Vespasian nor some of the families who had assisted him unscathed. Domitian's birth coincided with the marriage of Claudius to Agrippina, and the consequent lack of Imperial interest in Vespasian.[12]

This highlights the potentially disastrous reverse-of-the-coin effect inherent in the necessary search for connections at court. A person of influence who was in a position to dispense patronage could just as easily block the progress of a career. In the case of Agrippina, it was dangerous ever to have had anything but friendly contacts with her, for she had a long memory for the smallest insult and her rancour extended to the friends and acquaintances of those who had injured her. Suetonius says that she hated any friend of Narcissus; consequently when Narcissus fell from power, Vespasian found himself *de trop* at court, and without any official post. The disfavour seems to have been purely personal and not life-threatening – he was not, after all, invited to remove himself by falling on his sword, nor was his family under any threat. His son Titus was still educated at court and his brother Sabinus remained in office. After Agrippina had dispatched Claudius in 54, she still held sufficient sway over Nero to exclude Vespasian from court, an exclusion which seems to have continued for some years even after 59, when Nero's second attempt to murder his mother succeeded. Vespasian obtained the proconsulship of Africa by lot, at some unspecified date in the early 60s, most probably in 63 or 64.[13]

Throughout Domitian's earliest years, therefore, his father was at home, in leisurely retirement (*in otio secessuque*). Exactly what this means is not quite clear. Vespasian was still a senator as well as a priest and so perhaps did not withdraw altogether from public life. Whether he found his exclusion from court burdensome and whether there was any financial hardship at this period of his life is debatable. Suetonius depicts his trepidation at being denied access to Nero's circle but does not state that he was financially embarrassed. This idea derives from the life of Domitian, where Suetonius says he was brought up in poverty. There are two episodes in Vespasian's life where this charge of poverty could have had some basis in fact, one being his fall from favour between 51 and 59, and the other on his return from Africa when, having neglected to enrich himself, he was forced to mortgage all his property to his brother. In both instances, since he was allowed to remain a senator, he presumably still held the requisite financial resources for otherwise he would have been ejected from the Senate. Furthermore, official posts in the Roman Empire did not bring with them any remuneration, except whatever could be obtained by personal initiative, so that to be without appointments cannot be compared to modern forms of redundancy.[14]

Even so, on his return from Africa, Vespasian was forced to engage in trade in order to keep up his position (*sustinendae dignitatis causa*). The exact nature of his business is disputed. Taken on face value from his nickname *mulio*, it is likely that he sold or hired out mules for transport, but some scholars have suggested that we should read between the lines and that in reality Vespasian was engaged in the slave trade. Ancient and modern aversions to this trade stem from completely different standpoints. Modern disapproval on moral and humanitarian grounds would have no place in the ancient world, where disapproval would have been reserved for the shocking spectacle of a member of the senatorial class actually engaging in this sort of work. There is, however, probably no need to read between the lines at all. Had Vespasian been a slave-trader, the post-Flavian authors would certainly not have demurely drawn a veil over his activities. Transport contractor is the most feasible translation. It is natural to wonder what had happened to Vespasian's fortunes in the early 60s, and why the situation then was any different from his earlier return from Britain. After all, he had probably derived no personal or financial profit from his tour of duty in the new British province and had presumably lived on the proceeds of his estates. If these estates had for some unknown reason ceased to be profitable it is not likely that he would have been able to mortage them to Sabinus, unless his brother simply bailed him out of an awkward situation. According to Tacitus, the episode created bad feeling between the brothers. The tale of Vespasian as mule vendor is probably not entirely untrue, and is not without a certain panache. Suetonius' description of the guile, not to mention sharp practice, that Vespasian employed leaves the reader in no doubt that in modern times the future Emperor would have been quite successful in selling used cars. The degree of hardship incurred in this episode and the possible effects upon Domitian are difficult to estimate. Poverty is a relative term, subject to varying shades of inference, depending upon the background and way of thought both of those experiencing it and of those merely observing it.[15]

Suetonius uses the poverty theme as damning evidence against Domitian, as though he had brought it all on himself, with neither his grandfather Sabinus nor his father Vespasian having anything to do with it. This is not blind acceptance of Flavian propaganda. It is a sneer, of the snobbish senatorial kind, presenting poverty as a shameful crime. The lack of silver plate to which Suetonius refers should be laid at Vespasian's door, not the youthful Domitian's, but in his portrayal of Vespasian, Suetonius absolves both him and his family from all blame, without neglecting the opportunity to condemn Domitian for avarice and cruelty. The fact that Domitian was brought up in a house which could not boast a single piece of silver is not included to demonstrate Vespasian's inclination for the simple, unostentatious life, nor his inadequacy as a provider for his family. It is intended as a slur on Domitian, to account for his venality and cupidity.[16]

Domitian's childhood was presumably spent in the house on Pomegranate Street in Rome, and probably in the rural properties that his father had either inherited or acquired. Vespasian was born at Falacrina and brought up by his grandmother at her estates near Cosa. Throughout his life he visited his grandmother's house whenever he could, so it is permissible to assume that he owned it. He had estates at Aquae Cutiliae, near Reate, where he spent his summers and where he died. It is quite possible that he owned more lands and farms than those listed in the ancient sources. When he was forced to mortgage all his lands and his house to his brother Sabinus, Suetonius merely descibes them as *omnia praedia*, while Tacitus writes of a house and fields (*domo agrisque*). It is conceivable that Domitian accompanied his father to their summer residence each year when he was a boy. If he had not acquired the taste for country life in his boyhood he had certainly acquired it at some time before he became Emperor, retreating from Rome whenever he could, mostly for the purpose of sulking and stabbing flies, according to the hostile sources. When he was Emperor, he showed marked preference for residence at his Alban villa, roughly a day's journey from Rome.[17]

The relationship between Domitian and the rest of his family must remain conjectural and therefore open to widely divergent interpretation. It would be useful to know his attitude towards his father and brother, and in turn their opinion of him, at various significant times during their lives. Perhaps one major failing of any biographical study, even of relatively recent persons, is the tendency to assemble all the known facts into a comprehensible and consistent pattern. Thus the characteristics most loudly documented become the yardstick by which to measure the whole person. These traits are then sought for, and found, in every other aspect and all phases of the subject's life: geniuses are considered to have been endowed with brilliance whilst still in the cradle and despots are depicted as tyrannical even in childhood. Inconsistency and progressive change often go unobserved even during a subject's lifetime, and the surviving record bears witness only to what the person became, ignoring how he or she came to be that person. Suetonius detected a change in Domitian in his later years, blaming the revolt of Saturninus for the cruelty he displayed thereafter, but still subscribes to the theory that mildness of manner and modesty were part of Domitian's master plan to deceive the world until he held power in his own hands.[18]

During most of Domitian's early childhood, his father was living quietly at home, probably an active senator and priest, but without any specific office and with no reason to be absent from Rome for long periods. This does not mean that father and son were particularly close. Vespasian was hard-headed and determined, shrewd and calculating, possibly ruthlessly self-seeking, but also full of sound and practical common sense and possessing an earthy wit. He appreciated a joke, even if it was made at his own expense. He did not lack education and had obviously read all the right books – or had at least learned apposite quotations in Latin and Greek to drop into conversations at apt moments. External appearance, however, is no reliable guide to the internal man. The most affable, witty, clever people who function brilliantly in their social milieu can be abysmal parents, and vice versa the most detested, cruel people, seemingly with no social conscience whatsoever, can make excellent mothers and fathers. There is no information to elucidate the interaction between Vespasian and Domitian in the years before the Civil War of 69. The ancient sources merely take note of their supposedly strained relationship when Vespasian returned to Rome from Alexandria in 70. This episode will be discussed in its proper place; it suffices to note here that there is no absolute proof that Vespasian was displeased with his younger son because of his conduct in 69/70. The story derives from later interpretations formed at a time when nothing could be tolerated if it reflected creditably upon 'the monster'.[19]

When Domitian was born, his brother Titus was two months short of his twelfth birthday and already being educated at court with Claudius' son Britannicus. He would probably have been a distant figure evoking either admiration or jealousy. The latter is what the sources would have us believe. As a comparison, especially if his accomplishments were always drawn to Domitian's attention, Titus was perhaps quite sickeningly outstanding. He was a striking figure even as a boy, he was a good horseman, skilled at arms, graceful, majestic and so on and so forth: in short, all the things one would expect of a man who later turned out to be a reasonably good Emperor. There is presumably some truth in all this and, being so much older, Titus would achieve some modest military distinction as tribune in Germany and Britain, some successes in public life, two marriages and a child or children while Domitian was still a boy. Jealousy, in the form of a wish to emulate or to live up to and seek approbation from Titus, might well have been the result. Suetonius portrays Domitian as constantly plotting against his brother and sulking because he had not received his full share of power either after 69 or while Titus was Emperor. In return, both Suetonius and Tacitus portray Titus as merciful and considerate, advising his father to be lenient with Domitian because of his youth, and quite unable himself to punish his brother for his trangressions. The chillingly efficient and ruthless manner in which Titus disposed of Caecina in 79 when he suspected him of treason belies the suggestion that Titus simply neglected to punish Domitian. The sources have nothing definite to say about what Domitian actually did, the nuance being that all these plans were permanently in his mind but were not brought to fruition. His accusers declare that he 'almost explicitly' (*paene ex professo*) stirred up the troops, and considered fleeing to the army and bringing about the downfall of his brother and his own elevation by means of military force. Domitian's plotting, though, remains nebulous and unproven – names, dates and events are significantly absent in the written record. If there had been solid, irrefutable evidence that Domitian seriously intended to depose him, Titus would simply have removed his brother, at least by banishment and closely guarded confinement, if not by clandestine execution. The man who calmly executed 2,500 Jewish prisoners at a time, by way of honouring his brother's and then his father's birthdays, cannot have been so squeamish. The early relationship between Domitian and Titus was probably neither extremely hostile nor extremely affectionate, though when real power was at stake the flames of accumulated small resentments may have been fanned into a conflagration. Left to themselves the brothers might have come to a stable agreement, but they probably had more to fear from their associates, who flattered one at the expense of the other, manufactured gossip in order to instil suspicion, grasped at favours and vigorously advocated the cause of either one or the other for the purpose of consequent self-advancement. Apparently it was not possible to be a mutual friend of both brothers; Pliny records that Julius Bassus was afraid of Titus as a consequence of his association with Domitian (*Titum timuit ut Domitiani amicus*). This says as much about Titus as it does about Domitian and carries with it also the positive idea that Domitian could inspire loyalty in at least one of his friends. The reliability of Pliny's statement is unknown, but it must be allowed that as Emperor Titus could not be too careful about his choice of associates, nor about those of his brother, and this factor may have played its part in keeping Titus and Domitian at an emotional, if not physical, distance from each other.[20]

Domitian's relationship with his father and brother is therefore quite uncertain, unelucidated by reliable, unbiased evidence. It is even more difficult to evaluate how much influence Vespasian's brother Sabinus may have exerted on his nephew. Sabinus was already well advanced along the path of his senatorial career by the time Domitian was born and, if the sources are to be credited, he was much more energetic in seeking his fortune, both financial and political, than was his younger brother, though this rumour was really directed at Vespasian, and says much more about him than it does about the elder of the two Flavians. Sabinus may have been away from Rome at the time of Domitian's birth. According to Tacitus, Sabinus was governor of Moesia for seven years but it is not established beyond doubt exactly which seven years are meant, except that it was probably at some time during the 50s, perhaps during the first years of the decade, or perhaps extending as late as about 60 or 61. It is not of vital importance in this context to sift through the fine detail of the dates when Sabinus held his various offices. Various career structures have been postulated for Sabinus and the arguments have been summarized; each theory meets with one problem or another, so it is perhaps best simply to enumerate the salient facts, which are that Sabinus had held a succession of magistracies and military posts, not all of which are known, and that after his consulship in 44, he had gone on to become governor of Moesia. He would have been an element of unknown potency in Domitian's life, first as a distant relative governing an outlying province, and then as a physical presence as soon as Domitian reached the age of about eight, or at least by the time he was ten years old. Under Nero, Sabinus was made city prefect, an honourable and elevated post, which Tacitus informs us that Sabinus held for twelve years. Thus, at second hand, Domitian was perhaps afforded in his early youth a slight foretaste of political prominence. How close he may have been to Sabinus and his family is unknown, but the possibility should not be ruled out that he lived within the household of his uncle during his father's governorship of Africa, and again perhaps when Vespasian was absent as a member of Nero's entourage on the famous tour of Greece. Immediately after that the Jewish command was handed to Vespasian and so, from the age of about fifteen, Domitian was deprived of both father and brother. To some extent he seems to have compensated for this by retreating into himself, perhaps developing that taste for solitude and self-sufficiency that his later detractors found unforgivably offensive. For roughly a decade, then, at intervals, Sabinus and his family may have acted as substitutes for closer relatives and, if this is so, chroniclers who merely gloss over the murder of Sabinus in 69 have perhaps not taken sufficient account of the emotional factors that may have played an important role in Domitian's later development. It should be borne in mind that he had seen someone uselessly cut down – someone who had tried to keep order and to deal fairly and honourably with men who were not worth the trust so erroneously placed in them.[21]

Flavia Domitilla, Domitian's mother, died at some time before 69. She was probably already dead before 66, when Vespasian took up the Jewish command for if she had died during his term of office in Judaea, Josephus would probably have recorded the fact. There is almost complete silence about Vespasian's wife. It is thought that she was not deified after her death, unlike most of the other members of the Flavian dynasty. Evidence, albeit circumstantial, for this statement is found in Statius' *Silvae*, where he lists all the members of the Flavian family who had been deified but makes no mention of Domitian's mother. The coins of Titus' reign which bear the legend *memoriae Domitillae* could have been issued in honour of the mother, but those with the legend *diva Domitilla* are usually assigned to the younger Flavia Domitilla, the sister of Titus and Domitian. The absence of Vespasian's wife from most of the documentation could support the theory that she died while Domitian was still very young. It is not certain whether the younger Domitilla was born after Domitian, as Suetonius implies when he lists them in that order, or whether she was born in the long gap of almost twelve years between the two boys. The conjectural date of her birth must allow her to reach marriageable age and give birth to a daughter, also called Flavia Domitilla, before 69, by which date she was dead. It has been suggested that she married Q. Petillius Cerialis, as his second wife, since she was too young to have been the mother of Q. Petillius Rufus. This suggestion has much to commend it. Cerialis was certainly close to Vespasian, whether or not he was briefly his son-in-law. His relationship with Domitian has perhaps been obscured by Tacitus, who would inevitably look unfavourably upon those whose association with the tyrant had been remotely friendly. Cerialis may have been as incompetent and grasping as Tacitus portrays him but, as Birley points out, Tacitus loathed Cerialis, probably on behalf of his father-in-law Agricola. If Cerialis was indeed married to Flavia Domitilla he would have been to some degree influential, for an unknown length of time, in Domitian's youth and their interaction during the Civil War and after Domitian became Emperor demands close inspection.[22]

It is not known when Vespasian's wife died; all that can be stated with certainty is that she was dead before 69. The effect of his mother's death upon Domitian may have been negligible if he was so young that he could not remember her, or catastrophic if he had known her well and loved her. On balance, it is likely that he had no memory of her at all, and felt nothing except an impersonal loss and a vague feeling of something missing that could never be replaced. This perhaps provides a partial explanation for his later affirmation that he was the son of Minerva, his own particular tutelary goddess. Far from being a repudiation of his real mother, it may have arisen from a sense of abandonment and isolation, deeply felt from a very early age. Deep emotions do not have to have any basis in solid fact; they are personal truths of tremendous conviction. Domitian clearly derived support and comfort from his worship of Minerva and his insistence on his relationship to her demonstrates, among many other things, an increasing isolation and detachment that may have begun too early for him to analyse and understand. It may have been snobbish detachment, tinged with love and respect for the memory of his mother, that led Domitian to repudiate his father's mistress, Caenis. Suetonius relates how Caenis approached Domitian to kiss him as usual, after she had returned from a journey, but Domitian offered her his hand instead – a blatant attempt to put her in her place, since a person of inferior status would kiss the hand of a superior. The story may be fabricated, of course, or relayed and embellished by the gossip of household slaves; one wonders otherwise how such a personal and private incident should have become public property, to be related years later by Suetonius. It is impossible to estimate how long Caenis may have lived under the same roof, if at all, and there is no way of knowing whether Domitian was brought up in her company after his mother died or if he was left in charge of his nurse, Phyllis. This person is mentioned in no other source except Suetonius, and then by Dio, in passages describing Domitian's death. Phyllis burned his body and mingled his ashes with those of his niece Julia, Titus' daughter. She had reared both Domitian and Julia, which is the single, rather barren, statement about Phyllis that has been preserved. Presumably she remained loyal to the end, loving Domitian as only nurses and mothers can. Just as heroes are not heroes to their wives and valets, perhaps tyrants are not tyrants to their nurses.[23]

Domitian and Titus' daughter Julia had grown up together, reared by the same nurse, most probably in the same house. She was born in the early 60s, the exact date being uncertain, but it is known that her birthday was 10 August, recorded in connection with the fall of Jerusalem to Titus on that date in 70. Facts about her are sparse. It is not even established beyond doubt which of Titus' wives was her mother. His first wife Arrecina Tertulla died and he then married Marcia Furnilla, whom he divorced after she had given birth to a daughter, not named but generally assumed to be Julia. The divorce may have been necessary for political reasons, possibly because Marcia Furnilla was too closely associated with the conspirators compromised by the events of 65–6. No further details are available about Julia, and Jones makes the sensible suggestion that her mother was Arrecina Tertulla, whose family bore the name Julius in its ancestry. Acceptance of this theory involves either an outright rejection of the story that Marcia also bore a daughter to Titus, or the assumption that this second daughter died quite young. Perhaps the ancient authors themselves were uncertain as to Julia's parentage; when she was born Titus would not have been so prominent a figure as he later became, and in any case the birth of a daughter would not excite so much interest as the birth of a son. If Arrecina Tertulla was Julia's mother, she may have died in childbirth, or at least while the child was very young. The nurse Phyllis perhaps brought Julia up from earliest infancy. Domitian would have been about ten years old when she was born, and may have regarded her as a sister rather than a niece. This may explain why he refused her when she was offered in marriage to him, though at the time he was embroiled in his affair with Domitia, whom he afterwards married, having arranged that she should divorce her husband. In later life Domitian, it is said, conceived a passion for Julia, keeping her with him in the Imperial palace after he had executed her husband, Flavius Sabinus, a cousin of theirs. The scandal does not belong to a description of Domitian's youth, and will be dealt with in a later chapter. [24]

Though he was not educated at court like his brother Titus, Domitian's schooling was not neglected. It can be deduced from descriptions of his behaviour and the few *bon mots* attributed to him that he was soundly educated, just like any member of the senatorial élite. As Jones points out, the implication that Vespasian neglected his second son's schooling is nonsense. Whilst very young, Domitian may have been educated at home, or he may have attended classes held by a *magister* or *litterator* who would have taught the basic skills of reading and writing. The usual procedure, after this preliminary training which lasted until the age of about ten or eleven, was to attend the classes of a *grammaticus*, who taught Greek and a more refined style of speaking and writing in both Latin and Greek. The father of the poet Statius was a *grammaticus* and it has been suggested that he was Domitian's teacher, or one of his teachers. This is drawn from stray inferences in Statius' works, and is nowhere stated directly. It may be that Domitian wanted to dissociate himself from such lowly and mundane connections in later life. There is some slight evidence that he had attended lessons along with other boys at some time, in that Suetonius affirms that after his escape from the Capitol in 69, Domitian went to stay with the mother of one of his schoolfriends (*condiscipulus*) who lived across the Tiber. Presumably Suetonius' readers were prepared to accept the idea of the young Domitian having attended school along with other pupils, with at least one of whom he had maintained cordial relations.[25]

It is not known whether Domitian went on to the tertiary stage of education for the senatorial order. This meant attending the classes of a *rhetor*, basically to prepare for a career as an advocate. Public speaking and debating would thus have been very prominent in these studies, and though Domitian made creditable appearances in public and dealt admirably with the Senate in 69/70 it is perhaps not likely that he intended to take up a career as a lawyer. Unfortunately, for us, since he had not yet embarked on his career when he suddenly found himself the second son of a reigning Emperor, there are no real clues as to where his ambitions lay nor what preparations he had made, if any, to realize them. [26]

Both Tacitus and Suetonius refer to Domitian's love of poetry, insisting that it was feigned, mostly as a blind for his avarice for power. When thwarted in his attempts to share power after 69 he went off to the country, burying himself in reading and writing poetry, to try to deceive everyone that his pursuits were literary and innocuous. Even modern scholars decry his interest in literature, claiming, along with Suetonius, that it was merely politically motivated. After he became Emperor, he reputedly read nothing except the memoirs of Tiberius (of dubious and sinister reputation), delegating to others the writing of his speeches and his letters. One may inquire first of all how many Emperors actually sat down with writing tools and both composed and then wrote all their pronouncements and rescripts, and one may wonder, furthermore, whether the abandonment of his literary pretensions after becoming Emperor might not be accounted for by the fact that he was rather busy. Whatever the truth about his literary pursuits, Domitian had received a rounded education, could speak well, and was not without wit. He was also, whatever his other faults, not a fool; had he been so, posterity might have dealt more kindly with him.[27]

To sum up: towards the end of Nero's reign, as the second son of a Roman senator who had seen successful military service in Britain and had been rewarded with the consulship, Domitian was in an advantageous but not unusual position. There could be little to indicate that Domitian's future would be anything out of the ordinary, and his upbringing and education were no doubt geared to the normal senatorial career structure. He grew up in the shadow of his father and brother, perhaps without the influence of his mother from an early age, but with a sister possibly only a little younger than himself and latterly with his niece Julia. As a child he may have been sickly; the evidence is slight, but his physique in later life, as described by Suetonius, was one of protruding stomach and thin legs, though they had become thin through a long illness. Admittedly, this passage refers to Domitian as he was towards the end of his life, and the comparison with the physical appearance of both Caligula and Nero, both of whom had spindly legs, may merely indicate that this particular attribute was *de rigeur* for tyrants. But if the thinness of his legs really was the result of a long illness, the most likely occasion when this may have occurred is during his childhood, since it is not recorded that he was ill for any length of time after 69.[28]

These few facts and several inferences are all that are known of Domitian up to his eighteenth year, when a cataclysmic series of events elevated him from relative obscurity to Caesar.

II

BELLUM JOVIS

Towards the end of Nero's reign the Flavians were in a favourable position. They had achieved some creditable successes and were closely bound up with the court circle, ultimately dependent, like everyone else, on Nero's goodwill. This dependency was two-edged. It could bring worthy rewards but, equally, could lead to a swift downfall. There was no foolproof protection against intrigue and suspicion, which do not require the slightest foundation of truth for their existence and, once activated, can be fuelled by malicious gossip. It was necessary to choose one's friends with care and to act with circumspection. In this climate the Flavians seem to have conducted themselves prudently, avoiding involvement in the conspiracy of Piso in 65, and that of Vinicianus which followed shortly afterwards.[1]

The conspiracies were suppressed and executions followed. After the colleagues of Vinicianus had been eradicated the net was spread wide for Neronian victims. Very few facts are known about this plot, save that Vinicianus' father-in-law Corbulo was invited to fall on his sword, as were the governors of Upper and Lower Germany, Scribonius Rufus and Scribonius Proculus. The names of other conspirators, and their intentions, remain obscure. The surviving record is anti-Neronian, and throws all the blame on the Emperor. Nero, however, was not exactly innocent. By 66–7 it was not just selfish, power-hungry maniacs who opposed him – even reasonable, intelligent, conscientious people were beginning to wish for his removal.[2]

The Flavians presumably kept their own counsel. It would have been unwise to exhibit anything less than strict neutrality. Whether they indulged in the slightest sycophancy cannot be ascertained. The Flavian-approved historians of Vespasian's reign emphasized the apparent dissociation from Nero, and also from Gaius (Caligula). But the historical facts cannot be denied. Under Gaius the Flavians rose to prominence, while under Nero, Sabinus was city prefect and Vespasian was appointed to the Judaean command. Since it was patently impossible to deny that both the brothers held posts that implied high standing and trusted status, it was necessary to deny that their attitude was positively favourable towards Nero. The middle path was thus to represent them as cautiously neutral, so that it would be taken as read that they possessed the good sense to recognize a tyrant when they saw one but that, *faute de mieux*, it was necessary to survive, and they survived by serving the Empire rather than the Emperor.[3]

In 68 the reign of Nero came to its inglorious end. The story of the Civil War has been told many times, not least by Tacitus, and in several modern works. Lack of space precludes an enumeration of the finer details, except where they have implications for the Flavian house and for Domitian.

Very little is known of Nero from December 67 until April 68 when Vindex raised the standard of revolt in Gaul. While the Emperor was absent in Greece, Sabinus exercised some authority as city prefect but real power rested with the freedman Helius, acting as Nero's chosen deputy. At the end of 67, Helius asked Nero to return because there was 'a great conspiracy afoot in Rome'. It is not known whether this was merely a bluff, or whether Helius had actually got wind of events in Gaul. At any rate, Helius even decided to go to Corinth to ask Nero to return.[4]

At the end of 67 and the beginning of 68, Nero's relations with the Senate were at a low ebb. He was not particularly bothered by the revolt of Vindex, who was a Romanized Gaul and governor of an unarmed Gallic province with no access to a large army. It was only when the latter chose Servius Sulpicius Galba, governor of Nearer Spain, as Emperor that Nero began to feel insecure. At first all went well. Verginius Rufus, the governor of Upper Germany, defeated Vindex at Vesontio. The troops then hailed Verginius as *Imperator*, an honour which he consistently and wisely refused. Unlike Vespasian, Verginius had not had time to formulate long-term plans, to devise a strategy for survival if he should fail, to canvass support or to accumulate money. He lacked the greatest coercive advantage that Vespasian had, which was the control of Rome's corn supply from Egypt. For many reasons, Verginius was right to refuse to embroil himself in civil warfare.

In Rome the Senate obligingly declared Galba a public enemy. But by now things had gone too far, and the tables were turned when the praetorian prefect Nymphidius Sabinus joined hands with the Senate, declaring Nero a public enemy and the Republic restored. On 9 June 68 Nero committed suicide, reputedly lamenting 'What an artist dies in me'. The Empire was now open to Galba, who had been hovering in Spain wondering whether to commit suicide himself. When he heard that Nero was dead and the Senate and the praetorians had accepted him, he set off for Rome.[5]

It is not known precisely when Galba arrived in the city. One of his first acts was to remove Sabinus from his post as city prefect, possibly at the end of October 68. In Judaea, Vespasian administered the oath of allegiance to Galba to his troops, and it may have been then that he sent his son Titus to Rome, perhaps to negotiate a settlement with the new Emperor now that Sabinus was deprived of power. Tacitus reports that there was gossip that Titus was to be adopted by Galba, which story can probably be discounted since the dismissal of one Flavian in the person of Sabinus, followed by the adoption of another Flavian, Titus, can be construed as a contradiction in terms. Before Titus reached Rome, however, the world was once more turned upside down. On 15 January 69 Galba was killed and Otho took his place, while at the same time the Rhine legions raised revolt and saluted Vitellius as Emperor. Titus turned around and went back to Judaea.[6]

From now on, events in Rome directly concerned and involved the Flavians. The soldiers of Otho chose Sabinus as city prefect, and Otho acceded to their request, perhaps to re-establish continuity via links with the previous reign, most probably to be able to rely upon the expertise of the man who was best suited to the post. Tacitus says that the soldiers had one eye on Vespasian when they made their choice, which raises the question of how powerful Vespasian was considered to be at the beginning of 69. Though he dated his accession from 1 July 69, it is clear that he made plans long before that date. When it became obvious that civil war was inevitable between Otho and Vitellius, Vespasian would have needed to make cautious plans simply in order to survive, but he may have decided very early that survival of the fittest meant winning absolute supremacy before being eliminated.[7]

The inevitable clash between Otho and Vitellius took place in April 69. Vitellius' generals Caecina and Valens defeated Otho at Bedriacum, or the first battle of Cremona, on 14 April. Two days later, Otho committed suicide, and on 19 April, the Senate voted all the usual honours and privileges to Vitellius as Emperor, dispatching a delegation to meet him and his troops, still on the way from Germany.[8]

In Rome, all was quiet, largely thanks to Sabinus. The death of Otho was announced at the theatre without causing riots, and Sabinus administered the oath of allegiance to Vitellius to 'all the soldiers in the city' (*quod erat in urbe militum*), which may mean that he did so to more than just the urban cohorts under his direct command as city prefect. Sabinus presumably administered the city peacefully from April until mid-July when Vitellius entered Rome in triumph.[9]

By this time events had moved on apace in Judaea. Troops in the whole of the east had already sworn allegiance to Vespasian as *Imperator*, in Egypt on 1 July, in Judaea on 3 July and in Syria by 15 July. To review briefly how this had come about it is necessary to return to 66/7 and Vespasian's first contact with the eastern army. It is possible that for a short while Vespasian commanded the Syrian legions as well as those of Judaea, until Licinius Mucianus took over as governor of Syria. Thus Vespasian was not unknown to the eastern troops, especially *III Gallica*, which was later transferred to Moesia, where it played its part in the Flavian cause. Through the medium of Titus, Vespasian and Mucianus kept in touch from about 67 onwards.[10]

When news of Otho's accession and Vitellius' acclamation reached Titus, he was at Corinth. According to Tacitus, he debated as to what he should do, reflecting that whatever his course of action he was in danger from one party or the other. To continue his journey to Rome, or to break it off, would cause offence to either Otho or Vitellius, and at this stage it was not possible to predict who would emerge the victor. On the other hand, if Vespasian were to make a bid for the throne as well, then everyone would be concerned with survival and would forget offences. There were presumably, in addition, rather more serious debates than this. Tacitus makes it seem that the initial urge to power was brought about by a sudden whim of Titus, whose only consideration was to extricate himself from an awkward situation. If the impulse to power did originate with Titus, which is very likely, it would have been meditated as coolly and carefully as the plan was put into operation by Vespasian and Mucianus. The supposedly spontaneous acclamation of Vespasian on 1 July was the result of months of careful planning; it was a painstakingly engineered situation brought to fruition after much background work had been undertaken.[11]

Josephus gives no hint of all this forward planning in his account, claiming that it was only when Vespasian heard of the turmoil caused by Vitellius in Italy that he began to think of winning the Empire for himself. This is in line with Flavian propaganda, which proclaimed that the war was fought for a just cause. It goes without saying that it is much more honourable to fight for the state than to gain power for oneself. Tacitus, however, was not bound by ties of friendship to the Flavian cause, and makes it clear that Vespasian was already organizing for war while Otho and Vitellius fought.[12]

The first firm news of Vespasian's defection reached Rome in September, when Vitellius received a letter from Aponius Saturninus, the governor of Moesia, reporting that *III Gallica* had gone over to the Flavians. Exactly how much of Vespasian's plans were known to Sabinus and Domitian before this date is debatable. Both Josephus and Tacitus detail the advantage that Vespasian enjoyed as candidate for the throne in having two sons. This cannot have escaped the notice either of potential supporters or of potential opposers of the Flavian cause, so some attention must have focused upon Domitian whether he was party to the scheme or not. Josephus, in an imaginative reconstruction of the gossip among the eastern troops just before they proclaimed Vespasian Emperor, says that Domitian would be able to recruit many young men of rank, as though such a process was already in operation. This may be merely retrospective rewriting of history in order to imbue Domitian with a larger share in the legend than he actually had at the time, but he cannot have been kept entirely in the dark. It would not have been impossible for Vespasian to keep his relatives in Rome briefly informed, and the more they knew in advance, the more tense their lives would have been before the truth was revealed in September, since even in the days of Galba and Otho, there had been rumour and suspicion about what Vespasian might do. Now that it was no longer rumour, the Flavians in Rome were in an unenviable position. They were not harmed by Vitellius, even when the Flavian armies were marching towards Rome, but the knowledge that the current Emperor harboured no violent wishes was probably small comfort. Domitian and his uncle Sabinus were kept under guard, but it is alleged that when Flavian troops were close to Rome, Antonius Primus sent messengers to them, and that they could easily have escaped. It is possible that Sabinus considered himself much too old for adventurous projects of this sort, but it is much more likely that he felt compelled to remain in Rome because he was by this time trying to negotiate a peaceful settlement with Vitellius. As for Domitian, Tacitus affirms that he was not lacking in courage, but he did not trust the guards who promised not only to let him go but also to accompany him. That would have made an ideal scenario for summary execution while trying to escape, and Domitian had nothing to gain by an early martyrdom to the Flavian cause. He was probably safer under the public gaze in Rome. It is naive to say that there was no need for suspicion in an age when no one could trust even close family members, and when there was so much at stake.[13]

Troops began to converge on Italy from the east under Mucianus who set off in August, and from Pannonia under Antonius Primus, who argued passionately for a rapid spearhead march through the Alps before reinforcements could reach Vitellius from Germany. This was, or was later represented as, a direct contradiction of Vespasian's instructions. Officially, according to Flavian propaganda, the original plan was to blockade Italy by hemming in the whole country with troops watching the Alps in the north, coupled with a strangulation of the corn supplies from Egypt. Since this is not what actually happened, it is merely academic to debate whether such a blockade would have worked.[14]

By October 69 Flavian troops were at Padua and Verona. Vitellius and Valens were both ill, and it was left to Caecina to organize resistance. Convinced by now that he was on the wrong side, Caecina tried to negotiate with Antonius Primus, only to fail and be arrested by his own troops before Primus won the second battle of Cremona. This was followed by the infamous sack of Cremona, a blot on Primus' career that would later make it much easier to dispense with him. After Cremona, Vitellius' forces peeled away from him, until the remnants of his troops were defeated on 16 December at Carsulae, less than 100km (62 miles) from Rome. Vitellius, hearing the news two days later, finally accepted the inevitability of abdication. Sabinus accordingly set in motion the procedure for the transfer of power from the outgoing to the incoming Emperor. While Vitellius convened his followers to announce his abdication, Sabinus allowed a crowd of Flavian supporters to gather outside his house, confident that power would be formally handed from Vitellius to Vespasian and be ratified by the Senate.[15]

From then on everything went wrong. Sabinus had reckoned without the refusal of Vitellius' supporters to accept the abdication. Flavians and Vitellians clashed, and by the evening of 18 December, Sabinus and his party were barricaded on to the Capitol Hill, besieged by a Vitellian army over which Vitellius himself had absolutely no control. During the night Sabinus sent for Domitian, who evaded the careless guards and joined the party on the Capitol. Messages were sent to Antonius, encamped at Ocriculum, to allow his troops to celebrate the Saturnalia.[16]

On 19 December Sabinus sent Cornelius Martialis to Vitellius to protest against the violent disruption of negotiations, not realizing that Vitellius could exercise no authority over his troops, and the time for formal negotiation was at an end. Meanwhile Petillius Cerialis arrived from Fidenae. Though he had too few troops to effect the rescue of the Flavians in Rome, he attacked from the north–east, hoping to storm through the city with the advantage of surprise. He was beaten off, and the angered Vitellians responded by storming the Capitol. Sabinus had not summoned the urban cohorts, so the defenders were a motley collection of adherents, only some of whom had any military experience. Statues were used to block entrances to the hilltop, and stones and tiles were used as missiles against the attackers. It is not established who was responsible for the first use of firebrands, but in the course of the attack temples and houses were burned down. Sabinus had not the authority to quell panic and restore order so that it was only a matter of time before the Vitellians broke in. Several people who resisted were killed; Sabinus was taken prisoner and put to death; Domitian escaped.[17]

Domitian's part in the débâcle of the Capitol and his subsequent flight to safety generated a quantity of literature both ancient and modern, far in excess of the importance of the actual events. Flavian propaganda and Domitian's own emphasis on his miraculous survival elevated the episode to epic proportions. Tacitus and Suetonius present different versions of the story, which Wellesley attempted to reconcile. According to Suetonius, Domitian lay concealed all night by one of the temple attendants and escaped in the morning by disguising himself as one of the followers of Isis, thus crossing the Tiber and reaching the house of the mother of one of his school companions, accompanied by one other person, not named in the narrative. According to Dio, this was his cousin, the younger Sabinus. Tacitus tells a slightly different tale: Domitian was already in the house of the temple attendant when the Vitellians breached the defences of the Capitol. In a religious costume, a disguise improvised by an unnamed freedman, he escaped to the house of Cornelius Primus, who lived near the Velabrum and was one of Vespasian's clients. The two versions of the escape are not irreconcilable if it is assumed that Domitian quickly moved on from Primus' house – not the safest of hiding places given that the owner was an associate of the Flavians. Wellesley suggests that Domitian spent the night of the 19/20 December with the temple attendant, moved on during the morning of

20 December to Cornelius Primus and from there across the Tiber in the afternoon to the house of his friend's mother until 21 December, when he judged it safe to show himself in public. This reconstruction incorporates all features of more than one ancient narrative, but not all modern scholars agree with the interpretation.[18]

During the reign of Vespasian, Domitian built a small shrine to Jupiter Conservator on the site of the house of the temple attendant who had concealed him. When he became Emperor he enlarged this shrine to become a temple of Jupiter Custos, with a statue of the god bearing Domitian in his arms. From references made by Martial, it is known that Domitian himself composed a poem about his defence of the Capitol. The court poets, Martial, Statius and Silius Italicus followed his lead, taking up the theme and referring to the episode in suitably heroic terms. Clearly it had made a lasting impression on Domitian but then, human nature being what it is, the prospect of imminent annihilation generally does. The danger was vividly real. Suetonius' statement that there was a search for Domitian is not corroborated elsewhere, but is only to be expected, since the son of Vespasian would provide a valuable hostage and would have given the Vitellians some bargaining power. For two days Domitian could not be sure of his fate. Even though Antonius Primus was close to Rome and Sabinus had sent a message to him on 19 December, it was not certain that he had received it, nor that he had acted upon it, nor that he would achieve rapid success once he had entered Rome. During that agonizing period Domitian could have been discovered at any moment. Vitellius himself may have wished no harm to either Sabinus or Domitian but by this stage in the proceedings Vitellius' goodwill was null and void – the Flavians were facing an angered and leaderless mob which was out of control. Sabinus was murdered brutally, an event which cannot have failed to make a very deep impression upon Domitian, even if he was unaware of the death of his uncle until two days afterwards when he met the troops of Antonius Primus. If he had lived with his uncle while his father was absent then the death of someone so close would have been deeply affecting, even if they had actually disliked each other. The memory would have been difficult to eradicate, not least for the purely selfish reason that the same fate might have awaited Domitian himself. The true legacy of the siege of the Capitol was perhaps more sinister. Domitian had witnessed the violence of which an enraged mob was capable, and had seen how easily passions could be roused and in an instant expand beyond the control of the leader in whose name the mob fought. Thus there was a dual danger implicit in rebellion. The intentions of the leader were to be feared, naturally; but potentially more damaging were the various expectations of the supporters, fickle, faceless and difficult to identify. Rebellion was not over when the leader was removed, nor even when a few ringleaders were executed. Real security, therefore, was impossible to attain.[19]

After Domitian's death, the verdict on the episode of the Capitol was predictable. Tacitus avoids an outright sneer, but implies that Domitian took no part whatsoever in the defence of the Capitol, but scurried into hiding even before the Vitellians scattered the Flavians. What has survived in the literature is polarized into two extremes, adulatory and derogatory. During his own lifetime Domitian attached great importance to his experience of mortal danger – even as much as 13 years later he wanted to remind the world of it. The building of the temple to Jupiter Custos may have been both a declaration of gratitude and religious faith as well as a statement that while the Emperor was fully aware that not all his subjects supported him either in the past or in the present, his opponents should bear in mind that in taking on the head of state they were also taking on the supreme god himself.[20]

After the Vitellians were defeated by Antonius Primus, Domitian presented himself to the troops. There are two versions of this story, subtly different in detail. According to Tacitus, it was the troops of Antonius who acclaimed Domitian Caesar and led him in triumph to his father's house. Suetonius' version is similar. Josephus, the mouthpiece of the Flavians, and Dio, who had no particular reason to follow the Flavian party line, dissociate Domitian from Antonius Primus and put him firmly in the camp of Mucianus. Josephus affirms that it was Mucianus who brought Domitian forward and recommended him to the people as their ruler in Vespasian's absence. This emphasizes the peaceful and lawful aspects of the situation, while ignoring the military rule and recent turmoil in the city. More pertinently, Dio says that Mucianus presented Domitian to the soldiers and made him deliver a speech. Real power still lay with the army, and Domitian was caught up in the power struggle between Antonius Primus and Mucianus.[21]

Antonius had done more than anyone else to win power for the Flavians in the last months of 69, and could expect to be rewarded. He was to be rapidly disillusioned. He had made two mistakes, in that he had been embarrassingly right about the need for speed in crossing the Alps, and had allowed, or at least not prevented, the sacking of Cremona. Vespasian later claimed that Antonius had acted contrary to orders, thus offloading all the blame for the disaster. In Rome itself, there was considerable disorder as Flavians hunted down and killed Vitellians. Most probably many people used the lawlessness to settle old scores or to go on profitable looting expeditions. This is not a scenario that redounds to Flavian credit. No military commander would have been able to halt the troops immediately in a city the size of Rome, and Antonius was doubly unfortunate in that Mucianus arrived in time to take all the credit for restoring order. Tacitus makes much of the carnage, implying that Domitian condoned it and idled away his time in pleasures of the flesh. The unwritten subtext is that all this went on for some considerable time, but according to Josephus, Mucianus arrived in Rome on 21 December and took charge, which would mean that the disturbances lasted for only one day. Unfortunately the date of Mucianus' arrival is not established beyond doubt. Either Josephus or Tacitus bent the truth to suit their own purpose. The Flavians had a vested interest in glossing over the bloodshed and disturbances in Rome, just as Tacitus had a vested interest in exposing the truth, but in this case he may have exaggerated a little. With Antonius Primus already in Rome, all-powerful and likely to take the credit for ending the war, Mucianus would certainly waste no time in getting there himself.[22]

Mucianus was the man of the moment, to whom the populace turned immediately and to whom the Senate offered deference while swallowing its distaste. The readjustments began. The Senate had elected Vespasian and Titus consuls, while Domitian was appointed urban praetor with consular powers so that he could expedite business in the absence of his father and brother. The urban praetor Frontinus stood down for him to take up this post on 1 January 70. Even Tacitus admits that Domitian acquitted himself well in the Senate. It was on his suggestion that Galba's memory was honoured, and when it was mooted that the files should be opened on *delatores*, Domitian tactfully refused, saying that this was a matter that should be referred to his father. At the next meeting of the

Senate, he proposed that the enmities of the past be forgotten. Thus he received the credit for putting forward the idea and provided the opening for Mucianus to follow up with an appeal for the end to persecution of informers and for the cessation of their use. A few days later Domitian addressed and calmed the near-mutinous troops of Vitellius, now integrated into the Flavian army and demanding reinstatement and back pay. Mucianus had done the groundwork in restoring order, while Domitian played the part of reconciler. The apparent spontaneity of some of their actions presupposes careful rehearsal, where they presumably discussed business in advance and then performed their respective roles. Most modern authors assume that Mucianus would have had some difficulty in controlling the impetuous Domitian, but at this stage such impetuosity need not have arisen from an overweening desire for power. It is a commonplace that youth knows all the answers, and the irritation that this causes is in direct proportion to the amount of persistent enthusiasm displayed. Having just survived an enraged mob and being now faced with the reconstruction of the entire state, it is likely that Domitian's enthusiasm knew no bounds. Mucianus worked skilfully and tactfully. In their dealings with the Senate and the army, Mucianus and Domitian presented a united front and where possible Mucianus allowed the credit to fall to Domitian. The young Caesar himself could perhaps be forgiven if his sudden elevation went to his head. Privately he may have compared the situation to that of Octavian and Agrippa, but if he was under any illusion that he was in charge, he was quickly apprised of the truth. Mucianus had almost *carte blanche* to do whatever he considered necessary, if Dio is to be believed. He could issue orders in the Emperor's name and possessed a ring which Vespasian had given to him so that he could set the Imperial seal on documents. The story may be exaggerated but, given the distance between Rome and Vespasian in 69/70, some such method would be necessary to expedite urgent business which could not wait for the transmission of a message and its reply.[23]

With Domitian as figure-head, Mucianus took the reins. There were certain dangerous elements that needed to be eradicated. Suspicion, justified or not, fell on the son of Gaius Piso, who was executed 65km (40 miles) outside Rome. Julius Priscus, Vitellius' praetorian prefect, helpfully committed suicide. Antonius Primus and the praetorian prefect Arrius Varus survived but were deliberately deprived of powerful influence. Gradually, troops were removed from Rome and sent back to the provinces, thus depriving Antonius of support. He was prevented by Mucianus from approaching Domitian personally; perhaps he had some influence over the young Caesar, having been the first friendly face that Domitian saw after his ordeal on the Capitol. Mucianus presumably overruled Domitian too, if he chose to speak up for Antonius. Abandoned and snubbed, Antonius went eventually to Vespasian to appeal for better treatment, received short shrift, and retired to Toulouse, remembered only by Martial.[24]

No sooner had the situation in Rome been calmed than there was a revolt in Germany. Civilis, the commander of the Batavian auxiliaries attached to the Rhine legions, had fought against the Vitellians in 69, but it was now plain that he was wholly anti-Roman, not simply anti-Vitellian. Not only had his forces grown, but he had now joined up with Classicus of the Treveri. Petillius Cerialis was sent with seven legions to deal with the rebellion, followed by Domitian and Mucianus. Before they had crossed the Alps news came that the war was almost at an end. Josephus' account of Domitian's heroism in this war can probably be discounted as literary licence and Flavian propaganda, since the young Caesar took very little part. For the same reasons, Suetonius' comment that Domitian began an unnecessary war in Gaul and Germany can also be dismissed. The charge that he was eager for military glory is a little unfair: as Jones points out, it was *de rigeur* for Roman youths to desire military glory. But what is really being criticized here is not his desire for glory but his supposed presumption that without the slightest experience he should take command of an army. He seems not to have argued too strongly when Mucianus persuaded him that he should go to Lyons rather than become involved in the tail-end of the fighting, which would have been undignified for the Emperor's son. Tacitus reports the rumour, without exactly vouching for its veracity, that from Lyons Domitian sent word to Cerialis to ask him to turn over the command of the army to him. This may well be true, especially if the surmise that Cerialis was his brother-in-law is correct. The affair may have seemed to him to be a family concern, where he could win some experience and maybe a satisfactory military reputation in congenial circumstances. On the other hand there may have been more at stake. Tacitus reports that Domitian wanted command of the army because he was plotting rebellion against his father – an idea designed to show that he was power-hungry from the start and would stop at nothing, even the overthrow of his own family. Tacitus slots this unproven suggestion into his narrative to back up the assertion. There are no definite facts to substantiate or refute what was supposed to have been in Domitian's mind, and after the years of terror no one would have the least inclination to exonerate the so-called monster in defiance of the historians' accusations. The tale continues that when his scheming came to nothing, and he saw that he was ignored, Domitian sulked, withdrawing from his duties and refusing to carry out even the unimportant ones he had been performing before. Dio also accuses Domitian both of unwarranted ambition and of fear of his father because of what he had already done and even more so because of what he was secretly planning. Strange that unproven plans, made in secret and, more importantly, never carried out, should be such common knowledge to authors writing about him later on. [25]

Criticism was levelled at Domitian both for his actions and his inaction. As early indications of his dissolute character, it was said that while he was not commiting adultery and seducing other men's wives, he was sulking in solitude, stabbing flies. Dio says that such information is not worthy to grace the pages of history but includes the fly-stabbing all the same because it was too good to waste. Whatever he did during this episode of his life Domitian could gain no credit. He was accused of both idleness and over-zealousness in making appointments – two contradictory accusations. Anything that tended towards virtuousness was discounted as silent scheming, whilst most of his achievements were represented in the worst possible light. It is difficult to ascertain how much of this criticism is purely retrospective and how much of it, if any, was current during Domitian's own lifetime. Tacitus turns his behaviour into the excuse for Vespasian's return to Rome. After he had made several appointments, presumably with Mucianus directing events, Domitian reputedly received a message from his father thanking him for allowing him to remain Emperor, a phrase which humourless commentators have taken seriously as an indication of Domitian's treachery and Vespasian's suspicion of it. In the light of other anecdotes about Vespasian's sense of humour, it is possible to view this comment in a completely different sense: it means in rough translation, 'Well done, you have dealt with absolutely everything below the rank of Emperor and I can safely assume you are not going to replace me.' Since it was quite clear that it was Vespasian himself who wielded all the power and that in Rome it was Mucianus and not Domitian who executed it – both facts of which contemporaries and later authors were surely aware – Vespasian's comment can be seen as a fatherly pat on the back for his younger son in his first administrative role.[26]

Vespasian's supposed displeasure with his younger son is extended from the events of 69–70 in Rome throughout Domitian's life. The evidence for this is slight, perhaps owing its origin to the fact that the divine Vespasian, though not faultless, was a man of profound common sense and shrewdness. In order to dissociate him from the reign of his son, of damnable memory, it was necessary to maintain that he knew all along how depraved he was, but made allowances for him while keeping him in check. This neatly accounts for later developments: once removed from his father's benign influence, Domitian finally showed himself in his true colours. In 70, however, as more than one author has suggested, it is at least as likely that Vespasian was concerned about the growing influence of Mucianus as he was about the behaviour of his son. Before his arrival in Rome, Mucianus had proclaimed in a letter to the Senate that he held Imperial power in his hands and had made a present of it to Vespasian. This was possibly a pre-emptive declaration to the Senate, a warning of what he could do if he chose, and that he had chosen to take the subordinate role. Depending on the circumstances and the light in which Vespasian viewed it, this statement could have given some cause for disquiet. Some scholars have made a case for rivalry between Titus and Mucianus, beginning in 69/70 and enduring throughout Vespasian's reign. Tacitus reports a conversation between Titus and Vespasian before the latter departed for Rome in which Titus implored his father to be lenient with Domitian despite his shortcomings and spoke of changing affections among friends, which could be read as distrust of Mucianus. If this was so, the distrust remained in the background, for Mucianus did not fall into disfavour. The opprobrium therefore falls solely on Domitian. Accepting this, Jones represents the speech as a plea for family solidarity, but this is to imbue it with a Flavian rather than a Tacitean purpose, giving it a slant that would sit more comfortably in the pages of Josephus. The conversation may actually have taken place and may have been scrupulously and accurately reported, but it is at least as likely that it is a clever insertion fulfilling one purpose only, that of presenting Domitian in the customary manner. The purely practical reasons for Vespasian's return, however, have not been much considered. It is usually intimated that the new Emperor left Titus in charge of the Judaean war as an emergency measure while he hastened to Rome, reluctantly leaving the task unfinished. In fact, Vespasian himself may not have considered that he was taking a risk. He had successfully overseen the resumption of the corn supply from Egypt which he himself had disrupted, and quite probably considered that the proper time had come to attend to affairs in Rome. He would need to set sail before the season was ended and travel became hazardous if not foolhardy. Hence his arrival in Italy in October; to travel any later would have been difficult.[27]

Domitian met his father at Beneventum, where no one knows what was said either in public or in private, which allows malicious gossip free rein. The story of Vespasian's disapproval is so entrenched that it is probably hardly worth contradiction, but some slight evidence has been adduced to refute it. In his interpretation of the sculptured panels discovered in the 1930s near the Palazzo della Cancelleria (pls. 2–4), Hugh Last suggests that the scene depicting Vespasian and Domitian together represents an episode in Rome shortly after Vespasian's arrival in which Domitian is being thanked and rewarded. If this is so, it means that in 70 their relations were good. Unfortunately it cannot be proved that this is either the event or the date that the reliefs were intended to depict. Furthermore, since they are a product of Domitianic propaganda, it could be argued that they were intended to manipulate public opinion in Domitian's favour. This uncertainty weighs against the use of these sculptures for the development of any theory about Domitian's position in 70. More telling is Vespasian's subsequent treatment of his two sons during his reign, which is the subject of the next chapter.[28]

III
AUGUSTI FILIUS

With the arrival in Rome of his father at the end of 70, Domitian's position changed from superior to superfluous. Dio and Suetonius relish the fact that Vespasian brought his arrogant younger son to heel by making him live in the same house with him. This put Domitian firmly under the control of his father, underlined his subordinate position and prevented him from sullying the family name by retiring to the Alban villa to indulge his various anti-social passions. Chastisement is all that the hostile sources can see in Vespasian's ruling, but the new Emperor may have had a completely different motive. With Domitian close to him at all times, the world could be kept informed of his presence and witness his proper and adequate training for government. Vespasian intended to found a dynasty. Few scholars would dispute this, but it is less certain whether he intended to limit his full attentions to his elder son. Those who regard Domitian as the unmitigated monstrosity portrayed by Tacitus and Pliny cannot reconcile themselves to the possibility that Domitian was all along intended for the throne, second only to Titus.[1]

Domitian was certainly not kept in the background whenever there was pomp and ceremony. Suetonius says that he followed his father and brother in a litter when they appeared in public. At the joint Triumph of Vespasian and Titus he accompanied them, dressed in fine clothes and mounted on a white horse. Josephus describes the scene rapturously, but his rhetoric should not obliterate the fact that this was the normal procedure for a young prince. Vespasian's treatment of his younger son was neither unprecedented nor outrageously abnormal.[2]

Despite Titus' prodigious activity in the business of government attested by Suetonius, from 69 to 79 Vespasian, and only Vespasian, was officially in control. His authority, won initially by means of armed force, rested on the legal basis of the *lex de imperio Vespasiani*, which probably dates from the last days of 69 when Mucianus and Domitian directed affairs in the Senate. It is not known whether the law simply granted to Vespasian all the usual powers, or whether there were some unprecedented clauses which were necessitated by the unusual circumstances obtaining after the Civil War. Debate about the problems raised by this document would fill several pages without great reference to Domitian, but it is important to note the main points. Brunt's conclusions on this matter, in answer to questions about the purpose of the law, were that 'the Senate did no more nor less than vote to Vespasian at one stroke all the usual powers of a Princeps', and that there could be no question of the Senate trying to limit Vespasian's powers by closely defining them.[3]

Vespasian made no hypocritical attempt to hide the military origin of his power. He used the title *Imperator* more than previous Emperors had done, and his *dies imperii* was 1 July to commemorate the day when the troops had proclaimed him, a constant reminder that he had the support of the army. This blatant centralization of power could not be masked. At the conclusion of the Civil War Vespasian was in a situation similar to that of Octavian in 31 BC, but in 69/70 Vespasian lacked the advantage of youth to sustain him through the necessary programme of reforms and repairs. He was already sixty years old and could not foresee, still less guarantee, that he would still be active a decade from his accession. If the whole edifice was to remain intact after his death it was necessary to choose someone to succeed him peacefully in order that the work could be continued, his elder son being the obvious choice. Restoration of the Republic and supremacy of the Senate were not options which Vespasian entertained, to the constant irritation and eventual extinction of Helvidius Priscus. It may have been in connection with one of the latter's provocative attacks in the Senate that Vespasian declared that either his son, or his sons, would succeed him, or no one would. There are differing accounts of this episode. Suetonius relates the tale at the end of his life of Vespasian, and reports that he said 'sons' in the plural. Dio's account links the declaration with Priscus' behaviour in the Senate, thus setting it more plausibly perhaps in the early part of Vespasian's reign, but only one son, in the singular, is mentioned. The story is probably based on truth and even on the actual words of Vespasian, perhaps uttered more than once. But the discrepancies in the accounts that have survived serve only to add to the confusion about Domitian's position both in the eyes of his father and in the opinion of contemporaries. At the end of Domitian's reign most people would presumably conveniently forget that while Vespasian was alive, they had acquiesced in his intention that he should be succeeded by Titus and then Domitian. [4]

Second in command to the Emperor was Titus (pl. 5), clearly highlighted as successor to his father and possessed of more powers than ever Tiberius had been granted under Augustus. He was consul six times in nine years with his father as colleague; he was censor with his father in 73–4; he received 14 salutations as *Imperator* before he finally became Emperor; he held tribunician power from 71 onwards and was praetorian prefect as well. Despite the accretions of all these real powers, however, he was still only second in command, and never co-Emperor, certainly not in the sense in which later Emperors shared power with their colleagues. As Jones has pointed out, Titus, like Domitian, was always *Augusti filius*, never Augustus. [5]

Viewed in this light, the position in which Domitian (pl. 6) found himself was not quite so bitterly subordinate as it has been portrayed. He himself may have felt that it was so, but he would presumably have felt it even more keenly had Titus been co-Emperor in the fullest sense, leaving him honoured but powerless. For honoured he undoubtedly was. He was Caesar, *Augusti filius*, and *princeps iuventutis*, titles by which he was known on inscriptions and no doubt in flimsier documents which have not survived. He was consul six times under Vespasian, keeping pace with his brother and father, being always three consulships behind Vespasian and one behind Titus. Thus he did not lag behind at any time in honorific titles and positions. No one can prove how he was treated in private, but it is unlikely that, having been brought to live under the parental roof, he was excluded from all political discussion. His opinions may have counted for nothing, but it is highly probable that Vespasian ensured that he had a good grounding in administration and finance. According to Suetonius, Titus used to deliver Vespasian's speeches for him in the

Senate, while Dio says that Domitian undertook these duties as well. If so, it presupposes some collusion and discussion about the matters in hand, a rehearsal of the speech perhaps, or at least some familiarity with the thoughts behind it. Most of all it involves trust. Vespasian had a decade in which to observe his younger son and was shrewd enough and honest enough to recognize any signs that Domitian was unsuitable to govern the Empire. Vespasian probably cared about the welfare of the state sufficiently to take the appropriate measures to prevent Domitian from coming to power if he judged it necessary. This would have been effected by much more definite means than half-heartedly keeping him in the background in Roman affairs. Exile, imprisonment and sudden disappearance of even close relatives were methods not unknown to the Caesars from Augustus to Nero, and there is no evidence to suggest that on important issues Vespasian could be swayed by sentiment.[6]

Domitian's administrative experience cannot be doubted. Gsell's assessment of him as chafing at his enforced idleness has been rightly questioned, since it is unlikely that he was left with nothing to do for long intervals. The consulship was not simply an empty honour. It was the highest of all the magistracies. From the time of Augustus onwards, the number of consuls each year had increased from two to as many as six. The first pair to take up office opened the year, and were styled *consules ordinarii*. They were the most prestigious of all the consuls of the year, the others being the *consules suffecti*. The ordinary consuls usually resigned after a short period (six months under Augustus and Nero) to allow the suffect consuls to take up their posts. This procedure allowed more magistrates to reach the office and to gain experience in the post, which they held for two to six months, depending on the number of suffect consuls appointed for that particular year. Even so, probably only half the men who embarked on a senatorial career could ever hope to attain the consulship. In the Flavian period there were sometimes as many as ten consuls in one year, succeeding each other for a short time only, but few men ever held more than two consulships in their career under Vespasian, Titus or Domitian. Mucianus held three consulships, the reward for his support from the beginning, but he was a rarity. The fact that Domitian held six consulships under his father, without having held the preliminary offices demanded of other candidates, must therefore be seen as exceptional and important in any assessment of his position as designated successor. He was *consul ordinarius* only once under Vespasian, in 73. Since this was probably the year in which Vespasian and Titus became censors, Suetonius' disparaging comment, that Domitian was allowed this honour simply as an afterthought when Titus stepped aside for him, can be disregarded. As suffect consul in 71, 74, 76, and 79, Domitian would be involved in administrative procedures and senatorial debates which would give him valuable experience. The consuls were presidents of the Senate, and retained some judicial functions. They acted jointly, possibly deciding in advance which of them would preside over the Senate at a particular meeting. Some of Domitian's colleagues in the consulship were distinguished men, such as L. Valerius Catullus Messalinus, Caesennius Paetus and Ti.Plautius Silvanus. More important, as Jones points out, Domitian would be able to form alliances during his years in the Senate. By the time he became Emperor, after more than a decade of observation and participation in the Senate, he would have had a fully developed opinion of most senators, possibly tainted by his first experience of their behaviour in 69/70. Accurately or distortedly, he would have made up his mind about their capacities and weaknesses, both of which could be exploited.[7]

Against the honours and experience gained from 69/70 onwards must be set the absence of any real power for Domitian during the reigns of both his father and his brother. Though the consulship was the highest magistracy, it was not the seat of power. Executive power lay with the *tribunicia potestas* and proconsular *imperium*. Domitian received neither until his reign began, whereas Titus undoubtedly received tribunician power and probably *imperium* as well, implicit in his acclamations as *Imperator*. Tribunician power gave the holder the right of veto, including the right to veto any decrees passed at meetings of the Senate at which he had not been present, as well as bestowing the right to convene the Senate. Before the accession of Vespasian *tribunicia potestas* had been granted to Agrippa and Tiberius under Augustus, and this is the example that Vespasian followed. After the Flavian period, the possessor of tribunician power was regarded as the heir to the throne, with senatorial recognition, but this is not necessarily indicative of opinion during the reign of Vespasian. The times were exceptional and demanded exceptional measures, and in the 70s it was Titus who was exceptional – only one other Emperor in half a century had adopted this method of marking out his successor. It was also exceptional that there were two adult sons in line for the succession. These factors must be taken into account before it can be said with any certainty that the exclusion of Domitian from tribunician power definitely indicates that he was never intended for the throne.[8]

In the reign of Titus, Domitian (pl. 7) was *consul ordinarius* in 80, but still had no powers. This may signify no more than that the succession was secured and obvious to everyone. According to Suetonius, Titus himself described Domitian as his *consors successorque*. These are of course mere words with no legal obligation behind them, and apart from continuing to honour Domitian on his coinage Titus did not back up his words with anything more than empty air. Domitian is said to have complained that he had been left a share in the Empire according to his father's will, but that Titus had altered it. Titus' acknowledged skill as a forger would admit of this possibility. The story may have gained acceptance by a process of wishful thinking developed after Domitian's reign, along with the story that Titus' one regret, expressed on his death-bed, was that he had not assisted Domitian out of life. Both stories, if true, would have prevented Tacitus' rhetorically exaggerated 15 years of misery that resulted from Domitian's having been allowed to survive. There was probably no real affection between Titus and Domitian, but on the other hand the rivalry between the brothers may not have been so extreme. Titus may have intended gradually to admit his brother to a progressively greater share of power, but his reign was so short that no one could risk making this assertion. Only if Titus had lived for another 20 years, keeping Domitian firmly shackled to a subordinate rank throughout, could it be said that he never intended him to share the Imperial throne.[9]

In reality, Domitian could not hope to become Emperor himself for a very long time. Vespasian's reign of ten years may have been unexpected, but Titus was young, fit for another 20 years at the very least. While his father was still alive Domitian could only reconcile himself to the duties assigned to a younger son. With his brother as Emperor, if he had hoped to take the place that Titus had held as second in command to Vespasian, the disappointment would have been most vividly experienced. The parallel with Tiberius, who had to wait until he was in his fifties before he succeeded, cannot have escaped Domitian. Perhaps it was now that his interest in his predecessor developed, or intensified if it had its antecedents in an earlier phase.[10]

He may have found some consolation in his marriage. Domitia Longina, daughter of the famous Corbulo, was only one of his mistresses if the sources are to be believed, but she was the one about whom he was most passionate, and he eventually married her, as soon as her husband Aelius Lamia could be persuaded to divorce her. The marriage may have taken place late in 70, perhaps just after Vespasian's return to Rome. Few scholars doubt the intensity of Domitian's passion for his wife, despite her infidelity to him and his involvement, sexual or otherwise, with Julia, at a later time. There may have been political elements in the marriage as well as passion. Corbulo's followers would be attracted to the Flavians by this alliance, which Vespasian may have allowed for dynastic reasons. Domitian could now produce heirs, whereas Titus was not at that time married. His liaison with Berenice in Judaea in the end came to nothing and, though he may have hoped in 69/70 that he could marry her eventually, his father Vespasian perhaps wanted to make sure that at least one of his sons would provide successors. In order to reconcile the marriage to Domitia with the story in Suetonius's account that Domitian refused to marry Julia, Titus' daughter, Jones suggests that at first Vespasian tried to prise Domitian away from Domitia to make a more suitable match, but relented when he saw how genuine were Domitian's feelings. None of this can be proved.[11]

Domitia gave birth to a son in 73, during Domitian's second consulship. The child died very young, possibly in the next year. Some confusion arose over a lacuna in Suetonius' text, in which it is clear that something unknown happened in the year after the birth of Domitian's son. Some scholars preferred the emendation that a daughter was born in 74. Mooney accepted it reluctantly, while Scott rejected it altogether. Currently, most translations emend the text to read that the son born during Domitian's second consulship died in the following year. The exact dates of the birth, of the death and of the consecration as a god, of Domitian's son are not established. One alternative is to date the birth to 80, which partially explains Suetonius' text, reconstructed from a corrupt assortment of words, which seems to equate unrelated events, one the birth of Domitian's son and the other that he hailed his wife as Augusta, which he could not have done until 81. But this involves rejection of the specific date of Domitian's second consulship which Suetonius gives for the child's birth. All that is known for certain is that the child, already deified (*Divus Caesar*) appears on coins where Domitian does not hold the title Germanicus, which he took after his victory over the Chatti in 83 or 84 (pl. 8). Even this date is disputed, but discussion is left until the relevant chapter. All that can be discerned is that the son born to Domitian may not have been consecrated as a god until Domitian himself was Emperor. The poets Statius, Silius Italicus and Martial all refer to the child in eulogistic terms as a divinity. One of Martial's epigrams is quite touching, where he describes the child scattering snow from Heaven on his father's head, and Domitian smiling with pleasure. Whether this is pure flattery, otherwise empty of sentiment, cannot be determined. Domitian's pleasure at his son's birth and grief at his death are not attested. He may have felt nothing at all, or hidden his feelings and endured the tragedy with fortitude. Privately he may have reflected that not only power, influence and military glory, but also a son, were alike denied him.[12]

It is sometimes stated that Domitia was pregnant once again in 90, and that since no child was born, she must have suffered a miscarriage, but there is no support for this idea. It owes its origin to Martial's epigram exhorting the great child to be born, successor to the Emperor, to be trained as the next ruler. It is no more than a wish. There is no evidence that Domitian ever had more than one child by Domitia or anyone else.[13]

An opportunity for Domitian to display his military talents arose fleetingly in 75, when Vologaeses or Vologaesus, King of Parthia, sent a request for some auxiliary troops, commanded by one of Vespasian's sons, to help him defend his kingdom from the attacks of the Alani. Vologaeses had sent envoys to Alexandria in 69 to offer Vespasian the help of 40,000 soldiers, and when Titus had finally taken Jerusalem, he sent him a gold crown. Vespasian refused to send any troops, not wishing, he said, to interfere in the affairs of others, but the threat posed by the Alans could not be ignored, and this may be the context of the inscription, dated to 75, from Harmozica (Mtzhete, Georgia) attesting that the Romans built or rebuilt walls for Mithridates, King of the Iberi. Beyond the fortifications, there was no military expedition with Domitian at its head. The unspoken inference is, of course, that Vespasian could not afford to let his troublesome younger son anywhere near troops in case he developed ideas above his station. Domitian therefore remained in Rome. Disappointed, according to Suetonius, he wrote letters to other eastern kings, trying to persuade them by gifts and promises to ask for Roman help. Mooney suggested Tiridates as a recipient of one of these letters. Tiridates, the brother of Vologaeses, was king of Armenia by grace of Nero, and a Roman ally, whose kingdom was also threatened by the Alans. Since nothing came of the supposed letters, it is not of foremost importance to debate the truth or otherwise of Domitian's scheming. He probably thought that he had nothing to lose except his life and reputation if he failed, and everything to gain if he succeeded, including equality with Titus and esteem in the eyes of his father. The readiness with which, as Emperor, Domitian waged war on the frontiers in person gives some credibility to this report of Suetonius.[14]

For the next four years there is little to report. The Empire was peaceful, except for wars of expansion in Britain. The frontiers were being rationalized and strengthened. The army was under control after the disturbances of the Civil War. The foundations had been laid for financial stability, one of the greatest of Vespasian's achievements. As censors Vespasian and Titus had overhauled the Senate, introducing many provincials into its ranks. Grants of Roman citizenship were widespread. Latin rights were bestowed on the *civitates* of Spain and Romanization progressed in Africa. Peace and prosperity, however, did not eradicate opposition to the regime. Philosophers and astrologers were banished from Rome on the advice of Mucianus; Demetrius the Cynic was also banished, and though he hurled abuse at Vespasian when they met by chance, he was not otherwise punished. Helvidius Priscus, who repeatedly opposed Vespasian in the Senate, was another matter altogether. If his opposition had been limited to impersonal matters, or had been aimed at justifiable and attainable ends, then perhaps his behaviour could have been tolerated, simply as creditable evidence that there was still a spirit of independence in the Senate. This was something that Claudius had tried to encourage, but he had been disappointed by the slavish bending to his will. Galba had said that the Senate could not help responding to his rank as Emperor instead of to him as a person. Helvidius Priscus, though, responded to Vespasian as a person somewhat too vigorously – his personal attacks could not be condoned, because they undermined authority and wasted time. In the early years of Vespasian's reign, therefore, Helvidius became one of the few victims of a regretful Emperor who tried too late to recall the executioners.[15]

There was probably no reason to fear that either the so-called philosophers or Helvidius Priscus and his associates would ever have taken the ultimate step to remove the Flavians, but no one could be sure. Their actual intentions were not the most dangerous aspect of their opposition. It was rather that their words and actions could give rise to revolutionary – or simply hysterical – actions on the part of others who, once stirred up, would not listen to reason. Suetonius talks of incessant plots against Vespasian, without elaborating on the theme. Vigilance could not be relaxed even in an outwardly affable and forgiving regime. Titus seems to have kept his finger on the pulse of public opinion, both overt and clandestine. His preferred method of pre-empting rebellion was to install his agents in the theatres and at the circus where they could publicly demand the punishment of persons whom he suspected. Political opinions were often expressed in this way and Titus exploited the custom in order to gain spurious approval for the removal of opponents seemingly without recourse to due legal process. There may be some exaggeration in Suetonius' account, both about the number of plots and about Titus' methods of disposing of suspects. He outlines the most serious plot, or perhaps the one that made the worst impression because of the brutality of Titus' way of dealing with it. Aulus Caecina Alienus had become an *amicus* of Vespasian after the Civil War. His reputation was not of the best: he had supported Galba against Nero, then gone over to Vitellius, and then in turn deserted him for the Flavians when Antonius Primus entered Italy. Such a pronounced instinct for self-preservation is at odds with altruism or blind loyalty, so he was probably not deeply mourned when Titus had him killed at a dinner party in 79. The odium that Titus incurred from this barbarity probably arose not so much from concern over Caecina's fate as from nervous apprehension as to what might follow. Men feared that Titus would prove to be a second Nero.[16]

Nothing was ever proved against Caecina, nor was anyone given the chance to defend him. It was said that Titus had discovered a speech written in Caecina's own hand that he intended to read to the troops to incite the overthrow of the Flavians. Once again Titus' penchant for forgery comes into question. The document could have been fabricated and planted on Caecina, or produced later to give some credence to the existence of a plot. On the other hand, the danger could have been very real. Suetonius does not protest Caecina's innocence, while Dio strongly approves of Titus' prompt action, adding the dismissive comment that not even kindness can guarantee loyalty. Dio complicates the issue by including Eprius Marcellus in the plot, a most unlikely accomplice for Caecina, as Jones has pointed out. Marcellus had been a *delator* in the reign of Nero, and had made a profit from his denunciation of Thrasea Paetus. He had been well treated by Vespasian, becoming consul with Petillius Cerialis and then proconsul of Asia. How his grievances found accord with those of Caecina will never be known. He was brought to trial but – conveniently perhaps for the Flavians, if inconveniently for the historians – he committed suicide. The possibility that there were two plots which Dio has conflated does not signify much. It still implies that two very different members of Roman society were discontented, possibly because as Vespasian advanced in age, the reality of rule by Titus loomed large. It may have been in fear of this potential second Nero that rebellion grew.[17]

The effect on Domitian of Caecina's and Marcellus' plotting can hardly have been negligible. Whether they were guilty or innocent is not the point at issue. Titus obviously believed that there was some danger to the regime, no doubt involving removal of all three Flavians. Caecina had been, if not a friend in the modern sense of the word, then an acknowledged associate of Vespasian with no outward cause for complaint. If he was opposed to the accession of Titus, then it probably follows that he was opposed to the accession of Domitian as well. In this sense, Domitian would be entitled to interpret the plot as a personal threat. Marcellus could be said to have owed Domitian a small favour, if Tacitus' account of senatorial proceedings in 69/70 is correct. Helvidius Priscus bore a grudge against Marcellus because as informer Marcellus had brought about the condemnation of Thrasea Paetus, Helvidius' father-in-law. In the chaos of 69/70, Helvidius began to hope for revenge and tried to bring Marcellus down, starting a furious row with him in the Senate, at a meeting where Domitian himself was clearly present. At the next meeting, Domitian suggested that old hostilities should cease and Mucianus spoke in defence of informers. Marcellus ought to have been grateful – he had been rescued by the timely intervention of Domitian and Mucianus, and rewarded by Vespasian with the consulship and then the proconsulship of Asia. Caecina and Marcellus presumably did not act completely alone, but Domitian could never know for certain who had conspired with them. When the danger was past, he may have attended meetings of the Senate with tremendous interest in those who protested too loudly for his welfare, and those who would not quite meet his eyes.[18]

Shortly after the suppression of this plot, Vespasian succumbed to a fever contracted in Campania. He returned to Rome and then went to Aquae Cutiliae, where he died in June 79. Dio, discounting the story as false, reports that Hadrian believed that Titus had poisoned his father, but this rumour does not seem to have been current when Titus succeeded to the throne. The succession appears to have been smooth and without hindrance. If there is no recorded senatorial activity to grant him his powers, then equally there is no record of anything like the dilemma that Tiberius, the clearly designated successor of Augustus, found himself in when Augustus died.[19]

The reign of Titus took most of Rome by surprise. The ruthless tyrant turned over a new leaf, dismissing all his unsavoury friends and even his paramour Berenice, who went back to the east. If his kindness and benevolence was but an act, then at least he took his role seriously and played the part to the full. Jones suggests that though the ascertainable facts are limited because of the short duration of the reign, what evidence there is permits of the conclusion that Titus was very much his own man, independent of slavish devotion to Vespasian's ideals. He adapted his policies to suit the changed circumstances. As for Domitian, while the charges that he plotted to overthrow his brother may possibly be dismissed, those of rivalry over equality have perhaps more substance. It is quite possible that the peculiar tales attached to many of Titus' and Domitian's acts, whereby everything that either of them did is construed as detrimental to the other, are based on genuine evidence of discontent that has been exaggerated and distorted. For instance, it was said that Titus had cuckolded Domitian by sleeping with Domitia and that Domitian forbade castration of young men in protest against Titus' fondness for eunuchs, while Titus promoted

Domitia Longina's ex-husband merely to annoy Domitian. These petty squabbles are ridiculous when it is considered just how much capacity for real mutual harm the Emperor and his brother possessed.[20]

When Titus died, on 13 September 81, at Aquae Cutiliae like his father, Domitian was probably with him, till shortly before the end. If he had been elsewhere at the time, the rumours that he had ordered his brother to be left for dead, or that he had ordered the servants to place him on a bed of ice, could not so readily have flourished. The implications that Domitian killed his brother might have gained acceptance if any of the stories had coincided at any point with the others, but the number of methods that he was supposed to have employed read more like a penny dreadful magazine. Suetonius says that Domitian ordered Titus' attendants to leave him before he died, but makes no accusation of murder. It is only in Dio's account that Domitian is portrayed as dashing straight for the Praetorian camp even before Titus was dead. If this is true, Domitian may have anticipated the allegations of poisoning or otherwise arranging Titus' death, in which case it was vital to ensure his supremacy by reaching the army before the allegations started. He may also have distrusted the members of his own family, possibly with justification but maybe merely because of unfounded suspicion. It has been pointed out that Flavius Sabinus, the husband of Titus' daughter Julia, would have been a prominent member of the Flavian clan for some time. This Sabinus was probably the grandson, and not, as was thought until Townend challenged the theory, the son, of Vespasian's brother Sabinus who was killed by Vitellian troops in 69. There had been glimmerings of ambition here already, for according to Suetonius, Titus' son-in-law (not actually named in this passage) had caused Domitian offence by dressing his attendants in white, an Imperial prerogative, and one presumably adopted by Sabinus as an indication of his status. When Titus died, unexpectedly and in dubious circumstances, Domitian may have feared either an attempt at a *coup d'état* by Sabinus himself or, just as detrimental, an attempt by parties unknown in Sabinus' name, because of his connection to Titus by marriage. In the early part of his reign Domitian made Sabinus consul, but later executed him, taking Julia to live with him in the Imperial palace. The seeming inconsistency may indicate at worst Sabinus' guilt or, at an unfortunate best, suspicion on Domitian's part. This will be discussed in more detail in its proper place. As regards the accession of Domitian, it is worth pointing out that the very existence of Sabinus, son-in-law of Titus, may have rendered the transition of power rather less facile than most modern authors have assumed. Perhaps it is too difficult in the twentieth century to enter the minds of younger brothers who were the heirs to eminently contestable thrones. In the same way and for the same reasons as Domitian, the shrewd and practical Henry I of England wasted no time mourning William Rufus or making arrangements for the funeral. His brother had just died in very mysterious circumstances, and another member of the family, Robert Curthose, was still eligible to rule. Not being encumbered with a Senate, but without the advantage of a Praetorian Guard, Henry rode straight for the Treasury at Winchester.[21]

Domitian's hatred of his brother is said to have continued after Titus' death. Domitian awarded him no honours save deification, say the hostile sources. One may wonder what earthly honours are left after becoming a god. There seems to have been little delay, perhaps less than a month, in Domitian's deification of his brother, whereas Titus' deification of Vespasian seems to have taken longer. No one accused Titus of lack of filial devotion, yet Domitian was not even credited with genuine grief when he read the funeral oration for Titus with tears in his eyes – it was said to be all sham. The senators assembled without being summoned when news of Titus' death reached Rome, and 'heaped such praise on him after death as they had never done when he was alive and present'. Too late, the senators realized what they had had only when it had gone. It is much more difficult to assess whether they knew precisely what they were getting when, probably on the next day, they confirmed Domitian as Augustus, *pontifex maximus, pater patriae* with *imperium* and tribunician power.[22]

IV
DOMITIAN *IMPERATOR*

One of the most serious problems in reconstructing the events of Domitian's reign is the lack of a firmly established chronology. An Emperor who suffered *damnatio memoriae* tends not to be well attested epigraphically. The coinage and the surviving inscriptions can provide a loose framework for Domitian's offices and titles, together with the names of the consuls and other magistrates for the years 81 to 96, but none of this information is complete. In many cases this loose framework suffices for the more wide-ranging topics, but there are many more occasions where the establishment of an exact chronology, down to months and even specific dates, is crucial to the proper understanding of events, especially where those events run in tandem. An illustrative case is that of the wars in Britain and Germany in the earlier part of Domitian's reign, where the broad general outline is known, but a more detailed timetable would solve many problems, extending beyond the end of the wars and also retrospectively into the reign of Vespasian.[1]

A chronological outline is provided by Dio, if the extant arrangement of his work is taken at face value, but that is a hazardous undertaking. Since it is hardly ever advisable to accept words at face value when dealing with the often mangled works of ancient authors which have survived only by having been copied many times, Dio's supposed chronology is not reliable. Most ancient sources lack the sort of precision and explanatory detail that would settle arguments once and for all, yet that is hardly a fault to be laid at the doors of the ancient authors, for their purpose was quite different from that of modern authors. In many of his biographical studies, including that of Domitian, Suetonius groups his facts thematically, providing scarcely any timetable at all. What is needed is Tacitus, but his full commentaries on Domitian as Emperor are not available to us. Neither the subtle inferences nor the direct statements in the biography of Agricola are the most useful of tools with which to assess Domitian. In a work such as the *Histories* or the *Annals*, despite his distortions and senatorial bias, and his clever manipulation of words, it is likely that Tacitus would have married facts to dates with greater clarity than most other writers.[2]

For some years in the early part of his reign, Domitian was not inordinately cruel or rapacious (pl. 9). Even the hostile sources such as Eutropius, Aurelius Victor and his Epitomator agree that Domitian was at first restrained, though they damn with faint praise, insinuating that this restraint was exactly what the word implies, a successful and deliberately fraudulent suppression of Domitian's true character. When he could no longer keep himself in check, his savage nature emerged and his cruelty knew no bounds, as if he needed to make up for lost time. Suetonius is less scathing; in three separate sections of his biography he makes it clear that the later version of Domitian, the character he eventually became, contrasted sharply with the behaviour of the younger Emperor. At first he was fair and just, liberal and generous, unmarred by greed. His administration was a little uneven, influenced by a mixture of virtues and vices, but later, contrary to his inner nature, he became rapacious because of need, and cruel because of fear. Among the few fixed points that Suetonius does provide, there is the revealing statement that after his victory in the civil war, by which is meant the suppression of the revolt of Saturninus in 89, Domitian's cruelty increased. This does not entirely absolve him of cruelty in the years 81 to 89, but it surely permissible to interpret Suetonius' words as indicative of a discernible turning point, which would make sound psychological sense. The hypothesis cannot be proven conclusively, so its acceptance or rejection rests as always upon opinion. Either Domitian was merely pretending at first, or his genuinely humane nature underwent a drastic change, perhaps sudden, perhaps cumulatively progressive. The motives are perhaps less important than the facts: whatever the interpretation to be placed upon his behaviour and character as it emerges from the pages of the ancient authors, it seems beyond doubt that during the first part of Domitian's reign there were no presentiments of the terror of the last years.[3]

On the day of Titus' death, 13 September 81, the troops hailed Domitian *Imperator* for the first time. He was to receive 21 further acclamations in his 15-year reign. This has been labelled excessive, being interpreted as a pathetic attempt to shore up his authority, but when Domitian's 22 acclamations are compared to Vespasian's 20, and Titus' 15 from his wars in Judaea to his death after only two years as Emperor, the total perhaps does not seem so excessive. Claudius received no less than 27 acclamations; it is true that he added the province of Britain to the Empire, but he did not have to journey to the Rhine and Danube to fight Chatti and Dacians to earn his titles. Domitian ruled for 15 years and waged several wars, yet still the hostile sources begrudge him his 22 acclamations.[4]

The Senate confirmed Domitian's political powers on the day after Titus' death. There may have been some ulterior motive on the part of the Senate in the very slight delay, but the most likely explanation is that by the time Domitian had secured the support of the Praetorians, the day was over. When Tiberius succeeded to the throne he used his tribunician power to summon the Senate; Domitian did not yet possess this power, and to summon the Senate, as it were at the point of a sword, perhaps late at night, may have seemed to him somewhat too peremptory and, moreover, unneccessary. The exact procedure cannot be known, but the retrospective wishful thinking of some modern works would have it that he must have spent a restless night worrying whether the Senate would comply and do the decent thing. This may have been so, but with the troops at his back to protect him from attempted usurpation, he probably slept soundly, anticipating little trouble and secure in his judgement of what the Senate would do.[5]

The date from which the new Emperor reckoned his tribunician power was from then on 14 September. His full titles are attested epigraphically on an inscription dated 19 September 82: *Imp(erator) Caesar divi Vespasiani f(ilius) Domitianus Augustus pontifex maximus tribunic(ia) potesta(s) II imp(erator) II p(ater) p(atriae) co(n)s(ul) VIII designat(us) VIIII.* After the Chattan war he added *Germanicus* after *Augustus*, and from about 85 the title *censor perpetuus* appears, usually placed after *consul*. *Imperator Caesar Domitianus Augustus* became the most usual form of his name, with slight variations occurring from time to time in the order of words. Following determinedly in the Flavian tradition, Domitian was consul every year of his reign except in 89, 91, 93 and 94, and 96, reaching the hitherto unprecedented number of 17 terms of office, always as *consul ordinarius* while he was Emperor. Statius versified Domitian's glory on taking up his seventeenth consulship: he rose with the sun and the constellations, even brighter than they. While he was in office, he presumably attended to business with characteristic meticulousness, relying on his influence to direct affairs after he had stepped down for the suffect consuls to enter office. He held none of the consulships beyond 1 May, giving up most of them in mid-January. Pliny manages to disapprove both of the number of consulships that Domitian held and also of the fact that he relinquished them so rapidly, sometimes after only a few days.[6]

At some time before 1 October 81 Domitia Longina (pl. 10) was granted the title Augusta. The use of this title dates not surprisingly from the time of Augustus, who granted it to Livia in his will. Claudius' mother Antonia refused the honour from Caligula but received it posthumously from her son. Agrippina, Claudius' wife and Nero's mother, set the precedent by accepting the title in her own lifetime. Julia was styled Augusta by her father Titus, and after Domitia Longina accepted it the wives of Emperors regularly took the title.[7]

Clearly, titles were important to Domitian. It is possible that his insistence on their use really does reflect a deep inner insecurity that required constant reassurance. In theory, titles ought to have conferred on him a certain *gravitas* and created a respectful distance between him and his subordinates. With his need for solitude and privacy, perhaps he felt that he could not operate successfully without this distance. In practice, the use of titles became merely one more piece of evidence to be ranged against him. In his own day, or at least after his death, he was derided for his adoption of the name Germanicus as a victory title. Previously, Caligula, Claudius and Nero had adopted the name to indicate descent from Germanicus Caesar. Some time later, Domitian caused even more offence by his arrogant demands to be addressed as lord and god (*dominus et deus*). Later Emperors employed these titular baubles with impunity. Severus' fulsome titles probably kept stone-carvers all over the Empire busily employed for years, and a cursory glance at them makes nonsense of the fuss over one puny Germanicus. But Severus (*c.* 145–211) brought order after civil war, just as Vespasian had done, and apart from determination and a capacity for self-advertisement, he had years of precedents upon which to fall back. Aurelian (*c.* 215–75) with his cloth of gold and jewelled crown did not find it difficult to persuade the Romans that he was lord and god, but then his subjects were perhaps too preoccupied with the barbarians at the gates and potential usurpations in other parts of the Empire to worry over much about forms of address for the man who might put a stop to it all. Domitian was both ahead of his time and in quite the wrong position in the queue for the throne: he succeeded after a decade of peace and prosperity, when men had enough to eat, time to think and, more important, no need for a leader to save them from anything.[8]

Titus was a hard act to follow – he had taken everyone by surprise by his character reformation and had not reigned long enough to make mistakes. He never put to death any Senator, declared the ancient historians, conveniently forgetting Caecina's fate since that belonged to Vespasian's reign. When two patricians were found guilty of conspiring against him, Titus let them off with a warning – a calculated risk, certainly, designed no doubt to gain credit and influence, but probably based on a shrewd assessment of the efficiency of the guilty parties and their capability of causing serious harm. It was one of

Domitian's sayings that Emperors who did not have to punish several men were not necessarily good Emperors but were merely lucky. In this respect Titus was indeed lucky, not least because his reign was short. His anxiety threshold may have been higher than Domitian's, but if he had lived longer there would surely have been a point at which his security demanded more than a conscious display of clemency. His clemency was matched by his generosity, to the extent that some authors have speculated that he would have bankrupted the state if he had been in charge for much longer. Dio indeed was aware that Titus might not have enjoyed such popularity if he had survived.[9]

Domitian's inheritance can be broadly assessed. He was heir to an administrative and financial system that worked, on the whole, and in which he seems to have involved himself meticulously and minutely. If the Treasury was under threat from Titus, it seems to have been sufficiently robust for more than mere survival during Domitian's first few years. There was an ongoing war in Britain under the legate Agricola, but the rest of the Empire was for the time being peaceful. The city of Rome was emerging from a disastrous fire that had occurred in 80, in which many buildings had been damaged or totally destroyed. The temple of Jupiter Capitolinus and several surrounding shrines and lesser temples had been burned. Clearance of the sites and possibly initial rebuilding presumably began under Titus, but the completion of the new Rome must be credited to Domitian. A fourth-century document lists the monuments that he restored or built anew; modern scholars accept that he probably repaired all the buildings that Dio says were consumed by the fire. Suetonius recounts that he restored the Capitol and other monuments, but put his own name on them, without any mention of the original builder. There may be more to this statement than meets the eye: Suetonius wrote his biographies in the reign of Hadrian, who completely rebuilt the Pantheon but scrupulously placed Agrippa's name on the finished version. Work on the baths of Titus and the Colosseum would have been commenced before Titus' death and would still have been in progress on Domitian's accession; these buildings were completed by him. It is not certain whether work had already begun on the new temple of Jupiter Capitolinus, but it is quite likely that the rebuilding would have been given priority and that it was a product of both Titus and Domitian; it was dedicated in 82, a building of supreme magnificence, according to the fragmentary sources, but traces of Domitianic work do not survive. The shrine to Jupiter Conservator which Domitian built in the reign of his father was almost certainly a casualty of the fire. It was replaced by the far grander temple to Jupiter Custos, which has been identified with the sculptured representation on the second-century panel relief depicting Marcus Aurelius in his triumphal chariot.[10]

As part of this rebuilding, Domitian attended to the promulgation of the Imperial cult. His father was already deified; the deification of his brother is not dated precisely. The *Acta* of the Arval Brethren of 1 October 81 record Titus without his distinguished title *divus*, but Domitian probably deified him soon after his death. Perhaps at the same time, he dedicated the Arch of Titus on the Velian in the Forum in Rome. Exact dates are lacking for this monument. The assertion of the ancient authors that Domitian rendered no honours to Titus has led some scholars to suggest that the arch was completed and dedicated by either Nerva or Trajan, suggestions which can probably be safely ignored, along with the implication that Domitian can have had nothing to do with the arch because of his hatred of his brother. This is patent nonsense. It is much more likely that the arch owes its origin to Titus, and was completed in the early years of Domitian's reign, with the declared intention of glorifying his family. In his study of the arch, Michael Pfanner considers that the dedication of the monument and the deification of Titus are closely associated. If Pliny is remotely justified in his statement that Domitian deified Titus merely so that he could be the brother of a god, then it goes without saying that it was even more prestigious to be the brother of a god whose triumphal arch stood as a perpetual reminder in the Forum.[11]

Glorification of the Flavii extended to other buildings in Rome. Titus had begun to build the temple of the divine Vespasian, and it was completed by Domitian. His work and that of Titus cannot be clearly distinguished, but the interior decoration was almost certainly Domitianic. The *templum gentis Flaviae* which Domitian founded on the site of the family home on the Quirinal may have been an early creation associated with the beginning of his reign. Martial writes of the cleared house-site, fortunate in that it knew Domitian as a child; he describes the glorious edifice of gold and marble now appearing in its place. Little is known about this temple. It was intended as a mausoleum, where Domitian may have removed the ashes of his father and brother, and where his own remains may have been placed, but there is no proof for this. The building is attested in the earlier written sources, but it disappears after its mention in the fourth-century list of Domitianic buildings, leading to the conclusion that it must have been destroyed at some unknown date. Platner and Ashby suggest that it was altered in the short reign of Claudius Gothicus in the third century. Its ultimate fate is unknown. The date of foundation of the *templum Divorum*, the temple of the divine father and son, is not known, except that it was one of Domitian's new constructions. Contemporary evidence for the appearance of this work is lacking: the earliest representation of it comes from the *Forma Urbis Severiana*, about a century later. There were probably two identical temples, one dedicated to Vespasian and the other to Titus, and there may also have been a monumental gateway of Flavian date leading into the sacred precinct. This may have been built to mark the spot where the sacrifices took place before the triumphal procession of Vespasian and Titus began. A further suggestion is that the Cancelleria reliefs (pls. 2–4, 14) were associated with this gateway. None of this can be proved. Domitian has been accused of employing this group of buildings purely for reasons of self-promotion, as though he tolerated the presence of temples to his father and brother only in so far as they aggrandized his own reputation. All this building activity on behalf of the Flavians cannot be closely dated, but the early establishment of himself as heir to this tradition would probably have been of foremost importance to Domitian. The fire in 80 would have provided an excellent opportunity to embellish Rome on his own terms and to his own advantage.[12]

Among Domitian's first acts must be numbered the edict confirming all gifts and privileges granted by Titus, Vespasian and other Emperors. According to Suetonius, Titus was the first to do this in one single edict without being asked to do so, and without limiting his assent to those favours he approved while arbitrarily rejecting others. Naturally, Titus gained credit for this but while Domitian may have done so at first, he lost it quite quickly. Dio dismisses his generosity as feigned display and in view of the confiscations which began a short while later – perhaps as early as 85 – it no doubt seemed as though Domitian was indeed biding his time until the fruit was ripe for picking. As far as he was concerned, though, there may have been no connection between them, for if a week is a long time in politics, then four years is an eternity, and in each case he did what was necessary to suit the circumstances. His conscience would be a matter for himself alone.[13]

The humane side of his character is revealed in his law forbidding the castration of males and the deliberate suppression of the trade in eunuchs in the slave market. Humanity, however, does not enter into the calculations of the ancient authors, who condemn him for effecting this law merely for the purpose of posthumously deriding Titus' memory. There is also the charge of hypocrisy, since Domitian himself favoured the eunuch Earinus. Obviously, then, according to the hostile critics, there was one law for him and another for everybody else. The fate of Earinus was outside Domitian's control, the operation not being reversible, but the fate of other slaves could be ameliorated. Domitian's purpose may well have been truly compassionate – there is some evidence that he shrank from unnecessary bloodshed, an aversion which even extended to concern for animals, since he considered forbidding the slaying of oxen at sacrifices. Squeamish distaste does not always owe its origin to self-centered fastidiousness, though this is one possible interpretation of Domitian's actions. Unfortunately, over-sensitivity either for oneself or on behalf of others was not foremost among Roman virtues. From the very beginning Domitian may have found himself at odds with his contemporaries.[14]

The way in which he treated his contemporaries has been the subject of considerable distortion. The sources state that from the outset Domitian pursued a vendetta against the associates, or *amici*, of his father and brother. No doubt the sources were strongly influenced by the executions of the years of the terror, which were understandably rather more vivid than any number of placid years. *Amici* of the Emperors are described as advisers or sometimes as counsellors, loose terminology at best which gives the impression that there was an official cabinet of chosen personnel, permanently sitting in the debating chambers of the Imperial palace. The organization was in fact much more fluid than that. *Amici* were not appointed officially to a post of adviser, nor given a fixed term of service. They could be summoned for specific purposes, to give advice or to fulfill any related function that the Emperor thought fit. Though senators predominate, some *amici* were drawn from the ranks of the equestrians while yet others were *liberti*. Expertise, knowledge and experience were the determining factors, rather than social rank, in an Emperor's choice of 'friends'. The group was not finite or permanent. It was not necessary to utilize the services of the same men at all times, so that their absence and then reappearance does not always mean that they had fallen temporarily into disfavour and had then been forgiven and reinstated. To produce lists of the *amici* of various Emperors is fraught with difficulty. In this respect, Juvenal's fourth *Satire* is especially useful: Domitian calls his counsellors to his Alban villa, where a huge fish, a turbot, has just been delivered, too large for any of the Imperial platters. Discussion ensues as to the advisability of cutting up the turbot or having a special dish made that would be large enough. The participants are introduced one by one, with a descriptive line or two illustrating the evils of the time, and sometimes with a word about an individual's ultimate fate. They are a mixed group of lawyers, politicians and soldiers, together with informers. Pegasus the city prefect arrives first, then Vibius Crispus, portrayed as an honest man repressed by tyranny, silent in order to survive. Next come Acilius Glabrio the elder and his son, then an unsavoury four: Rubrius, Montanus, Crispinus and Pompeius 'whose gentle whisper could cut men's throats' (line 110). The praetorian prefect Cornelius Fuscus, Fabricius Veiento and Catullus Messalinus make up the complete party. There may have been more members of this select group whom Juvenal does not name, among them the future Emperors Nerva and Trajan, probably Cn. Julius Agricola, Petillius Cerialis and Sextus Julius Frontinus, perhaps L. Julius Ursus and A. Lappius Maximus. For several reasons – political correctness, prudence and tact – Juvenal would not list everyone who had been associated with Domitian. Presumably his readers would not need assistance to remember the most famous, or infamous, of Domitian's *amici*. The satire comes back down to earth with the wish that Domitian had devoted all his time to such follies, instead of to cruelty.[15]

Continuity of *amici* when Emperors succeeded each other was probably always problematic even in optimum circumstances. Completely new regimes have always to face this problem, throughout history. A study of the ministers and counsellors during the Protectorate and the reign of Charles II in England, or those of Napoleon I and Louis XVIII in France, perfectly illustrates the point. Without exception, those men with useful talents, not least perhaps a talent for survival, crop up under succeeding regimes, fame and fortune intact. Ancient Rome witnessed the same procedure. Nerva had been closely associated with Nero, and had been rewarded by him after the Pisonian conspiracy had been suppressed, but his Neronian connections were not held against him. A new Emperor was not bound by law or tradition to retain all his predecessor's advisers, but it goes without saying that to rid himself of absolutely everyone who knew what had happened and what might happen, and moreover how to deal with it, was ill advised to say the least. Trajan survived the transition with an admirable turn of phrase, by admitting that whilst Domitian was the worst of Emperors, nonethless he had possessed good *amici*, which at one stroke condemned Domitian, absolved his friends of the sin of association with him, and brought them over to Trajan's side with the least fuss. An appropriate colloquialism may be justifiable: 'Nice one, Trajan!' By the same token, Domitian could not afford to dismiss all his father's and brother's friends, even though the new Emperor and his inherited *amici* may have entertained strong mutual dislike for each other. Suetonius praises Titus for his choice of friends, who were retained by succeeding Emperors on the grounds that they were indispensable to themselves and to the state. The idea that Domitian regarded as his enemy anyone who had enjoyed the affection of Vespasian or Titus perhaps originates from the pages of Cassius Dio, who was far removed from events. Suetonius was closer, and perhaps would not have wasted so golden an opportunity to sink one more nail into the coffin of Domitian's reputation.[16]

The balance has been restored by the researches of several modern authors. Crook detected a considerable degree of continuity in Flavian policy, until the terror began at the end of Domitian's reign. The direct references in Juvenal's *Satires* to the members of Domitian's entourage reveal that he associated with several of the men from the immediate circles of Vespasian and Titus. They were from different backgrounds – military, political and legal – and some of the Imperial *amici* survived several reigns. The services of M'Acilius Aviola, for instance, were utilized by Vespasian, Titus, Domitian and Nerva. Fabricius Veiento survived from Vespasian's reign to Trajan's. M.Cocceius Nerva, the future Emperor, served with all three Flavians. The theme of continuity was examined by Jones, whose conclusion was that Titus tried to strike out independently, with his own *amici* rather than his father's, while Domitian reverted to tried and tested policy. This may well be true, but Titus did not live long enough to provide definitive proof for this theory. Neglect of some senators in a two-year reign cannot be attributed solely to Titus' disapproval; as Devreker points out, some of those supposedly ignored by Titus had reached the second consulship, and would need to be exceptional men to be rewarded further in such a short time. Only if they had languished in obscurity for years could it be said that they had fallen into disfavour. Perhaps it is not quite so important to establish the nuances of Titus' attitude so distinctly since the salient point is that Domitian inherited – and did not dismiss – a number of *amici* who were prominent under both Vespasian and Titus. Relations between the Senate and Domitian may never have been friendly, but whatever it was that went wrong at the end was not overtly detectable at the beginning.[17]

The Imperial family was another matter. It was almost inevitable that family members with even the remotest claim to the throne should be eliminated, unless they could display a miraculous and consistently attested loyalty and detach themselves completely from almost all the rest of humanity. The destruction of the Julio-Claudians under Nero is a case in point. It may have been quite early in his reign that Domitian encountered difficulties with both his wife and his cousin Flavius Sabinus. At some unknown date he quarrelled with Domitia and sent her away, initially under threat of her life, if Dio is to be taken seriously. Perhaps around the same time, Flavius Sabinus was executed, along with a few senators. Whether these two quarrels shared a common origin is debatable. The dearth of chronological evidence only exacerbates the problem, allowing of no firm solutions and increasing the opportunities for endless permutations of opinions. Some authorities have interpreted these events as evidence of a family conspiracy in which Sabinus and Domitia were somehow allied for their own ends or for the state. It has been postulated that the followers of Titus, bitterly opposed to Domitian from the first, were plotting to remove him and then install another Flavian on the throne, more compatible with their aims and a legitimate choice because of his relationship to Titus. Jones dismisses this quite properly as rubbish, but leaves unsolved the problem – or problems if the dismissal of Domitia and the execution of Sabinus were in fact entirely separate incidents, one domestic and the other dynastic.[18]

The real reason for Domitia's disgrace is not known. The literary reason was supposed to be retaliation for her mad passion for Paris, an actor (*pantomimus*) who had reached a position of influence at court. How he had obtained this influence is not recorded, nor can it be discerned whether he was part of Domitian's inheritance from Titus. Dio renders an implausible account of Domitian murdering Paris in the street, then executing the actor's friends and admirers for placing flowers on the hallowed spot. Attempts to make Paris into a hero are not very successful and Martial's verse about his tomb can be interpreted as satirically dismissive. Only slightly less implausible is Suetonius' assertion that Domitian murdered one of the pupils of Paris who closely resembled him. Paris, it seems, had, at the least, overstepped the mark according to the Domitianic standard of behaviour but unfortunately his crime remains unknown, and even the connection with Domitia is not firmly established. The events may have been separate but contemporary, and it may therefore have seemed to onlookers that they must have been related.[19]

Domitia Longina's part in all this is shadowy. Suetonius recounts that Domitian repudiated her and then recalled her shortly afterwards, declaring that the people demanded it. This is thinly disguised political expediency, but for reasons which cannot be known.

An exact time-scale is not given by either Suetonius or Dio, so it is not known how long the separation endured. It was probably not very long, a matter of months only. The crucial year seems to have been 83, when Domitia does not appear on the coinage. She is represented on the coins of 81 and 82, and reappears on the coins of 84 to 87. It may be because of some other problem that Domitia is not honoured on the coinage of 83, but the coincidence is very strong. It is not known where Domitia went to live; she may not have left Rome, being banished from court but not the city. In Suetonius' version of the story there is no mention of divorce. By the time of Dio's treatment of the tale, not only is divorce taken for granted, but Domitian is so angry that he is determined to execute his wife, and is only persuaded to desist by Ursus, who has not been definitely identified. He was probably the same Ursus who was later spared from execution by the intervention of Julia. He may be of no importance whatsoever in the case of Domitia, or he may hold the clue as to what had really happened.[20]

Domitia has found few defenders to reinstate her moral standing. Suetonius, speaking of her with distaste, discounts the story that Titus had seduced her only to use it as a vehicle to blacken her character even further, because if it had been true she would have boasted of it. By implication therefore, she had several lovers and made no secret of the fact. It has been suggested that she led an empty life in the Imperial residence and naturally diverted herself to compensate for her marriage to a husband who notoriously preferred his own company. On the other hand it has also been pointed out that she had been married for ten years, as far as can be known without major problems, and the divorce story contains several commonplace literary themes, mostly designed to highlight Domitian's hypocrisy in enforcing moral legislation while acting immorally himself. Imperial ladies, for instance, were often accused of dalliance with 'actors of Hellenic extraction', so the accusation in this case may be worthless. This strips the episode of some of its top dressing but does not answer fundamental questions. The search for political overtones may be mistaken – adultery may in fact have been the only transgression. Too often simple things are imbued with mystifying complication generally because in the circumstances in which Domitian and other rulers found themselves, private and public affairs are irretrievably intertwined. The moral legislation aspect may have been uppermost in the Emperor's mind, on the basis that Caesar's wife must be above suspicion. Such rectitude may have been what prompted Domitian to dismiss his wife, to create the impression of the stern Emperor living up to the standards he would like to set for everyone else. Perhaps he intended from the first that the separation should be short and salutary, or perhaps he intended it to be permanent and then found that he could not live without Domitia.[21]

According to Dio it is now that Julia enters the scene. Suetonius' information gives no clues as to chronology. He records that as a youth, Domitian refused the offer of marriage with his niece, preferring to legalize his passion for Domitia, but some time later, while Titus was still alive, he seduced Julia, even though she was by this time married to an unnamed husband. Then when both her father and her husband, still not named, were dead, Domitian took her into the palace to live with him. Dio lists the events in the following order: Domitian planned to execute his wife, divorced her instead, took Julia to live with him as man and wife, then recalled Domitia but kept Julia with him as well. The narrative continues with various executions, contrived deaths, and the punishment of the Vestals. Neither of these two authors mention Sabinus as Julia's husband, that information being derived from Philostratus. These links have led to the conclusion that the Domitia and Sabinus episodes must be related, but dates and times, not to mention facts, are simply not available. [22]

Sabinus was *consul ordinarius* in 82, with Domitian as colleague. He was Domitian's own choice, rather than an inherited option of Titus. At some time between 82 and 89, Sabinus was executed for reasons which are obscure. All that has survived in the literary sources is that on the day of the consular elections the Imperial herald announced Sabinus as *Imperator* instead of consul, and so Domitian, suspicious as well as superstitious, had him killed. The flaw in this argument is that he did not act immediately, because Sabinus survived long enough to hold office. Gsell tried to circumvent this difficulty by proposing that there was another consulship for Sabinus some time after 82, and that it was on this occasion that the herald's mistake led to immediate vengeful retribution and Sabinus' death. This mistake is surely not sufficient for such a punishment, even for a monstrous tyrant like Domitian, and to postulate a second consulship is unnecessarily tortuous. Such attempts to exonerate Sabinus from all blame are designed to condemn Domitian for unreasoning cruelty. On the other hand, to try to find a reason for Sabinus' fate compels Domitian's supporters to stretch the facts slightly. Waters, for instance, tries to link Sabinus with the revolt of Saturninus in 89, which causes fresh difficulties. Suetonius places the execution last in a substantial list of names, but it is not a chronological arrangement. It is a gradual ascent via names of lesser importance to the final heinous crime of the execution of Domitian's own cousin. Suetonius would probably have been severely disappointed in a reading public who displayed less interest in his literary special effects than in precise chronological order. The execution of Domitian's cousin was more likely to have occurred in the early part of his reign, at the same time as the executions of certain senators to which Eusebius refers, dated between October 82 and September 83. Further support for this date can be derived from the writings of Dio of Prusa, also known as Dio Chrysostom. He was exiled by Domitian, most probably in 82. Reflecting on his banishment, he states that he had been a friend of a man who lost his life on account of his connection by blood and by marriage to high officials who were 'Fortune's favourites'. This is all very enigmatic, but Flavius Sabinus fits the description of the man related by blood and by marriage to Domitian although other candidates have been put forward for this friend of Dio's, and it has to be admitted that the identification of Sabinus is tenuous. The balance of probability, however, is that Sabinus was executed after he had held the consulship, but not long after, and certainly before the end of 83. Jones concludes that Domitian had removed Sabinus before he set off for the Chattan war. If this is true, it contrasts with the judgement that the early part of the reign was peaceful. Perhaps there is some support for the theory that the executions were fully justified, supported by legal process, though record of trials and passing of sentence is lacking.[23]

Domitian may have acted from any one of a number of motives, ranging from unfounded suspicion to definite knowledge of a plot to overthrow him. He may have forestalled a hastily arranged attempt at a *coup d'état* timed to seize power while he was absent in Germany. The existence of a plot can be neither proved nor disproved. Marginal evidence suggests that there was a very real danger. There seems to have been no contemporary reaction against Domitian for inhuman behaviour. Julia seems not to have demanded rescue, and Sabinus' brother Clemens seems not to have become troublesome until much later. Fear may have silenced them and made them compliant, but it is equally possible that they had no justification for an outcry. Negative evidence such as this is never strong, but the possibility that Sabinus represented a threat to Domitian should not be dismissed. There was never universal acceptance of the Principate in general, nor the Princeps in person. Philosophers and ideologists talked about *libertas*, which they considered to have been curtailed by the Emperors. Dio of Prusa wrote speeches about freedom, which cannot all have been new products of his imagination after his exile. The ideals of the philosophers may have been lofty and noble, but it was dangerous talk in the wrong brains and in the wrong hands. Noble schemes such as the restoration of the Republic, or less nobly the replacement of the existing Emperor with another man considered more suitable would be all the same to Domitian – neither scheme represented long life to him. Sabinus may have been just as much a victim of loose talk as he was guilty of rebellion. Perhaps he had not chosen his friends carefully enough, or perhaps he imagined that he could indulge in philosophical discussions about liberty and still carry out his duties as cousin of the Emperor, unaware that others had cast him in an altogether different role. History is strewn with examples of prominent personalities set up without their consent as figureheads of rebellion.[24]

Despite the controversy over dates and reasons behind these ill-documented events, it is likely that as he set out for the war in Germany, Domitian's confidence and sense of security, perhaps never very strong, had suffered a severe setback. His disappointment would have been directly proportionate to the degree of trust he had placed in Sabinus, and the affection he felt for Domitia – both of these are unfortunately immeasurable commodities. Depending on his philosophy of life at this stage, the quarrel with his wife and the execution of his cousin may have been only what he expected, or deep personal blows. A penchant for solitude may indicate comparative independence of other people, but it is not proof against the isolation brought about by real or imagined hostility. The former is a restorative process; the latter is purely destructive.

V

IMPERIAL RULE

From 83 onwards a broadly chronological narrative can be given of the major events of Domitian's reign, but there are some topics which do not readily slot into such a framework and in consequence are best dealt with thematically. Domitian's administration, his financial and legislative measures, his relationship with the Senate and the equites, the people and the army, are matters which permeate the whole of his reign, and cannot be properly illustrated by a few chronological landmarks inserted into a year-by-year account.

Domitian's attitude to his role and the power he wielded is generally seen as authoritarian, autocratic to the point of despotism, even ridiculous. His real powers rested on his *tribunicia potestas*, his consulships, his appointment as *censor perpetuus* and, naturally, his command of the armies and his *imperium maius* which gave him supremacy over all military commanders and provincial governors. Augustus had been shrewdly capable of retaining all these attributes of power while still maintaining the fiction that his *potestas* was merely equal to that of any other senator. He relied on his *auctoritas*, authority without strictly coercive power, to preside over the Senate. Domitian did not subscribe to this fiction, and chose to emphasize, or at least not to disguise, his *potestas*. He underlined it in various significant ways, one of them highly controversial. He decided, perhaps in 86, upon the title *dominus et deus*. *Dominus* in itself was not so offensive; it probably meant nothing more than 'sir', without any connotation of autocratic mastery. Augustus had rejected the use of such a title, and though it seems that at first Domitian did so too, he was later accustomed to begin his letters in true autocratic style with the phrase, 'Our Master and God'. It cannot be known precisely what Domitian intended to convey by this means. As a written formula *dominus et deus* may have had less impact than it would have had as a spoken title, and it cannot be ascertained whether Domitian insisted on its use as a form of address. After the tyrant was murdered in 96, Pliny obviously found no incongruity in reviling Domitian for his use of the title, while at the same time addressing Trajan as *domine*; it is probable that had Trajan insisted upon it, no one would have found it difficult to address him as *deus* as well. The populace of Rome probably did not find it disagreeable to call Domitian and Domitia 'lord and lady': in the amphitheatre on feast days they shouted *'Domino et dominae feliciter'* without apparent coercion. It was the lengths to which Domitian went in insisting on respect and reverence that finally offended Roman dignity, or at least that of the upper classes. He demanded obeisance, if Pliny is to be believed, to remind people of their relative status. It is said that the Emperor Gaius Caligula had demanded the same obeisance – if true, this would have been an unfortunate precedent, given that by Domitian's reign the traditional opinion of Gaius was highly unfavourable. There are those who deny that Domitian ever insisted upon either the title of lord and god or the bowing and perhaps oriental style foot-kissing that went with it. There is no way of knowing; only that after his death, men remembered their real or imagined subjection with distaste.[1]

Further reminders of the supreme authority vested in Domitian and of the gulf between him and his subjects came in the form of the decree that no statues of him should be erected except in gold, and the renaming of the months of September and October as Germanicus and Domitianus. The literary sources cannot agree about the inception of these new names. Suetonius says it took place after Domitian's two triumphs, but the triumphs themselves are not without chronological problems. Eusebius, Hieronymus and Dio place the events early in the reign, but Martial and Statius only refer to the new names towards the end, about 94 or 95. There were precedents for appropriating parts of the calendar, of course, in that July and August owe their names to Caesar and Augustus. These names, however, are still with us whereas those introduced by Domitian were dropped after his murder.[2]

The Imperial cult was another means of underlining power, used by all Emperors and observed throughout the Empire. The Flavian *gens* had its own temple in Rome and its own cult with priests to observe worship. Deification and worship of dead ancestors was an accepted procedure with an established history. There is considerable epigraphic evidence for the activities of the priests of the Flavian cult, though the very abundance of inscriptions creates problems over terminology. There were *sodales Flaviales*, *sodales Flaviales Titiales* and *seviri Flaviales*, the latter presumably modelled upon the *seviri Augustales* – some display both titles, as in three inscriptions which mention a *sevir Augustalis Flavialis*. It is not known whether these represented successive amalgamations of the colleges of priests as first Vespasian and then Titus were deified, or whether there were different colleges all observing worship at the same time. Scott believed that Domitian was responsible for the establishment of the Flavian cult throughout the Roman world, and that worship was kept up until the close of the second century, despite the *damnatio memoriae* of the last of the Flavians. The cult included most members of the Flavian *gens*: an inscription from Padua attests a priest of the cult of Diva Domitilla, Vespasian's daughter, while another attests the cult of the divine Julia.[3]

It would seem that Domitian took his power very seriously, anxious lest anyone forget it or try to undermine it. The crucial factor in an assessment of him is whether or not he seriously believed in himself as Emperor and living god, son of Minerva and associate of Jupiter, or whether he was playing the role as he thought it should be played. The inhabitants of the eastern provinces were accustomed to the idea of worship of a divine ruler, and were willing to subscribe to the worship of a living Roman Emperor. Vespasian had made use of this device to shore up his power, but no one would accuse such an earth-bound realist of actually believing himself divine. Domitian's belief is another matter. Sober judgement dictates that he cannot have thought of himself as a god; to accept that he did necessitates a more detailed examination of his sanity. His adherence to Minerva was both sincere and profound, declared unequivocally on his coinage, in the temples that he built – one of them in the Forum Transitorium – and the festivals that he arranged in her honour. But in this he was unusual only in the degree of his attachment to his chosen goddess. There was a noble precedent in Gaius Julius Caesar's attachment to Venus, from whom he claimed descent. Since there was already a monopoly on this goddess, Domitian could have chosen no better alternative than Minerva, an important member of the Capitoline triad, goddess of war and the arts. In addition, as supreme ruler of the Roman world, Domitian equated himself with the supreme god, Jupiter Optimus Maximus. He had no objection to the regular custom adopted by the court poets of comparing him to Jupiter, Hercules and so on, but this does not mean that he believed what was said of him, only that he thought it a necessary part of statesmanship. *L'etat, c'est moi* is not a concept confined to Louis XIV of France. Preservation of personal authority and preservation of the state are closely intertwined and, for this purpose, external appearance is everything. Tiberius compared controlling the state to holding a wolf by the ears. Much later, another autocrat who rose to power after revolution and upheaval admitted in private conversations that he was playing a part and knew it. In exile on St Helena, Napoleon concurred with Tiberius, also describing himself as Emperor of the French struggling to hold a taut spring. In either case relaxation for one instant would bring disaster. Domitian would probably have sympathized. What he sought was absolute control, for which purpose power was indispensable. It is a narrow distinction, since control and power amount to much the same thing, but there is a world of difference between the exercise of power for its own sake and control intended, however misguidedly, for the ultimate good of the state. The tragedy is that the best intentions can cause untold suffering. It was Che Guevara who said that without power a regime cannot establish itself, and with power it rarely survives. Perhaps this is what Domitian discovered for himself.[4]

If he had been a little less distant and a little more flexible he might have been able to overcome the problems inherent in ruling the Empire. Trajan was no less authoritarian and autocratic than Domitian, but he struck the correct note from the first and never stopped sounding it; the changes that came about when he became Emperor were not profound, but seemed as if they were, because the whole of life changed its complexion. Augustus too was arguably just as much of an autocrat, but he had the tact and flexibility to accommodate the Senate – qualities which Domitian either never had or, more likely, abandoned as a lost cause. Modesty and simplicity in external appearance, in all its forms, were the key to Augustus' success, but there was just as much showmanship in this simplicity as there was in Domitian's magnificence. Domitian was concerned to do nothing sordid, in the sense both of corrupt practice and of shabbiness in appearance. He would have agreed with, perhaps he had even read, the sentiments expressed in Aristotle's *Nichomachaean Ethics*: 'The magnificent prince is interested in how he can achieve the finest and most appropriate results, rather than how much it will cost and how it can be done most cheaply. The magnificent man is a connoisseur, with an eye for what is fitting, and can spend large sums with good taste, not upon himself but upon public objects.'[5]

Magnificence extended to Domitian's rebuilding of the temple of Jupiter on the Capitol, already described, and to the Imperial residence on the Palatine, the Domus Augustana (or Augustiana) Domitiana, which rivalled Nero's Golden House in size and excellence. Construction probably went on all through Domitian's reign, the monumental entrance being built towards the end of his life. The palace was vast, incorporating some Neronian work as well as the older Tiberian palace. Perhaps the most impressive remains visible today are those of the so-called stadium, a sunken garden to the east of the private apartments. Dominating the centre of the main residential area was the peristyle described by Suetonius, richly decorated and lined with slabs of stone, highly polished to make their surfaces mirror-like, so that Domitian could see anyone coming up behind him as he walked there.[6]

The extent of the palace, covering most of the Palatine Hill, as well as its opulence, may have been one of Domitian's constructions uppermost in Tacitus' mind when he wrote that the splendour of the city did not lie in its buildings, things without life that come and go, but in the continued existence of the Senate. Domitian was not prepared to work closely with the Senate and kept the senators out of his private life. He never assembled them in his Imperial residence, as other Emperors had done in the past. According to Juvenal he admitted members of his *consilium* to the Alban villa but he may well have felt, having rebuilt the Senate House, that that was the proper place for meetings. This would be in keeping with his preference for doing things in the proper manner, and with his need for distance from the Senate.[7]

His relationship with this body is central to his reign and reputation, and has been the subject of a special study by Brian Jones. The surviving record of Domitian is almost wholly senatorial; there is no other literary tradition and no defence counsel for Domitian to present his own point of view. A biased account is of necessity selective, involving suppression of facts detrimental to the self-styled good party or favourable to the villain, and emphasis of those facts which enhance the virtues of the good and the wickedness of the villain. It is plain that Domitian and the Senate were not compatible, but they were not in a position to obtain a divorce and go their separate ways. There is very little evidence of how Domitian acted when attending meetings of the Senate. Epictetus describes a Senate paralysed by a tyrannical Emperor, while Pliny complains of the triviality of debates. There was a general feeling of powerlessness, which Domitian, unlike other Emperors, did not bother to alleviate.

Extraction of a balanced view about Domitian and the Senate is impossible without alternative source material. Complete exoneration of the tyrant is neither feasible nor realistic, nor on the other hand can the Senate be held up as a model of innocence. There are credits and debits on both sides, but whether either side was justified in its opinion of the other cannot be ascertained, especially since justification is so often dependent upon a pre-determined set of values. Modern scholars are constrained by the deficit of information, and by their understandable inability to escape their own social moulds and think like a Roman senator of the first century. It has been pointed out that at no time was the whole of the Senate opposed to the Principate in general or to Domitian in particular, and that when opposition came it was from a vocal minority, either the philosophers, or a group of men who did not object to absolutism as such, merely to its abuse. This is one reason why Domitian emerges as a tyrant and Trajan as a paragon; the dividing line is very fine. It is permissible to add that opposition arose when the system did not work to the immediate personal advantage of the objectors.[8]

Nevertheless, something went badly wrong between Domitian and the Senate, and continued to worsen. It cannot be accounted for merely by reference to the necessity under Nerva and Trajan of vilifying the previous regime. This form of discrediting the predecessor is quite normal when a new ruler comes to power in dubious circumstances involving the death of the previous incumbent, but the virulence of the post-Domitianic literary tradition, even when some of the wilder stories are discounted, leaves a residue of a problem, or at best a gross misunderstanding. In his study of this problem, Jones concluded that at first Domitian co-operated with the Senate and tried to conciliate the more distant elements in an effort to gain support. His attempts to overcome the opposition by friendly means are attested by his appointments to the suffect consulship of Helvidius Priscus the younger, at some date before 87 or possibly in 93, and of Arulenus Rusticus, a supporter of the renowned Thrasea Paetus, as late as 92. He admitted non-Flavians to the ordinary consulships, and promoted non-Romans in both equestrian and senatorial posts. Thus Jones concludes that Domitian showed no unreasonable bias in his appointments, but that he finally came to the conclusion that complete conciliation was not possible. The precise juncture at which this came about, and how his attitude changed, is not established. Even the ancient authors could not agree on this, since it is wholly dependent upon opinion.[9]

As censor, Domitian had control over membership of the Senate. Later Emperors exercised censorial functions without the benefit of the title. Little is known of how Domitian used the censorship. It empowered him to supervise the morals and financial status of all members and, in addition, both to dismiss senators who did not meet the specific requirements and to admit new men who did. He ejected one man for acting in pantomimes, unbecoming to senatorial dignity and, despite popular appeals, refused to reinstate Palfurius Sura, who had been expelled by Vespasian. In adlections to the Senate, he exercised some discretion. Vespasian and Titus had already admitted many new members, and Domitian encouraged the admission of provincials, especially easterners. This was not an innovation of his own but a continuation of Flavian policy. The first suffect consuls of eastern origin appeared in the reign of Titus, and in Domitian's reign there was a definite increase in the numbers of orientals gaining admission to the Senate.[10]

Though there were *Senatus Consulta* passed during his reign, the Senate as an instrument of power was largely ignored by Domitian. Its executive power at this date was negligible, and despite the reconciliation effected by Trajan it never regained any strong influence thereafter. There are cases where an Emperor wrote directly to a provincial governor or another official without conferring with the Senate first. In some instances, speed would be of paramount importance and there would not be time to debate the issue, but in 88/9 when Domitian wrote directly to the proconsul of Cyrene, authorizing him to delineate land boundaries, it is likely that the matter could have been presented to the Senate for consideration without jeopardizing matters in the province. Even Nero had managed to include the Senate in deliberation of a simliar matter of land divisions in Crete. It is highly likely that in senatorial business, the initiative always sprang from the Emperor, accompanied by all the attendant nuances of subtle control to ensure that the debate concluded in the way he wanted. But the tiresome drawbacks of waiting while points were constitutionally debated, even though there was only minimal risk of everything going contrary to his wishes, may well have deterred Domitian from submitting matters for consideration. Thus a circular, self-perpetuating problem could have been created, whereby Domitian's increasing impatience and unwillingness to submit important matters to the Senate would leave its members with only trivia to discuss, which in turn would decrease his respect for the senators and ensure that he left them with less and less responsibility. The situation is hypothetical, but probable. For some senators, a sense of powerlessness would be compounded by a feeling of uselessness. If Domitian had been able to foster the myth of autonomy among the senators, he might have enjoyed a better posthumous reputation.[11]

The proceedings of the Senate were not without some importance to Domitian. Perhaps in order to monitor debates, he may have revived the post of *ab actis Senatus*, the keeper of records of all that was said in debates. This post is first mentioned by Tacitus in his account of the year 29, so it may have been an innovation of Augustus or Tiberius. The latter was absent from Rome for much of his reign, and required some means of keeping himself up to date. The post seems to have lapsed after his reign, but since Domitian familiarized himself with all that Tiberius did, and since he too was absent from the city for long periods, it may have been one of his measures that revived it. The *acta Senatus*, which were deposited in the *aerarium Saturni*, were probably not verbatim records of debates, but were more likely written as synopses of the main points; their form is disputed. L. Neratius Marcellus, quaestor under Domitian and suffect consul in 95, is attested as *curator actorum Senatus* at some time in his career, suggesting that the terminology for his post was not yet established, for by the second century, it was more usually described as *ab actis Senatus*.[12]

It has been suggested that one factor which may have led to a rupture with the Senate was Domitian's advancement of members of the equestrian class, sometimes in preference to freedmen administrative staff, and sometimes in areas hitherto considered the exclusive preserve of senators. Domitian's measures with regard to the equites are described as the foundation of the equestrian career structure supposedly regularized by Hadrian. Various attacks have been made on this theory, questioning the historical development of equestrian careers and whether there was in fact a strictly regimented career structure at all. Another point for debate is whether there was serious rivalry between senators and equites. This is taken for granted in many modern works, but if there was a sense of competition and rivalry between the two orders, it does not find its way into the contemporary ancient literature. Though promotion of equites at senatorial expense may have disgruntled a few senators, there was no bar to social mobility – freedmen could be promoted to equestrian status, and it was accepted and perfectly legal procedure to allow equestrians to enter the Senate.[13]

From small beginnings in the first century, equestrians rose to greater prominence in governmental posts in the second century. The reasons for the choice of equites and the relative expertise they brought to their posts have been examined by more than one scholar. One theory is that equestrians were more loyal, and that this is primarily what Emperors looked for. Domitian's letter to Laberius Maximus, calling him to Rome to fill the vacant post of praetorian prefect, mentions *fides* and *pietas*. Other factors such as good character and ability were advantageous, but since initially most equestrians entered public life as unknown quantities, patronage would also pay a large part in their careers, followed by Imperial favour if this could be sustained. This favour could presumably be lost after transgressions. Brunt questioned the loyalty theory, pointing to the numbers of equestrians who fell from favour or were involved in plots. He also questioned the need for special skills or knowledge in holders of equestrian posts, concluding that this was not a prerequisite in an Emperor's decisions concerning appointments. Brunt demonstrated that the prefects of Egypt had no previous knowledge of the country, no special financial, legal or military backgrounds that would have suited them ideally to the post, and nor did their subordinate staffs. Indeed, from an account by Dio, it seems that equites were chosen as all-rounders, co-operative, willing and capable of doing anything. It may have been this quality that appealed to Domitian. Perhaps there were fewer 'prima donnas' among equites than among senators. The tasks given to some equestrians were frequently of a nature that would have been repugnant to senators, and so it cannot be said that equites encroached to any large extent upon senatorial preserve. Nor did Domitian employ equites in a wholesale removal of Imperial freedmen from the central administration; for some time the two classes worked side by side. Equestrians filled gaps in administrative procedures of all kinds, sometimes overlapping both low- and high-grade appointments. In so far as Domitian can be said to have adopted a definite policy towards equestrians, it may have been the purely practical one of appointing the best man for the job in hand. Some of these appointees happened to be equestrians, a fortuitous arrangement rather than a deliberate search for men of this class in preference to any other social rank. This is an egalitarian approach, possibly derived from genuine concern for equality, but just as likely to derive from a kind of indifference. Domitian has been accused of lack of sensitivity to senatorial feelings, a lack which probably extended to equestrians, freedmen, populace and slaves. He may have been totally insensitive to all ranks because as far as he was concerned they were all equally beneath him; on the other hand, if his sensitivity amounted to an understanding of social differences, he may have subordinated this to the overriding need to achieve his purpose, that of successfully completing the necessary tasks. He probably expected everyone else to subordinate their inner feelings to the same ends, and became impatient when they refused to comply.[14]

It remains to examine the evidence for Domitian's advancement of equites. The posts open to equestrians were varied. The four great prefectures, of the *vigiles*, the *annona*, Egypt and the praetorian guard were the loftiest and most prestigious posts, while in the army and in the provincial and central administration a number of places of greater or lesser importance were available. Domitian employed one or two equestrians in unusual ways. His promotion of L. Julius Ursus via the command of the praetorian guard to senator, and then to suffect consul in 84 hints at favouritism. The reconstruction of Ursus' career is based on evidence derived from three separate sources, considered by some scholars to refer to the same man. The letter from Domitian to Laberius Maximus promoting him from prefect of Egypt to praetorian prefect makes it clear that a certain Julius [Ur]sus, the outgoing praetorian prefect, had been asking for advancement for some time. He may be the same Julius Ursus who spoke on behalf of Domitia when she was banished from court, and for whom Julia interceded when he had temporarily fallen into disfavour. If so, then he is a special case, probably atypical of Domitian's attitude to equestrians. There is more to be derived from his appointment of Cornelius Fuscus, the praetorian prefect, to the overall command in the Dacian war, a post which would normally have been entrusted to a senator of consular rank. The choice of Fuscus is revealing: regardless of conventional procedure or the dictates of hierarchical rank, Domitian chose the man he considered best suited for the task. A few senatorial feathers may have been ruffled; they were probably sanctimoniously smoothed again when Fuscus met with disaster. Another instance where Domitian appointed the man best able to deal with the situation occurred in 87 or 88, when the equestrian C. Minicius Italus, procurator of Asia, took over the duties of the proconsul Vettulenus Civica Cerialis when the latter was executed for reasons unknown. The execution is a mystery. It is not known for certain how he was dispatched, or whether he killed himself in obedience to Imperial will. It will not suffice to assume that he was innocent, but the way in which he was dealt with is also suspect. Even if he had been blatantly guilty of some crime, he ought to have been subjected to due process of the law, and recalled to Rome to answer charges. Senators cannot have failed to remember parallels that had occurred under Nero, not least the fate of Domitian's own father-in-law, Corbulo. Domitian's arrangements to fill the post were novel. An inscription attests that Minicius Italus was appointed on the orders of the Emperor (*proc. provinciae Asiae quam mandatu principis vice defuncti procos. rexit*). In the circumstances, he was the man most qualified for the task, since he was in the province and presumably experienced in at least some of its business. He could be allowed to get on with the process of government until the affair died down, and the next proconsul could be appointed via the normal methods. This equestrian appointment would not be a permanent fixture but, even without the added scandal of the execution of the proconsul, it may have been regarded as an ominous precedent. Rivalry between senators and equites was not the keynote, nor the whole story; senatorial fear of redundancy would perhaps be nearer the mark.[15]

To label the central administrative posts as part of the Imperial civil service is convenient but misleading, for it evokes in modern minds a hierarchical, tightly structured and salaried organization which the Romans of Domitian's day would not have recognized. The central administration had grown up empirically from Republican times and the Imperial *officia* were reorganized by Claudius, who classified and then divided up most of the operations into sections. He did not create a completely new administration nor new officials, but rationalized existing procedures. Finances, that is the income from Imperial estates and other sources, were under an official called *a rationibus*; legal matters were the preserve of *a cognitionibus*, who prepared papers on all cases coming before the Emperor. There were three kinds of personal secretary, *a studiis*, who was in charge of the Emperor's private library, perhaps providing an immediate information service, *a libellis,* who took charge of petitions presented to the Emperor, and *ab epistulis*, whose title indicates that the holder took charge of letters, presumably both incoming and outgoing, and many other duties besides.[16]

These posts were initially filled by freedmen, of whose number Narcissus and Pallas, the famous – or infamous – Claudian secretaries, have become for modern scholars the archetypal examples. During his brief reign Vitellius appointed an equestrian to the post of *a libellis*. There was no time for Vitellius to pursue this further, so it cannot be said whether he had formulated a policy on this matter. Nor is the evidence extensive enough to draw definite conclusions about Domitian's policy, though there are some widely different examples of equestrian appointments made during his reign which seem to support the idea that he favoured and intended to promote the whole class. As for the central administration, Suetonius noted the appointment of both freedmen and equites to the same posts under Domitian, and in this context the fate of both classes must be discussed together.[17]

Early in his reign, perhaps in 82 or 83, Domitian dismissed the financial secretary, Tiberius Julius Augusti libertus, a freedman who had served Vespasian and Titus as *a rationibus*. This official was in charge of the income from Imperial estates and other payments into the *fiscus* or privy purse, but he also had responsibility for estimating public expenses. Statius indicates that both public and private expenses were within the brief of the *a rationibus* when he speaks flamboyantly of control of the revenue of the whole world and the wealth of every race, all submitted to the charge of Tiberius Julius. One of the most important functions of the financial secretary was to advise on the amount of coinage to be issued. The dismissal of Tiberius Julius provides one instance where Domitian was not content to perpetuate his father's arrangements. It is not known what had happened – embezzlement has been suggested, but there is no evidence. Punishment for something as serious as embezzlement ought to have been severe, but it has been suggested that Domitian refrained from such a step because of Tiberius Julius' family connections. He was probably related by marriage to Tettius Julianus and Tettius Africanus, respectively legate of the African army and governor of Egypt, and therefore in a powerful position, being in virtual command of Rome's grain supply. The implication is that Domitian would not risk antagonizing these two men. On the other hand it has also been suggested that he removed Tiberius Julius precisely in order to neutralize such a concentration of potential power. Such polarized speculation has not yet elucidated the reason why the experienced financial secretary was sent into a comfortable exile in Campania, being eventually recalled to Rome, where he died at the age of ninety. After his death Statius addressed a poem to Tiberius Julius' son, Claudius Etruscus, who had become an equestrian. No reasons for the exile or for the recall are to be found in the poem, save for the tactful hints of weary old age, exhaustion through work, or Fortune having temporarily departed, which may imply a slight transgression. Close connection with Titus is an unlikely reason for Domitian to banish him; the problem was more likely a personal clash between the two men.[18]

About seven years after the removal of Tiberius Julius, Domitian also dismissed the second in command to the financial secretary; Statius makes it seem as though the two events were related, but the lengthy time gap weighs heavily against any connection. This time the penalty was more serious – banishment from Italy, not just from Rome. The two dismissals indicate that Domitian was keenly interested in the finance department, and that he rigorously monitored its performance. It is not without interest that he also dismissed, early in his reign, the procurator *castrensis*, Tiberius Claudius Augusti libertus Classicus, the official whose domain was the financial accounting of the Imperial household. The incidents may have been purely coincidental, or they may provide strong hints of an absolute perfectionist at work. Domitian had high and inflexible standards, for which others perhaps did not display sufficient enthusiasm. He was liberal at first, cancelling debts to the Treasury (*aerarium*) and refusing inheritances payable into the *fiscus* where surviving children would be compromised, thus reducing potential income. Next he seriously increased expenditure, beginning to overhaul the mint towards the end of 82, less than a year after his accession, and raising the standard of the coinage to the level of Augustan times. Then he embarked upon his lavish building programme and, in 83, introduced a massive 33 per cent pay-rise for the army. Tiberius Julius had served under the careful and parsimonious Vespasian; his sharp intake of breath is very nearly still audible. His dismissal may simply be due to the fact that Domitian wanted total control and would not brook the slightest opposition, which by his definition perhaps included whispered doubts and disagreeable facial expressions. There is no hint as to who the replacement *a rationibus* was, but modern scholars have suggested a certain Atticus, another freedman. It cannot be stated that Domitian expressed any preference for equestrians in his financial departments until further evidence comes to light.[19]

In one of the other administrative departments, Domitian replaced the freedman Abascantus, *ab epistulis*, with the equestrian Titinius Capito. This belongs to a later period of his reign, and Capito continued in his post under Nerva and Trajan. It is not known for certain what happened to Abascantus. He may have been given another post, since an inscription attests a man of this name as *a cognitionibus*, but there may have been two Abascanti. The *ab epistulis* Abascantus is known to us from Statius' poem offering lengthy condolences on the death of his wife. The poet describes the duties of the *ab epistulis* – nothing less than keeping a finger on the pulse of the whole Empire. Allowing for poetic licence, there was probably a need for considerable and wide-ranging knowledge in this post, and also for continuity. As far as decision-making was concerned, it is not known how far the secretaries were involved. They certainly wrote letters, but there is little information as to whether they actually composed them or merely took notes from dictation and were then responsible for producing neat copies, sending out and receiving correspondence, and perhaps filing notes about decisions taken and replies received. This procedure could in any case have varied from reign to reign, depending largely upon the personalities of both the Emperor and his secretarial staff and the relationship between them. Millar assumes that dictation by the Emperor was the normal method of writing letters, thereby excluding the secretaries from any power of decision and preventing them from gaining too much influence. But this is such an insidious and uncontrollable matter that it would be surprising if there had been any hard and fast means of preventing personal influence from growing.[20]

All the departments of the central administration would have employed subordinate staffs of slaves and lower ranking freedmen, perhaps not very many, but there is little information about numbers. One or two names are known of other staff in the Imperial administration, but it is difficult to be certain of their rank. In some cases it is quite uncertain whether the named personnel were heads of departments or merely underlings working in that department. Another problem arises from the slight blurring of distinctions between the administrative staff and those of the Imperial household, much like the administrative and domestic systems of most European medieval kings. It is only in modern parlance, with its ready acceptance of job descriptions and strict demarcations, that any clear division is expected. The domestic side of Imperial administration is harder to understand, not only because the structure may have varied subtly from one reign to the next, but also because there is no complete list of all posts at any one time, and the hierarchy and duties of the ones that are known are not at all certain. A career inscription of Tiberius Claudius Aug. lib. Bucolas reveals that he had held a number of posts, possibly beginning his career under Vespasian or Titus: *praegustator, triclinarius, procurator a muneribus, procurator aquarum, procurator castrensis*. The first two in this list, food-taster and supervisor of the dining table, may have been quite lowly but Bucolas next became procurator of the Imperial games, was then put in charge of the aqueducts, and finally became *procurator castrensis*, possibly replacing Classicus, though the dating is not secure.[21]

From the literary sources, a few names of Domitian's palace staff have survived. Parthenius is attested in Suetonius and mentioned by Martial and the Epitomator of Aurelius

Victor. He was *cubiculo praepositus*, usually translated as chamberlain. This was an important and highly influential post for the incumbent would naturally be close to the Emperor, acting as a filter for anyone wanting to approach him. No one could expect to proceed to an interview or to obtain a favour without knowing the chamberlain. Since bribery was not so frowned upon in the Roman world as it is now, it was a prime post for personal enrichment. Martial addressed Parthenius to ask him to bring his poems to Domitian's notice, and he cannot have been the only author to do so. Parthenius was reputedly a favourite of Domitian's since he was allowed to wear a dagger, an honour normally granted only to generals. Nevertheless, he was one of Domitian's assassins. In the position that he occupied, Parthenius faced only two choices, to be killed to ensure his silence if he opposed the murder of his master or to join the conspirators and allow events to take their course. He survived until 97, when the Praetorians demanded revenge, and killed him brutally, taking great care to mutilate him first. Stephanus, the man named as the real murderer of Domitian, was not a member of the Emperor's staff, but was a procurator, or steward, of Domitilla, the daughter of Domitian's sister. Staff in the Imperial palace would no doubt have been very numerous. Domitia Longina would have employed her own establishment, and so would Julia when she came to live there. The higher ranking staff members would have had their own staffs, as well; Maximus, a freedman of Parthenius, was present when Domitian was murdered.[22]

Jones suggests that Domitian would not tolerate domestics who had been attached to Titus, and that this is the true meaning of Dio's statement that he 'regarded as his enemy anyone who had enjoyed his father's or his brother's affection beyond the ordinary'. The normal interpretation of this passage is that Dio referred to senatorial and equestrian officials, but perhaps the description was intended to embrace all categories of personnel. If Domitian removed Titus' domestic staff in favour of his own, it possibly reveals a lack of trust, but there may also have been an element of loyalty to his existing staff. As an Imperial prince, he too would already have employed a circle of slaves and freedmen and may have wanted to ensure that they still had a place when he became Emperor. He was thirty years old, perhaps not yet set in his ways, but surely more comfortable with staff he already knew. This hardly constitutes tyranny. Had his reputation emerged unsullied, Titus' associates would probably have been forgotten, and the retention of Domitian's own staff would have been hailed as an example of his constancy.[23]

Domitian's central and provincial administration has been both praised for its efficiency and philanthropic care, and discredited for its injustice and corruption. The existing evidence is neither extensive enough nor sufficiently unequivocal to draw firm conclusions entirely uninfluenced by opinion. Debate has focused on Suetonius' statement that Domitian restrained city officials and provincial governors, so that at no time were they more honest or just, whereas under later Emperors, many men were prosecuted for all manner of offences. This can be taken at face value or investigated more closely in an endeavour to reveal implications that are not immediately obvious. Lack of prosecutions for *repetundae* could indeed have resulted from a complete absence of extortionate practices. Empire-wide prosperity and contentment is what Statius would have us believe, all due to Domitian's shrewd choice of governors and provincial officials, who were either innately honest or cowed into obedience by the Emperor's all-seeing eye. Modern minds tend to be sceptical. There is only one trial known from Domitian's reign, when Pliny and

C.Herennius Senecio successfully prosecuted the governor of Hispania Baetica, Baebius Massa, in 93. If there were other trials, there is at present no evidence of them, but this may be purely accidental; absence of evidence is not evidence of absence. In any case, the lack of prosecutions is not necessarily a point to be used in Domitian's favour. Since such litigation was, in the main, politically orientated, it may be that Domitian's attitude discouraged the whole process. There must be an expectation of success to encourage prosecution. A stultifying inertia may have arisen; Pliny implies that Domitian neither punished offenders nor rewarded good conduct. It was all the more enterprising then of Pliny and Herennius Senecio to undertake the prosecution of Baebius Massa, who was allegedly one of Domitian's favourites. Here is the paradox: if Domitian actively discouraged prosecutions and oppressed the Senate, how did the oppressed feel free to prosecute one of Domitian's favoured officials as late as 93?[24]

Roman government was carried out mainly to the advantage of the provincial élite, who were usually the agents of Rome in their own territories. In order to protect the provincial population from unfair exploitation, legal machinery for the prosecution of governors who misgoverned had been instituted during the Republic and survived into the Empire, but for a variety of reasons was not always enforced. Whilst in office, an official could not be prosecuted. After the expiry of his term of service, the provincial council (*concilium*) could set in motion a case for prosecution which must face several hurdles before it came to court. Even if the outcome was successful, and condemnation of the official resulted, the provincials would not automatically gain restitution or compensation for their wrongs. The expense of sending representatives to Rome and waiting for a judgement probably deterred all but the most desperate from embarking on such a procedure. The lack of prosecutions in Domitian's reign may mean that the degree of extortion and other practices damaging to the provincials never exceeded a certain level. It is unlikely that Emperors concerned themselves with the lot of the common folk and, as Brunt points out, they generally turned a blind eye to exploitation provided that it was carried out intelligently. Therefore Domitian's all-seeing eye perhaps did not eradicate extortion in the provinces but merely ensured that everyone took greater care than usual not to be caught *in flagrante delicto*.[25]

The documentary evidence suggests that whenever he discovered injustices or inefficiency, Domitian responded correctly, and decreed in no uncertain terms that the practices should stop. He obviously prided himself on his legislation, and felt justified in thinking himself successful as a ruler. It is important to note that commensurate with the information that reached him, he probably was justified. Accurate information would have been of the utmost importance to an Emperor whose jurisdiction extended over such a large extent of the known world, and it is in this one vital aspect of his rule that Domitian's self-image was most vulnerable. Studies of the nature of power reveal that in any organization, promotion often depends on presenting a good case to the ruling body. The higher up one goes in an organization, the less realistic becomes the view of the outside world, because information is either finely sieved to remove unpalatable elements, or subtly altered in some way so that, on delivery, whilst not exactly full of untruths, it is still not accurate. Examples of this phenomenon include Stalin's completely unrealistic view of what was happening on Soviet collective farms, all due to fear of telling him the truth and the dire consequences meted out to those who tried. Stalin has a tyrannical reputation, but another case, hardly concerning a tyrant on the Domitianic scale, is the filtering of information about the Vietnam War before it reached President Lyndon Johnson. Such tampering with information is not always a result of the tyrant's inability or unwillingness to listen; it is a natural consequence of hierarchical organizations, however small, compounded in the case of the Roman Empire by factors such as the wide diversity of provinces and customs, and long, slow communications.[26]

A few pieces of documentary evidence have been cited in support of Domitian's benevolence towards provincials, but none of the documents constitute irrefutable proof. They all attest meticulous attention to detail, but this does not guarantee either efficiency or good and humane government. Running through each piece of evidence there is the constant theme of rigidly conservative respect for the absolute letter of the law. The direct, personal intervention of Domitian himself is not always obvious. One of the documents, the edict of the governor Antistius Rusticus, probably had nothing to do with the Emperor, except in so far as the author of it acted as his agent. Antistius was governor of Galatia-Cappadocia at a time of severe famine; the inhabitants of Pisidian Antioch asked him to ensure that the *coloni* and *incolae* of the city declared how much grain they held in store, so that it could be sold at a fair price. Levick has shown that the edict was quite unlikely to have originated with Domitian, since there would not have been time to send to Rome and wait for an instruction, but must owe its origin to the initiative of the governor. It displays fairness and concern for the provincials, but is only marginal proof of Domitian's pervasive influence. [27]

A Greek inscription from Acmonia (Phrygia) concerns the endowments left to his native city by Titus Flavius Praxias. The Emperor's ruling was sought to ensure the fair and correct usage of the money but this may be no more than a mechanical interest in proper practice. Even Domitian's apologists admit that there was no element of fostering the interests of the ordinary provincials, since the chief beneficiaries of the endowments would be the city councillors who had sought the Emperor's support. The document that is most revealing of Domitian at work is the record of his orders to the procurator Claudius Athenodorus in Syria. He refers to the laws of Vespasian concerning the requisition of transport animals and lodgings, laws which have not been enforced, to the distress of the provincials. If allowed to continue, the current illegal practices would create dangerous precedents. Domitian therefore decreed that there should be a return to the old order, reminding everyone that requisition was allowed only by written permit from the Emperor. The emphasis is on complete centralized control, adherence to the law and – mostly – upon sanctity of Imperial prerogative, but these are surely minor faults compared to the possible alternative of failing to do anything about abuses.[28]

The documents discussed so far derive from the eastern provinces. Perhaps even more widely known are the three municipal charters from the Spanish *municipia* of Salpensa, Malaga, and a town probably called Irni, though its name is not definitely established. The first two documents were found in the nineteenth century; the last one was discovered in the 1980s. All are dated to Domitian's reign, but they contribute much more to the knowledge of municipal and provincial administration than they do to knowledge of Domitian, except that it is clear that he was following Vespasian's policy with characteristic thoroughness. Vespasian had granted Latin rights, generally regarded as the half-way house to full Roman citizenship, to several Spanish towns and cities. The laws clarify in minute detail the rights and duties of the municipal officials and populace. The city laws were modelled as far as possible on Rome itself, and allow for a great deal of autonomy in the government of each municipality. This would not conflict with Domitian's authority, as long as the laws were obeyed. This is clearly stated in the so-called letter of Domitian at the end of the *Lex Irnitana* but, as the text is incomplete, it is not certain whether it is Roman law in general or the municipal law that Domitian wished to stress. It scarcely matters; the principle is the same.[29]

Domitian's interest in the well-being of the provincials is not abundantly attested, beyond a certain disinterested, routine application of the law. He probably did not differ from other Emperors in this matter. Where he showed concern about the common people at all, his attitude can be explained away by reference to the state as a whole. Crushed, oppressed people do not produce foodstuffs or taxes. Hungry people tend to riot or form longer term plans for rebellion. It is in any ruler's interest to pay attention to the food supply. The famous vine edict was passed, not simply to reduce wine production, but in an attempt to increase the grain supply. The edict, which was applicable throughout the Empire, forbade the planting of new vines in Italy, and ordered the removal of half the vines in the provinces. Suetonius begins his description of this episode with the observation that Domitian considered that grain production was being neglected in favour of vine growing. There are conflicting theories about this law. Some authors have seen it as a puritanical attack against drunkeness caused by excessive wine consumption; others have seen the problem in a more modern light, in terms of the overall reduction of a wine lake, comparable to the current crisis of over-production in the twentieth century; yet others insist that the legislation was intended to reduce competition from the provinces and encourage Italian wine production, even though it is unlikely that Italian wine producers were suffering from provincial competition. The problem was precisely what Suetonius says it was, and Domitian was trying to encourage cereal growing. The plan was not a success, as Suetonius admits in two separate passages. According to Philostratus, the *concilium* of Asia appealed directly to Domitian about the edict, which was repealed. Attempts to demonstrate that the edict was still in force in Africa in the third century have been refuted.[30]

It would be surprising if extortionate practices and other abuses were completely eradicated all over the Empire. The revolt of the Nasamones who invaded the Syrtic region of Africa during Domitian's reign was said to have been caused by the over-zealous collection of taxes, and there is no real reason to doubt this. The corruption of the tax-collectors cannot be personally attributed to Domitian, but he did not seem to feel the slightest contrition, if the sources report his actions accurately. Rebellion that called for punishment, not injustice that called for reform, was all that he saw. He displayed a callous indifference to the fate of the natives. 'I have forbidden the Nasamones to exist,' he is reported to have said. He has been ridiculed by modern authors for imagining that his word was sufficient to obliterate a race, but it is probably only in modern eyes that the enormity of such a concept would be seen. Romans probably appreciated the witty remark, whilst making a mental note to find out who the Nasamones were.[31]

Imperial indifference probably extended to the populace of Rome. The attitude was mutual. When Domitian was murdered, the people received the news with no emotion and left it to the army to demand a belated revenge. Affairs of state had long since ceased to interest them, as Juvenal noted: the people who had once bestowed commands, con-sulships and the like now thought of two things only – bread and circuses. These two things Domitian gave them. As has been said above, the motive in keeping the people contented was not purely philanthropic but was rather a by-product of ensuring that none of the prime causes of discontent grew to riotous proportions. Domitian gave three *congiaria* of 300 sesterces each to the people during his reign, in 83, 89 and 93, celebrat-ing victories over the Chatti, the Dacians and Sarmatians. Pliny describes the people eagerly queuing up to glimpse the Emperor, who ignored them all. This is to contrast the worthy Trajan who of course did this sort of thing properly. Suetonius describes a feast day given by Domitian in Rome at the Septimontium, and devotes a whole section of his book to the games, shows and regular naval battles (*naumachia*) that Domitian arranged, at least one of which the Emperor attended in pouring rain. The people were not affected by Domitian's death, but it seems that they never had serious cause for com-plaint while he lived.[32]

VI
THE COST OF EMPIRE

The distinction between the state treasury (*aerarium*) and the Emperor's private income (*fiscus*) had begun to fade by Flavian times, and by the second century the two terms were almost synonymous. The merger was reciprocal. The state funds had passed into the control of the Emperor, but equally the Emperor's own income and property was absorbed into the public domain. Financial administration was in the hands of the Emperor alone, with the Senate and people relegated to the background. The letters SC (*Senatus consulto*, by decree of the Senate) still appeared on Domitian's bronze coins, representing the authority of the Senate, but this was at best a token gesture. Nerva and Trajan tactfully restored to the people and Senate nominal control of certain funds in what was still merely a gesture but one which was more gratifying than the eminently realistic attitude that Domitian displayed. Certain of his financial measures could be labelled purely practical, but his uncompromising common-sense approach was not tempered with the necessary time-wasting tact.[1]

The control of the coinage was also the preserve of the Emperor through the medium of his financial secretary, one of whose functions was to advise on the amount of coin to be issued. Statius may have exaggerated the duties of the *a rationibus* in order to write with a poetic flourish, but 'the link between provision of coinage and the management of finances' is clearly demonstrated in the poem. For the first few months of his reign, Domitian never departed from the standards and the designs of coinage that he inherited from Titus. Towards the end of 81, or at the beginning of 82, unrestricted by the possible disapproval of the banished *a rationibus* Tiberius Julius, Domitian turned his full attention to the coinage. The first of the new issues are dated to the spring of 82, a date established by the legend showing Domitian as COS VIII on the old coins of the Vespasianic standard, and the legend COS VIII DES VIIII on the new ones, of noticeably higher quality. It may have been during preliminary discussions about the projected reform that Tiberius Julius and Domitian found themselves at loggerheads. This is to enter the realms of pure speculation, but it would be compatible with Domitian's solitary and fiercely independent character to dismiss the old man and push through his reforms alone and unaided. From 82 to 84, minting of bronze coins ceased, while the fineness of the new gold and silver coins was much improved, and new designs of reverse types replaced all the old ones, with the exception of one. Gradually, between 82 and 85 depictions of the goddess Minerva formed the dominant design on the reverses of the denarii and aurei (pls. 12, 13). A new, smaller head of Domitian appeared on the obverses, wearing, according to Sutherland, an expression of 'critical disdain, of a kind familiar to the medallists of Louis XIV'.[2]

For three years these high standards prevailed, then in 85 there was a debasement of the fine metal content that took the coinage back to the Neronian standard of 64, which was still higher than the standard with which Vespasian and Titus had operated. The coinage remained at this level for the rest of Domitian's reign. Carradice remarks upon the quite astonishing degree of care which Domitian devoted to the maintainance of his coinage from 85 until his death; the systematic organization of production and the rigid adherence to high standards reflect Domitian's efficient but inflexible administration. The reasons for the debasement are not attested in any ancient source, leaving the matter open to modern speculation. Some scholars have envisaged a link between the debasement of the coinage and Domitian's increasing rapacity. It is postulated that some crisis arose which demanded the threefold response of debasement of currency, more stringent collection of taxes, and confiscation of property. All three elements are attested, but not necessarily in association, nor contemporaneously. Suetonius says that Domitian descended into cruelty sooner than he succumbed to greed, but no one can be certain that this chronology of events is correct. The confiscations are too well attested (though they are perhaps exaggerated in scale) to deny that they occurred. They were certainly in evidence towards the end of Domitian's reign, as attested by Pliny's story of Corellius Rufus, old and very sick, but determined to live through his constant pain at least one day longer than the Emperor in order to deprive the robber (*latronus*) of the pleasure of claiming his property. Confiscations were probably not a regular feature of Domitian's early years, being more likely to have been associated with the years of terror and the executions of the late 80s and 90s, though there is no absolute dating evidence. As for the onset of ruthless tax-gathering, this too has been dated to 85, on the flimsy grounds that as an adolescent, Suetonius (born *c.* 70, therefore aged 15 in 85) witnessed the examination of an old man to discover whether he was circumcised and therefore liable to pay tax to the *fiscus Judaicus*. With regard to dating evidence, this is not a strong argument: firstly, adolescence can be said to span several years and the date of Suetonius' birth is not accurately known, and secondly, the court case that Suetonius witnessed was not necessarily the very first case to be heard. It is probable that Domitian's approach to the collection of tax revenue was totally uncompromising from the first, and there is no need to postulate a horizon round about 85 beyond which his attitude hardened – his attitude was probably of the consistency of tungsten all along. To sum up, Domitian probably attended to taxation consistently from the beginning of his reign, then in 85 met with a crisis which required debasement of the coinage, and some time later began to confiscate properties, for a variety of reasons, only one of which may have been financial.[3]

The crisis that gave rise to the decision to debase the coinage may have been the outbreak of the Dacian war. This is not accurately dated – some scholars believe that the Dacians crossed the Danube and defeated Oppius Sabinus in the winter of 85/6, while others date the event to the winter of the previous year. Karl Strobel argued that the disaster occurred in June 85, and that the news reached Rome in the summer. The coinage reform was instituted between April and September 85; by the end of September or the beginning of October 85 Domitian was at the scene of operations on the Danube with Cornelius Fuscus. This proposed timetable is not firmly attested, but it is not out of the question. Devaluation of the coinage may have been associated with hasty preparations for war in the summer of 85. In normal circumstances, the Empire perhaps operated on partial credit, or deferred payment schemes, with the constant influx of tax revenues to support the system. In an emergency, such a system would be inoperable, since financing war on credit, especially a war in which the Emperor with no unequivocal heirs intends to take part in person, is riskier to the lender than financing building programmes or gladiatorial games. Such an emergency would depend for its resolution upon measures independent of taxation. The imposition of higher taxes, or even the institution of new taxes, would not bring instant cash; benefits would accrue too slowly to pay for the immediate necessities of war; they would be useful to pay for the aftermath, but not the preparation. It would also take considerable time to convert confiscated properties into cash. Reduction of the silver content of the denarius, however, would provide an immediate solution, using reserves ready to hand and at the same time economizing on silver. Purchase of stores and war *matériel*, animals for food and transport, manufacture of vehicles and so on would be greatly facilitated. Frontinus describes how Domitian paid compensation for the crops that were destroyed in the Chattan war in the early 80s when camps and forts were laid out over them. If he continued this policy in the Danube provinces – and it is probable that he did not intend to lay waste territories under Roman rule – then he would need money rapidly. Unfortunately, this is not reflected in the output of denarii for the years 85 to 87, which was not extraordinarily high compared to the output for the years 88 to 96, but there are three hindrances to the calculation of exact figures for coinage output. Firstly, estimations are derived from investigation of coin hoards, but the circumstances of deposition of hoards, and also of their discovery by archaeologists, are at best arbitrary. Secondly, it is not known how much coin was already in circulation at any time, which would have a direct influence upon the output of fresh coins. Thirdly, in the case of Domitian's production of denarii, it is not known whether the shortfall in silver was made up in payments in gold.[4]

Domitian steadfastly refused to devalue the currency further after 85 but succeeding Emperors did so, beginning with Trajan in 107, shortly after he had gained the proceeds of the gold-mines of Dacia. The management of the Imperial finances was not startlingly or consistently successful at the best of times, and Domitian's attempts to maintain the standard of the coinage should be judged against this background. The real aberration was his revaluation in 82, a bold step that could not be sustained. His refusal to devalue even further probably led to the financial difficulties he faced later in his reign. Perhaps this was precisely what Tiberius Julius Augusti libertus tried to say before he went to live, involuntarily and at the Emperor's pleasure, in Campania.[5]

A study of the coinage in isolation cannot elucidate the wider implications of Imperial finance. This is a problematic subject, hindered by the sparseness of accurate and sufficiently detailed information. Scholarly opinion is once again divided into two opposite camps, on the one hand blaming Domitian for leaving the Treasury empty at his death, and on the other hand praising him for assiduous administration of revenue collection and efficient regulation of expenditure, which ensured the robust health of the state finances. One of the major problems is that not enough is known of the finances of Nerva and Trajan to be able to state categorically that these two Emperors inherited a stable Treasury. It has been argued that without substantial sums of money left over from Domitian's reign, they would not have been able to put into operation their various policies, such as the institution of the *alimenta*, public works in Rome and Ostia, and above all the wars that

Trajan undertook. Others argue that both Nerva and Trajan were forced to economize, and that it was only the profit from the Dacian gold-mines which saved the Roman state from bankruptcy.[6]

When Vespasian succeeded to the throne after the ruin of the Civil War, the finances were probably his most pressing concern. He did not mince words when he told the Senate that he needed 40 billion sesterces simply to make the state solvent. Thereafter he required a steady and guaranteed income, just as Agrippa advised Octavian, when he said that he would need vast quantities of money from wherever they could get it, because otherwise there would not be enough to cater for all future needs. The words were invented for him by Dio, but they were perhaps not too far removed from the sentiments of either Octavian or Agrippa. Suetonius says that Vespasian doubled some of the tributes levied on the provincials, and the famous story of the tax that he levied on urine is indicative of desperation as well as guile. Two disasters, the first in 79 when Pompeii, Herculaneum and the surrounding areas succumbed to Vesuvius, followed by the fire in Rome in 80, added extra, but incalculable, financial burdens to Titus' problems. There are also suggestions from some modern scholars that Titus was extravagant and would have bankrupted the Empire if he had not died so young. The truth cannot be known, because there are no complete figures of either income or expenditure from the accounts of any of the Flavians. Most arguments are based on preconceived opinions of the characters of Vespasian, Titus or Domitian, and the few ascertainable facts are dressed up and marshalled accordingly to support the opinion. There is agreement that Vespasian was a careful administrator, but then the argument runs either that Titus squandered all the accumulated wealth, thus leaving Domitian with problems that he never entirely overcame, or on the contrary that Titus followed in his father's footsteps and it was Domitian who wasted state money on wars and banquets. Hyperbole, most of it, but much more colourful and far less boring than the unrecorded drudgery of account-keeping and administration of taxes.[7]

Various attempts have been made to estimate Domitian's state income, which is presumed at least to have kept pace with that of Vespasian. The surviving information about taxation in Domitian's reign is vague; Suetonius merely says that Domitian collected taxes ruthlessly (*acerbissime*), but includes only one example to support this claim, namely Domitian's determination that no Jews should escape the tax of two denarii per head, imposed by Titus in return for the free practice of the Jewish religion. Dio links the revolt of the Nasamones with over-rigorous collection of taxes but the procedure need not have been directly attributable to Domitian himself, though he bears overall responsibility. It could be argued that this particular tax-yield was neither important nor substantial – when Domitian forbade the Nasamones to exist he was presumably not overly concerned about the loss of revenue that he had just eradicated along with the population. Both Suetonius and Dio are silent about other revenues, save for a reference to gifts to Domitian upon which Dio does not elaborate. Frontinus tells how Domitian reorganized the collection of rentals for water rights from the aqueducts, fountains and reservoirs, which was usually lost through mismanagement. The Emperor gained from this exercise nearly 250,000 sesterces for the *fiscus*, but it is not clear whether this sum represents net profit, since the *fiscus* had to provide funds for the payment of the labour gang of 460 men who worked on the aqueducts alongside the 240 men paid out of the state Treasury. Materials such as lead piping, water basins and tanks were also paid for from the *fiscus*. Frontinus admits that the administration of the water supply and collection of revenues had been lax, but implies that Domitian kept the money that he recouped for his own use. He then praises Nerva for restoring the rentals to the control of the people. Domitian is therefore dismissed and, while not quite labelled a thief, certainly receives no credit for the fact that without his careful attention to detail Nerva would not have had an income to restore to the people.[8]

Thus it is hazardous to try to estimate the state income under Domitian with only these few pieces of information. Even if firm figures could be ascertained, the picture would still be one-sided, because income alone is of little use without the concomitant figures for expenditure, accompanied by some knowledge of contemporary prices for staple commodities. Virtually nothing is known of these factors. Suetonius is the first to accuse Domitian of spending more than his income, saying that at first Domitian was mild in his administration but that, contrary to his nature, he was forced into adopting harsh measures by the continuing need for money and, in order to remain solvent, he confiscated properties, legitimately or otherwise. This has created another controversy over Domitian's motives. Syme argued that the confiscations were politically motivated, intended to undermine the economic base of the senators. Others insist that Domitian was more interested in upholding high moral standards and enforcing the law, and that the confiscations came about as an accessory after the fact. Some scholars have calculated that property confiscations would have made a substantial contribution to state funds. Others, however, insist that the only profit that would accrue to the Treasury would be from immediate sale of the properties at full market value, for if the estates were exploited for their annual revenue, then the proceeds would scarcely be sufficient to balance the budget. The financial motive in confiscating properties is therefore not established beyond doubt. The 'need caused greed' theory is not substantiated by Pliny, who insists that Domitian possessed far more than he required, but always wanted more, indicating that the confiscations came about as a result of some flaw in the Emperor's character, and not from financial embarrassment. This is further supported by Pliny's admiration for Trajan's policy of allowing new owners to enter into possession of the confiscated estates, which had apparently fallen into ruin. It is implied that they had been neglected for some considerable time. Evidently Domitian had not placed any reliance upon the income from these lands and farms, whereas if he had had pressing need of the money he would have ensured that the estates functioned efficiently. This supports Syme's argument that the motive for confiscation was not financial but political. Pliny also refers to Domitian's jealousy and there may be an element of truth in this. Later rulers fell victim to the same sentiment – thus Cardinal Wolsey surrendered Hampton Court to Henry VIII, and Nicholas Fouquet relinquished Vaux-le-Vicomte to Louis XIV. In neither case did the initiative spring from the original owner; each had made the mistake of becoming more magnificent than their ruling monarchs, who were both autocrats of the Domitianic stamp. There are probably multiple explanations for Domitian's confiscation of estates, but the subtle distinctions would not necessarily be apparent to observers, and the suffering of the victims perhaps precluded any detailed examination of the reasons behind their treatment.[9]

Precise figures for Imperial income from legitimate and not so legitimate sources cannot be established, which means that Domitian's defenders are forced to fall back upon his reputation for intelligent and efficient administration in order to refute the idea that he had miscalculated in some respect. Expenditure is no less difficult to establish than income, but here scholars are armed with a little more information. Suetonius mentions Domitian's finances in five separate chapters. In the third chapter he provides an overview of the whole reign, using the now famous phrase that Domitian became rapacious through need; at the end of the seventh chapter, he gives exact figures for the army pay rise early in the reign; in the ninth chapter he is full of praise for Domitian's leniency and lack of avarice, followed by a short remark in the tenth chapter that this did not last. In the twelfth chapter he comes to the point, informing readers that Domitian was reduced to financial straits by the expense of his buildings, games and shows, and by the pay-rise awarded to the army. Dio discusses the army pay-rise in a little more detail, but has little to say about buildings and shows.[10]

The cost of the building programme in Rome and Italy was without doubt enormous, but it cannot be discerned at what point it became onerous, if at all. Repair and rebuilding of the areas of Rome burned down in 80 will have been a constant factor in financial calculations, and even after the work was finished it is probable that Domitian's plans for Rome involved him in building expenses all through his reign. We are informed of the most spectacular costs, such as the gilding for the temple of Jupiter Capitolinus, but not of the mundane costs of brick and stonework. It is not known to what extent the costs may have been offset by subscription and gifts from private individuals, or if the Emperor bore the entire costs alone. For games, races and spectacles, contributions from individuals probably played a part. There is little evidence for this, save for Martial's references to the glory of contributing money to pay for the games. Without exact figures for the costs of games and public dinners, and without knowledge of Domitian's income, it is not possible to be certain that they did form a constant drain on the state finances. At worst they could be considered extravagant and wasteful, opinions which no one seems to have held of Nerva's and Trajan's expenditure on similar entertainments.[11]

The expenditure that seems to have caused the most resentment was the army pay-rise of one-third. The soldiers had received no such acknowledgment since Julius Caesar doubled army pay. Augustus established the *aerarium militare* in AD 6 to provide for the pensions of discharged veterans. He provided 170 million sesterces from his own funds, and, to ensure a regular income for military pensions, he diverted the proceeds of the taxes *centesima rerum venalium* and the *vicesima hereditatum*. The legions mutinied on Augustus' death in AD 14, demanding unsuccessfully of Tiberius that their daily rate of ten asses should be elevated to one denarius. It is from this figure of ten asses per day that the standard rate of legionary pay is derived: 3600 asses = 225 denarii = 9 aurei per annum. Pay was divided into three equal instalments of 75 denarii = 3 aurei. Domitian raised annual pay to 300 denarii = 12 aurei, by adding 25 denarii = 1 aureus to each of the three pay-days. It was thus equivalent to adding a fourth pay-day each year, and from Suetonius' phrasing about the pay-rise (*addidit et quartum stipendium militi auros ternos*), some authors have assumed that during Domitian's reign there were four *stipendia*. But an alternative explanation is that Suetonius may have been referring to an extra, one-off, payment inserted as the pay-rise was awarded, in order to backdate it, to use a modern term. Carradice links the high level of output of aurei of 82 and 83 with the pay-rise, suggesting that payments were made in both aurei and denarii, not solely in denarii. Alston endorses this, concluding that the Imperial authorities reckoned army pay in aurei, citing in support of this theory the payment in three gold coins of *viaticum*, or the travel allowance granted to new recruits. Actual payments at each pay-day, or at least the small percentage of pay that was left to the soldiers after all the compulsory deductions, would need to be converted into more manageable denominations of coin, to effect everyday transactions.[12]

It is difficult to estimate the overall cost to the state of the army pay-rise, because there are two imponderable factors which hinder any calculation. The total strength of the army is not established, and the rate of auxiliary pay is not fully attested. The problem of army strength has been investigated several times. The exact number of legions is not definitely known. Two legions disappeared and were not reconstitued, *V Alaudae* perhaps in 69 or perhaps as late as 86, and *XXI Rapax* at some time during the reign of Domitian. At the time of the Chattan war, Domitian raised a new legion, *I Minervia*. There may have been other fluctuations in army strength which remain undocumented. Within each unit, actual strength may not have equalled paper strength, a feature which defies calculation after a lapse of 1,900 years. Rogers attempted to produce figures for legionary pay for 30 legions in 84 reducing to 28 legions after 92. His figures are *HS* 198 million for the early part of Domitian's reign, declining to nearly *HS* 185 million in the last four years, exceeding Vespasian's outlay by 41 million. [13]

Additionally, auxiliary pay may have reached nearly the same figure. The documentary evidence for auxiliary pay derives in large part from Egypt and yields very detailed information, yet even this is not without its problems. The traditional view is that auxiliaries were paid at a lower rate than legionaries but there is no general agreement on exactly how much lower. This tradition has been challenged, first by Speidel, who suggested that there cannot have been much difference between auxiliary and legionary pay, and then by Alston, who thinks that there was no difference at all. It is too early to say whether this theory will gain general acceptance, with all its implications for estimating Imperial finances. Needless to say, the total auxiliary establishment is not known. Calculations of the wage bill are thus reduced to speculative floundering. It is perhaps more pertinent to point out that the army may have cost nearly half, or possibly even more than half, of the state revenues. Expenditure on the army dominated state finance. It was spotlighted by several ancient authors, who probably thought the expense wasteful. It may have seemed to many Romans, not yet threatened with destruction from beyond the frontiers, but perilously at the mercy of battling factions in civil wars, that the soldiers were a troublesome lot, not worth the taxes and other revenues that went towards their wages. This could be one reason why expansionist wars met with approval: in wars of conquest the army could be seen to be doing something useful, acting for the benefit of the state, contributing to its own upkeep, providing lucrative booty and the opportunity for career-minded men to pursue glory. When the Dacian wars were concluded in 88/9, Domitian was distracted by the revolt of Saturninus and did not have the opportunity to consolidate as he would have liked. In the event, he paid subsidies to the Dacian king Decebalus, which may have been cheaper in the long run than financing another war. But his critics would view it differently. The army had been given a massive pay-rise, then suffered two defeats in Dacia before it managed to emerge victorious at great cost in lives. Then, instead of triumphs, strings of captives, swelling cartloads of captured wealth, a general feeling of smug superiority, peace and quiet and a territorial advance, the only result was diversion of taxes to a barbarian king with an unpronounceable name from an unpronounceable capital. Added to that was the withdrawal from Britain, and the absence of large-scale annexation of territory in Germany. *Imperium sine fine* must have seemed far away. Perhaps if Domitian had gone crashing round the edges of the Empire conquering new peoples, his reputation might have been slightly improved. The fact that it took Trajan two attempts to defeat the Dacians was perhaps not considered relevant after Domitian was dead.[14]

Domitian made no secret of the fact that his power rested on military support, and so it was in his interest to look after the soldiers. The pay-rise could be seen merely as an attempt to buy their loyalty, an extension of the donatives given to the troops on accession, and Domitian probably considered loyalty to his person synonymous with loyalty to the state. On the other hand, his concern for the soldiers' welfare did not cease with the pay-rise. In an edict dated to 88 or 89 he granted tax exemptions to all veterans, and awarded Roman citizenship to those who did not already possess it. Parents, wives and children of the soldiers enjoyed the same privileges. The grant may not have been revolutionary but may simply have confirmed a situation which was already in existence, but not regularly applied throughout the Empire. If the edict dates to the period after the revolt of Saturninus, it may have been passed in an attempt to bind the troops to the Emperor. Domitian was associated with the army from the earliest possible date, from 69/70 when he addressed the troops under the supervision of Mucianus. The tradition that he tried to take charge of the army under Cerialis, and then to lead an expedition to help Vologaeses, serves only to illustrate his consciousness of the army and the need for association with it. Ensuring that the army was properly paid for its services was a part of this contract. Significantly it was the army and not the other divisions of society who were enraged at Domitian's murder. It was a few months after his death that the soldiers avenged him but, far from proving their dilatoriness, this shows that their attachment to the last of the Flavians was strong enough to survive undiminished throughout the delay.[15]

VII
PERDOMITA BRITANNIA

When he succeeded to the throne in September 81, Domitian inherited an ongoing war in Britain, documented by Tacitus in the biography of his father-in-law Agricola. This war was part of the Flavian forward policy in Britain, beginning with the two governors Petillius Cerialis, who subdued northern England, and Julius Frontinus, who subdued most of Wales. Agricola took over where Frontinus left off, completing the conquest of Wales. The extent of Cerialis' conquest of the north has been elucidated in recent years, as a result of excavation, coin studies and dendrochronological dating of timbers from the first fort at Carlisle, founded perhaps as early as 72. Scotland was next on the list for conquest. This is a subject that has been discussed in print many times already. With regard to the background and earlier history of the conquest of Britain readers are referred to a selecion of the most relevant literature cited in the notes, while this chapter will concentrate on events from Domitian's point of view.[1]

Agricola's life history is unusual in three respects. Firstly, he had a historian for his son-in-law, whose biography has survived, which has always given Agricola precedence over other governors, since the reconstruction of most military and civil careers is dependent upon scant mention in a few texts and the arbitrary discovery of epigraphic records. Secondly, Agricola served three times in Britain, as tribune of a legion, legionary legate and finally governor, whereas most men served in a wider variety of locations, thus gaining more diverse experience. Thirdly, Agricola was governor of Britain for an unusually long term of seven years, perhaps the last three of which, or much more likely the last two, were with Domitian as Emperor.[2]

Tacitus' narrative divides Agricola's term of office into summer and winter seasons, without providing any dating clues. Since the date of his appointment is not firmly attested, it is impossible to verify which season's work Agricola was engaged upon when Titus died and Domitian took over. Key factors which have been debated are the initial appointment and duration of Agricola's consulship, generally agreed to date to 77, but which could just as easily have belonged to 76, or to 78, and the date of the final battle of Mons Graupius. Scholars try to establish one or the other of these dates on epigraphic, literary or numismatic grounds, allotting relevant dates to all the other events. One date is firmly fixed, that of Titus' fifteenth Imperial acclamation in 79. This was specifically connected to events in Britain and is more likely to have been as a result of the third season's advance to the Tay than any other achievement.[3]

There is considerable support for the dates 77 to 83 for Agricola's governorship of Britain, as the most recent examination of the evidence by M.-T. Raepsaet-Charlier has shown. By this reckoning Agricola arrived in late 77, fought a brief campaign in Wales that same year, then turned his attention to the north, finally arriving at the Tay (*Tavum*) at the end of his third season in 79, when he even had time to build some forts. In 80, his fourth season, he consolidated his position by building forts (*praesidia*) between the Forth and the Clyde. Despite this unaccustomed exactness on the part of Tacitus, providing two of the very rare place-names of his narrative, none of these *praesidia* has been identified with any certainty. The fort at Elginhaugh may be one of them, and Barochan may be another, but the expected chain of posts between the two rivers has defied decades if not centuries of enquiry. It has been suggested that the halt on the Forth-Clyde isthmus was carried out on instructions from the Emperor, who would be Titus no matter which chronology is preferred for the date of the fourth season. Stretched resources are advocated as a reason for the halt, or if the late chronology is used, the reason that most readily suggests itself is the death of Titus, after which Agricola would halt to await further instructions. Neither of these reasons seem quite so compelling as military necessity with reference to the geography of Scotland, but this does not seem to have been considered. It is worth pointing out that an advance beyond the Tay without first securing communications, supply bases, and above all safe retreat, is to invite complete disaster should anything go wrong, simply because the position can be turned with ease, and troops advancing beyond the Tay can find themselves cut off by forces coming down behind them.[4]

Another debate concerns which Emperor finally gave the go-ahead for further advance the following year. If it is surmised that Agricola began his term of office in 77, then that Emperor would still have been Titus; if Agricola arrived in Britain in 78 the forward policy was Domitian's. It is more likely that the advance had already been made, and that at Domitian's accession, Agricola had probably completed his fifth season, the purpose and location of which is perhaps the most enigmatic and therefore the most disputed of all the seven seasons, save for the three or four centuries of theorizing about the location of Mons Graupius. Tacitus' hints about the fifth season are very brief. He reserves his main narrative for the account of the sixth and seventh seasons, and a large proportion of the book is devoted to the fictitious speeches of Agricola and the British leader Calgacus to their respective troops before the final battle. All that is known of the fifth season is that Agricola made a crossing by sea to an unnamed destination, that the army encountered hitherto unknown tribes, and that Roman troops were drawn up on the part of the coast that faces Ireland. The requirements of Tacitean grammar indicate that the crossing by sea was over the Clyde, and that therefore the scene of operations in the fifth season was the west of Scotland, which would account for the unknown tribes of Tacitus' narrative. Not a shred of archaeological evidence has been found to support this theory, nor for that matter to establish any convincing alternative venue.[5]

Reviewing the situation shortly after he became Emperor, Domitian could have recalled Agricola and replaced him with a new man to take over from where he left off, but he chose to allow the British specialist to remain in office, to complete his task and gain the credit for it. He may have taken advice from Agricola himself, who by September 81 probably felt certain that with communications and bases established in southern Scotland, and perhaps the west secured as well, the whole island was within his grasp, given one more campaigning season. Domitian presumably authorized him to complete the conquest. At this point the Chattan war had probably not yet begun, so the possibility of strain on manpower would not have been a problem, and it was probably envisaged that in another two years the new territory would have been annexed and pacification – coupled with exploitation – could begin. Unfortunately the sixth season did not prove as successful as Agricola had hoped. There was some fighting, involving a night attack on *IX Hispana*, but the Britons escaped, leaving the work to be done all over again in the next season.[6]

It is now that the events in Britain and Germany become inextricably intertwined, at least in the modern literature. Two inscriptions seem to indicate that when he began the war against the Chatti, Domitian took troops away from Britain while Agricola's campaigns were still going on. At some unattested date, vexillations were drawn from all four of the British legions and placed along with four other legionary detachments under the command of C.Velius Rufus. This individual would have been surprised at the amount of verbiage originated by his career inscription, and if he could have foreseen the anguish caused to archaeologists and historians by the lack of dates, he might have left instructions to have them included with every sentence. He might also have insisted that the precise number of vexillations should be carved in words as well as numerals, since nine (VIIII) are mentioned, but only eight are actually named. Various dates have been suggested for Rufus' special command, some with more likelihood than others. The eight detachments may have fought in the war of 77/8 in Germany, or they may have been assembled for the Danube war of 85/6, in which case Rufus will have been placed in command of them while they marched to that destination. Neither theory is convincing. Strobel suggested that Rufus played a very important role in the Pannonian war against the Marcomanni and Quadi, as leader of a strike force of eight vexillations marching through Dacian territory to attack from the west while the main army operated from Pannonia. This necessitates considerable readjustment of the text of the inscription. Most scholars interpreted the text as a roughly chronological account of Rufus' career, but Strobel points out that this is not necessarily so. The main elements are grouped thematically, beginning with the most prestigious posts and listing them in descending order of importance. This was perhaps the product of a highly organized mind, a theory which is borne out by the fact that the vexillations are listed in numerical order, and it is perhaps not accidental that *II Adiutrix* and *II Augusta* are listed alphabetically. Freed from the obligation to take each part of the inscription in strictly chronological order, Strobel united the list of vexillations (lines 3 to 6 on the inscription) with an apparently separate command where Rufus led an expedition against the Marcomanni and Quadi, marching through the kingdom of Decebalus (lines 15 to 19). In the text this expedition is divorced from the list of vexillations, perhaps because it is classified under the heading of Rufus' military awards, which are all grouped together. Strobel assigns the vexillations to the expedition against the Marcomanni and Quadi. This would place the special command and the withdrawal of troops from Britain in 89, long after Agricola's campaigns. The latter hypothesis seems the most convincing for it is highly improbable that Domitian would remove troops from all the legions of Agricola's army at such a crucial moment in the process of conquest. Even if he regarded Agricola with animosity, he could not allow that sentiment to override wisdom. When he embarked on the war against the Marcomanni and Quadi, Domitian had already abandoned Scotland and troops could be more easily spared.[7]

The second case for removal of Agricola's troops is more difficult to answer. Tacitus' statement that in the sixth season the *legio IX* was the weakest of the three battle groups has been married to an undated inscription attesting that a vexillation of *IX Hispana* served under the military tribune Roscius Aelianus in a German expedition. It is but a short step to the conclusion that Agricola's sixth season belonged to 82, that Domitian was collecting troops in 82 for the Chattan war fought in 83, and that he took a number of men from at least one of the legions of Britain. It has also been suggested that Roscius Aelianus' vexillation was taken from Britain at the time of the revolt of Saturninus in 89, to fight in the ill-documented war against the Chatti who had allied with the rebels. The counter-argument to this is that since Roscius was suffect consul in 100, his military tribunate could not have been held as late as 89. Marginally, it could be argued that since the Chattan war went on until 85, the vexillation of *legio IX* was withdrawn after the battle of Mons Graupius, and before the complete withdrawal from Scotland, but this is grasping at straws. An element of doubt remains, however. It is reasonable to inquire why, if *legio IX* was weakened on Domitian's account, Tacitus failed to wring every last ounce from such a 21-carat opportunity to tell a story which would at one and the same time enhance the sterling talents of his father-in-law, winning through in the face of adversity, and also magnify Domitian's black-hearted villainy. Still unanswered is the question as to why *legio IX* was the weakest of the three battle groups in the sixth season. One suggestion is that troops had been seconded to guard communications in the rear, or that a large part of the legion remained at its base at York in order to supervise the territory of the Brigantes, which had only recently been overrun and would therefore require more extensive policing than areas further south. Another possibility is that Agricola deliberately weakened one part of his forces to act as bait to encourage and precipitate a battle.[8]

Agricola's real achievement is not that he won the battle of Mons Graupius, but that he managed to bring it about at all. The exact location will probably never be established, and in consequence the run-up to the battle can only be surmised, since Tacitus gives few details. One of the greatest difficulties faced by an army in mountainous country is that the places of refuge afforded to the inhabitants by the geographical formation of the terrain allow the natives to vanish and wait for the invader to go away. It has been pointed out, in connection with Edward I of England, that in the end it is the invader who starves in Scotland, not the natives. Mountain peoples need not fight at all, unless they are forced to do so, having been harassed to a point where they have nothing to lose. For those who believe that in order to conquer Scotland, all that is necessary is to subdue the Lowlands and ignore the Highlands, blocking them off with forts to watch the glen mouths, as archaeology attests, this argument falls flat. Subscribers to this theory will never be swayed by words, but William I, Edward I, Cromwell, General Monck and Butcher Cumberland would disagree – if the Highlands are not subdued, then Scotland is not conquered.[9]

The huge monument at Richborough was designed to proclaim to the world that the whole island had been conquered, but it has been debated just how complete the conquest was, since archaeology has yet to demonstrate that there was any permanent Roman presence north of the Highland line. At the glen mouths, both temporary camps and permanent forts were built, confusing in their chronology. The forts may have been founded by Agricola, but some authors think that they belong to his unknown successor. Marching camps have been found, tantalizingly reaching into Moray, but there is no indication as yet that the armies of any of the various expeditions into Scotland in the Flavian, Antonine or Severan eras ever reached the Moray Firth. The fleet sailed round the country after

Mons Graupius, thus proving that Britain was an island. Ptolemy's *Geography*, the British sections of which were probably drawn up using evidence gathered during Agricola's campaigns, provides a number of place-names, which cannot be totally reconciled with the archaeologically attested sites. No place-names are given in Ptolemy's work for the far north, which indicates to some authors that this information was gathered by the fleet rather than by the army, which in turn implies that the army never penetrated these regions. *Perdomita Britannia* may have been written for effect, without due reference to the facts, or it may be that one day, at some previously unconsidered northern site, someone may come across a dated artefact, proving that Agricola was there.[10]

Tacitus emphasizes the victory of Mons Graupius, contrasting it unfavourably with Domitian's Chattan victory, and even going so far as to suggest that the Emperor was jealous of Agricola. The date of the battle was most likely 83, and the timetable proposed by Birley seems the most sensible, namely that the battle was fought in September 83, Agricola then made a slow progress into winter quarters to impress the natives by his nonchalance, and in October wrote his report, which reached Rome in December, by which time Domitian had celebrated his recent triumph, just as Tacitus says. Agricola survived for another decade after his British victory, recognized by the triumphal awards that Domitian granted him. But that was all he received, and the expected promotion did not happen. There may well have been some prejudice in Domitian's mind; perhaps he did not think that a man who had served three times in Britain had enough experience to govern another province; perhaps Agricola was not physically fit enough to do so; there may be any number of explanations.[11]

If Agricola was embittered by his lack of promotion, he was no doubt even more disappointed by the abandonment of all that he had gained within a very short time. It is an incontrovertible fact that Scotland was abandoned, but the date is disputed. It seemed at one time that the withdrawal was a gradual process, undertaken in successive stages, and thus giving the lie to one of Tacitus' most overworked statements that Britain was conquered and immediately let go (*statim missa*). This theory is now outdated. Coin evidence suggests very strongly that the withdrawal was not only sudden, but also that abandonment of the north occurred in a single stage, very soon after the conquest. In brief, the archaeological evidence suggests that with regard to Britain, the supply of bronze coinage of 81 to 85 was low, in contrast to the relatively high supply of coins of 86 and 87, which reached most British sites. Roman forts of the Flavian period (Fig. 1) in Scotland have yielded a number of coins of 86, one or two in mint condition, or with little sign of wear. No coins of 87 have been found so far, which implies that the forts were abandoned before supplies of coinage of 87 reached them. It is postulated that coins of 87 may have arrived in Britain at any time between August 87 and August 88, which in turn implies that the forts in Scotland were evacuated no later than the summer of 88. This is compatible with the abandonment of the legionary fortress of Inchtuthil, which was levelled before it had even been completed. A certain sense of urgency is indicated by the burial of over a million nails at Inchtuthil, which were presumably too much of an encumbrance to carry and too valuable to leave for the natives.[12]

The deliberate destruction of Inchtuthil and the transfer southwards of its legion (assumed to be *legio XX*) is probably related to the withdrawal of *II Adiutrix* from Britain. The legionary base at Wroxeter similarly yielded several coins of 86 but not many of 87; when the legion moved the site was given over to civilian development. *II Adiutrix* was definitely on the Danube by 92, and may have been transferred there in 87 or 88; Strobel affirms that it was in Moesia Superior by 87. *Cohors II Batavorum* may have been sent from Britain to the Danube at the same time, though it is not attested in Pannonia until 96. The scenario thus forming is that Domitian drew extra troops for the Dacian war from Britain, which measure rendered it imperative to abandon Scotland. This may have occurred as early as the winter of 86/7, not long after the loss of Fuscus and his army in Dacia. The date of this disaster is not firmly attested, but 86 is highly likely and the enormity of the loss would account for withdrawal of troops from the recently conquered parts of Britain. After the defeat of Oppius Sabinus by the Dacians, Domitian had already gathered extra troops for the expedition which he and Fuscus undertook probably at the end of 85. When the second disaster occurred, the previous sources of troops would have been already stretched, forcing the Emperor to look elsewhere for further supplies. A complete change of policy was called for. The armies of other provinces could provide legionary vexillations and perhaps some auxiliary units, but nothing more without compromising the safety of the Empire. Only Britain could rapidly provide an entire legion, and possibly some auxiliary units, without endangering the security of Rome. Geographically, Britain presented the Emperor with a choice of two locations (the Forth-Clyde isthmus and the Tyne-Solway gap) which could be utilized as a defensive boundary. Domitian chose to keep northern England and much of southern Scotland under Roman control, thus retaining the parts of the island which were profitable, while at the same time excluding undesirable intruders, and relinquishing those parts in which there had as yet been no concerted effort in civilizing and Romanizing the natives with a view to extracting profit from them (Fig. 2). Millett points out that the lack of a centralized authority in the far north of Britain would not have been conducive to the establishment of Roman forms of administration, and therefore the possibility of profitable exploitation would have been negligible. He wonders whether Domitian's decision to withdraw the troops was not after all correct, since there was nothing to be gained by remaining in Scotland. Whilst this is probably quite true, it is a narrow argument, confined to economic and social factors in a single province. It implies that the withdrawal was simply an option and makes no reference to events in the rest of the Empire. The need for troops was surely the primary consideration, with the impossibility of Romanizing the natives a secondary factor, making it easy to decide which troops to remove. If the new military arrangements in Britain failed, the loss of northern England would pose no threat whatsoever to Rome itself, since the Britons were hardly likely to sweep through Gaul and menace Italy. Another factor which probably influenced Domitian in making his decision, was the very important advantage that the British troops were trained and experienced.[13]

The theory that Scotland was indeed given up so rapidly after the conquest necessitates a readjustment of the interpretation of the archaeology of the region. In particular there must now be a revision of the idea that the so-called Gask Ridge watch-towers erected around the western edge of Fife served as a temporary frontier as the troops were pulled out in a phased withdrawal. In keeping with most Flavian sites in Scotland, there is no precise dating evidence from the towers themselves, nor from the forts at Ardoch, Strageath and Bertha, on the road connecting the towers. A rim of a mortarium from the tower at Gask House and a sherd from Westerton tower can be dated only very broadly to the

Flavian period. There were two Flavian phases at Ardoch and Strageath, but it is not known whether the watch-towers were designed to accompany each phase, or only one, and if only one, whether this would be the first or second phase. It has been suggested that the system was set up as Agricola embarked on his sixth season. Such detail would not concern Domitian, whose attention would be permanently focused on the larger issues concerning the safety of the Empire. His withdrawal from Britain was not undertaken in a spirit of malice. He could not have foreseen the outbreak of the Dacian war at the time when Agricola was completing his task in Britain, and he certainly could not have foreseen that there would be two disasters, the second probably worse than the first, within such a

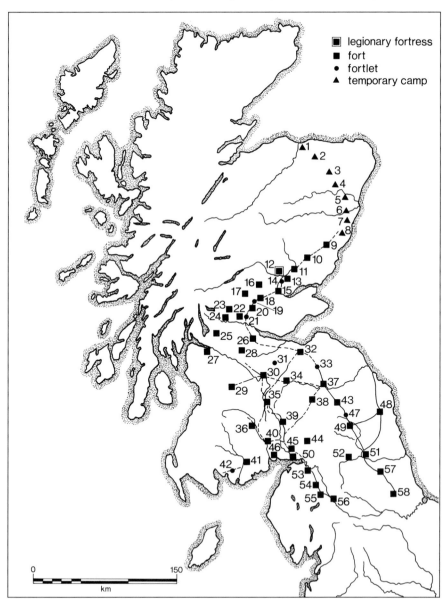

short time-span. In this context it is prudent to remember that trouble on the Danube affected Rome much more directly and rather more vividly than any amount of fighting in Britain, and so Domitian made the ruthless but realistic decision to abandon Agricola's conquests. If Scotland had possessed gold or silver, or other lucrative and exploitable resources in abundance, then he may well have found it more difficult to arrive at his decision. He may have shared the opinion of William I, who reached the Tay in 1072: many miles from his base at York, William refused to advance any further, made a treaty with Malcolm Canmore, and returned home, because once at the Tay, 'there he found nothing that he was any the better for', as the *Anglo-Saxon Chronicle* baldly and dismissively states. Agricola may have gained some small compensation from the fact that he had probably penetrated further north than any other general, but the rapid loss of all that he had achieved reduced his conquest to the status of a mere expedition. Coupled with his failure to win further promotion, his disappointment that all his efforts had yielded nothing tangible sowed the seeds of bitterness brought so expertly to fruition by Tacitus.[14]

Fig. 1. *(Opposite)* Map showing the first-century Roman occupation of Scotland. The glen-blocking forts skirting the southern edge of the Highlands may have been founded by Agricola at the end of his campaigns, or by his unknown successor. It is not known how far north Agricola may have penetrated; the marching camps at Muiryfold and Ythan Wells are generally agreed to date to Agricola's campaigns; Bellie is suggested as a base on the River Spey. There may be more camps in Moray which have not yet come to light. (Drawn by Graeme Stobbs)

Camps and forts:

1. Bellie	21. Glenbank	41. Glenlochar
2. Muiryfold	22. Doune	42. Gatehouse of Fleet
3. Ythan Wells	23. Bochastle	43. Cappuck
4. Durno	24. Menteith	44. Broomholm
5. Kintore	25. Drumquhassle	45. Birrens
6. Normandykes	26. Camelon	46. Ward Law
7. Raedykes	27. Barochan	47. Chew Green
8. Kair House	28. Mollins	48. Learchild
9. Stracathro	29. Loudoun Hill	49. High Rochester
10. Inverquharity	30. Castledykes	50. Annan
11. Cardean	31. Castle Greg	51. Corbridge Red House
12. Inchtuthil	32. Elginhaugh	52. Vindolanda
13. Cargill	33. Oxton	53. Carlisle
14. Cargill fortle	34. Easter Happrew	54. Old Penrith
15. Bertha	35. Crawford	55. Brougham
16. Fendoch	36. Drumlanrig	56. Kirkby Thore
17. Dalginross	37. Newstead	57. Ebchester
18. Strageath	38. Oakwood	58. Binchester
19. Kaims Castle	39. Milton	
20. Ardoch	40. Dalswinton	

By about 90, the most northerly forts in Britain were those at Dalswinton and Newstead. The latter was probably remodelled in 86/7 in connection with the withdrawal
from the north. Long-distance patrols may have served to keep the territory in advance of
these forts under control, and may account for the stray finds at sites much further north.
This arrangement qualifies for the title frontier only in the broadest sense, and the system
was not long in operation. Pottery evidence suggests that Newstead and Dalswinton were
given up by about 104. The early Trajanic arrangements for the north of Britain involved
pulling back as far as the Tyne-Solway line, thus making the Stanegate, the road that connected Corbridge with Carlisle, the most northerly in the island. It is precisely this period,

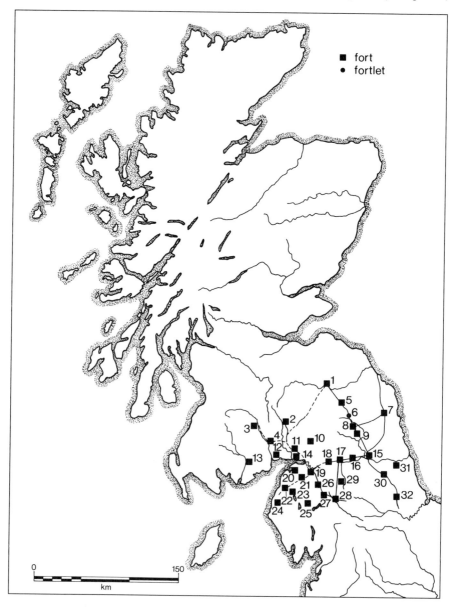

the end of the first and beginning of the second century, to which the Vindolanda writing tablets belong, illuminating the day-to-day details of life on the northern frontier.[15]

It is suggested that late in Domitian's reign there may have been a war in Britain, which necessitated this further withdrawal. The famous pits at Newstead, containing broken weapons and human heads, undated but suggestive of grisly events, can be interpreted in one of two ways – either that there was a battle after which the troops who tidied up buried the remains, or that the evacuation was orderly and the pits were dug to take old unwanted weapons that could not be repaired. In this case the heads are explained as trophies that had been dangling from the fort walls, taken by Romanized Celtic soldiers who subscribed to the head cult. The signs of a conflagration at the first fort on the Red House site at Corbridge can be interpreted in the same light, as deliberate destruction by the Romans who were already planning to build the new fort on the present site. It is unlikely that the destruction was by enemy action. [16]

Instead of, or as well as, a war against the natives, it has also been suggested that there may have been an attempt at rebellion against Domitian in Britain. Some of the evidence derives from an inscription recording an unprecedented series of awards granted to Gaius Julius Karus at some time between 89 and 128 for his part in an undated and unspecified British war. This may mean exactly what it says, referring to a native war, which may have occurred early in Hadrian's reign, or it may be a euphemism for a civil war, just as the revolt of Saturninus in Upper Germany was termed *bellum Germanicum*. It is suggested that the rebellious culprit may have been Sallustius Lucullus, who was governor of Britain when Domitian had him executed, allegedly for naming a lance after himself. Those who suggest that Sallustius Lucullus may somehow have been in collusion with Saturninus in 89 cannot reconcile the possible intervention of Karus, since the unit that he commanded was still in Germany at the time of the revolt, and was rewarded for its loyalty to Domitian. Thus the supposed British rebellion has to be placed after 89 and before 96, but there are no further clues as to the date of these events. The presence on the Danube at some time

Fig. 2. *(Opposite)* Very soon after Agricola's conquests, troops were withdrawn from Scotland, probably in connection with the Dacian wars. The map shows those forts still in occupation under Domitian, after most of Agricola's conquests were abandoned. Under Trajan, the forts north of the Tyne–Solway line were given up. (Drawn by Graeme Stobbs)

1. Newstead	12. Ward Law	23. Caermote
2. Milton	13. Glenlochar	24. Papcastle
3. Drumlanrig	14. Annan	25. Troutbeck
4. Dalswinton	15. Corbridge	26. Penrith
5. Cappuck	16. Vindolanda	27. Brougham
6. Chew Green	17. Carvoran	28. Kirkby Thore
7. Learchild	18. Nether Denton	29. Whitley Castle
8. High Rochester	19. Carlisle	30. Ebchester
9. Blakehope	20. Kirkbride	31. Whickham
10. Broomholm	21. Old Carlisle	32. Binchester
11. Birrens	22. Blennerhasset	

between 103 and 107 of a unit entitled *pedites singulares Britannici* has been linked to this probable affair. *Singulares* were bodyguard troops, and these men were probably in the bodyguard of the governor of Britain. Their removal to the Danube may have been punishment for their involvement in the supposed rebellion.[17]

If there was a rebellion, organized by Sallustius Lucullus or any other governor and eventually quelled with the assistance of Karus, or if there was a spate of serious fighting with the Britons at the end of Domitian's reign, news of it did not find its way into any of the surviving sources, a strange omission in view of the fact that in the eyes of some Latin and Greek authors, Rome's most northerly and outlandish province was perpetually barbaric and turbulent, with the result that trouble in Britain became almost as proverbial as trouble at t'mill in modern estimations of the northern English past.

VIII

CHATTI

The Chattan war of the early 80s has generated a vast amount of printed words, the quantity of which is in inverse proportion to attested facts. This is a logical development; had there been in existence epigraphic or literary sources providing incontrovertible evidence for the date, purpose, duration and result of the Chattan war, then controversy over these matters would have been stillborn.

The search for exact dates has occupied numerous scholars, without producing a solution satisfactory to everyone. The commencement of the war has been dated to either 82 or 83. Various pieces of evidence have been brought to bear in support of each theory, but in the final analysis there is nothing more than probability backed up by opinion in favour of any date between the end of 81 and the middle of 83 for the outbreak of hostilities. Dio's contribution, or rather that of Xiphilinus, depends upon the date of the punishment of the Vestals, which is described just before the account of the outbreak of the war. Dio provides no dating evidence. That is derived from Eusebius, who says that the Vestals were tried in the year 2098 *a Abr* ('post-Abraham'), or in modern terms between 1 October 81 and 30 September 82. The problem is that Hieronymous assigns the episode to the following year. It is unlikely that hostilities began in the winter of 81/2, partly because the outbreak of the Chattan war so early in Domitian's reign might have occasioned comment from the ancient authors about his misguided eagerness for military fame in embarking on a war only two or three months after his accession. The spring or early summer of 82 would seem more likely. Frontinus reports that the Chatti were preparing for war (*in armis*) but this need not mean that they had already attacked in the winter of 81. It is possible that information had reached Domitian of hostile spear-shaking among the Chatti, and that he decided to go to war to prevent an eruption into Roman territories (pl. 14). His thwarted ambitions in the war of 70 may have played a part here, in that he was determined to demonstrate, a decade later, what he might have achieved, given the opportunity. Then there was the general Roman dream of conquering Germany beyond the Rhine, perhaps as far as the Elbe, a project which may have been among Augustus' long-term plans, shelved after the disaster of Varus. The duration of Domitian's activity on the war front is not known, which makes it possible to argue the case for a number of theories. Some scholars assign the war improbably to 82, some with more likelihood to 83. According to others, hostilities did not cease until 85, but there is disagreement as to whether the fighting was continuous or whether there were two separate campaigns. Difficulties are encountered at all stages of discussion in favour of any of these theories. A major problem is a discharge diploma of 82, attesting that in September of that year, not only were veterans being discharged from the Upper German army, but also that whole units were operating elsewhere. The text of the diploma reveals that at least three auxiliary units, one *ala* and two cohorts, had been transferred from Germany to Moesia. It is thought that Domitian could not have taken such a step if he was either embroiled in a serious war already, or was about to embark on a new campaign in 83. The Chattan war and Domitian's participation in it therefore has to be slotted wholly into 82 to account for these measures, or another more probable explanation has to be found.[1]

There are a few pieces of evidence that lead scholars to suggest that the war was conducted wholly in 83 – the traditional date for the Chattan war. The discharge of veterans in the autumn of 82 can be accommodated if it is assumed that in September 82 there was no hint of the impending hostilities. It is postulated that the campaign of 83 was very brief, beginning perhaps in spring, and leading to Domitian's triumph possibly in mid-83. There are shades of Gaius Caligula's infamous campaign here, lending themselves to the assumption that Domitian's victory was nothing but a sham and his triumph laughable. This is a story spread about by Tacitus and Pliny. A Blitzkrieg of such short duration could denote either a fiasco such as the hostile sources depict, or a successful operation carried out by a gifted commander. But these are two extremes, whereas the reality may have lain somewhere along a middle path. For example, the preparation for the war may have begun in 82 with the campaign itself being conducted in 83.[2]

It is quite possible that the Chatti began to be troublesome in the early summer of 82, and that Domitian spent the latter part of the year getting ready for the campaign. Frontinus relates how the Emperor took care to disguise his preparations for the war, so as to gain the advantage of surprise when he finally attacked the Chatti. The official reason for Domitian's presence and the gathering of troops was the administration of a census in Gaul. In September 82 the discharge of veterans could have been part of this ruse to convey the impression of normality even to the Upper and Lower German armies, so that gossip could be curtailed and no hint of the impending attack allowed to leak out. The transfer of auxiliary units may have served the purpose of temporarily securing the Danube while Domitian attended to the Rhine. If the estimates of troop numbers (*c.* 50,000) at the start of the war are correct, the loss of veterans and three auxiliary units would not have been detrimental to the overall strength of the campaign army.[3]

This leaves the problem of precisely when the attack was launched. Most scholars would assert that a winter campaign in 82/3 would be out of the question, but it is worth pointing out that winter would be a most advantageous time to begin a war against an enemy such as the Chatti, whose territory lent itself to guerrilla warfare. Native food supplies would be low, and constant harassment and destruction of food stocks and refuges would be all that was necessary to wear the enemy down. A winter campaign is indeed severe on the attackers as well, but if sufficient preparation has been made and attention paid to supply lines, it can be very effective to attack unexpectedly in this way. Such a war is one without glorious pitched battles or even memorable achievements but, though it requires slow and thorough progress, it can be left to subordinates to complete after the initial onslaught. It is comparable to taking a city block by block; if external help can be eliminated, there comes a point at which the outcome is inevitable but the final capitulation takes time to bring about. This may explain why Domitian celebrated his triumph in 83 although the war itself was not finally concluded until 85. Vespasian and Titus celebrated a triumph over Judaea in 71, despite the war not being concluded at that date, so it is unjustified to suggest that Domitian's triumph was ridiculously premature. In the opinion of some scholars, Domitian truly imagined that he had finally and fully defeated the Chatti in 83. Thus he ended the short campaign on a glorious note, but his confidence in victory soon proved to be seriously flawed, so that the army had to be assembled once again for a second campaign, in which the Emperor took little part, and which lasted from 83/4 to the final victory in 85. This casts an unfavourable light on Domitian's expertise, with a sub-text that the army could manage its affairs much better without him. The problem of whether there were two separate campaigns, or one lengthy war, can probably never be resolved, but a continuous war of attrition and annihilation seems a more feasible solution to the Chattan problem, especially since the literary and epigraphic evidence provides no hint of a final battle, as happened at Mons Graupius in Britain and at Tapae in Dacia.[4]

Bound up with the questions of the date, duration and course of the war are the equally contested questions of Domitian's Imperial acclamations, and the adoption of the title Germanicus. The Imperial salutations between 81 and 84 cannot be closely dated, nor can they be definitely related to the German campaigns. The first two acclamations belong to September 81 and some date before the end of March 82. From January to 9 June 83, Domitian was IMP III, and by January 84 he had progressed to IMP V. In the next nine months between January and September 84 he received three more salutations, reaching a total of seven. The acceleration of Imperial salutations between June 83 and January 84 has been cited as evidence that the Chattan war was fought in 83, and that the triumph and the title Germanicus belong to late 83 or early 84. Since there was fighting in Britain and Mauretania at this same time, some of the Imperial acclamations presumably belong to victories in either of these two provinces. The problem is to identify which salutations belong to which victories at which dates, a debatable theme that is probably incapable of solution. The title Germanicus may have been adopted in midsummer 83, since according to Braunert it is first attested at some point between 9 June and 28 August 83, but the evidence upon which he bases this conclusion, derived from one coin, an inscription and two papyri, is disputed. Strobel dismissed the coin, and Kneissl was able to show that the appearance of the title Germanicus is by no means a consistent feature on inscriptions until 86, so its use is haphazard to say the least. The argument that the first known appearance of the title is also the date of its inception is unsound. The date of the triumph is no more clearly attested. Strobel argued that it took place in autumn 83, while Kneissl and Perl argue for late 83 or even early 84. The *congiarium* paid out in 84 influences some authors, who associate the triumph very closely with the payment, but the two were not necessarily contemporaneous. The triumph could have been held as soon as Domitian reached Rome, and the payment made in the following year. The suggestion that the triumph was not held until 84 causes an immediate difficulty for those who assign Agricola's victory at Mons Graupius to 83, since Tacitus affirms that news of the conquest of Britain reached Domitian after he had celebrated his recent (*nuper*) triumph. The choice is between doubting Tacitus' words, or juggling the dates of the battle of Mons Graupius, the time it would take for the news of it to reach Rome, and the date of Domitian's triumph. Logically, triumph and title ought to be closely related. The co-ordination of both events would certainly emphasize Domitian's part in the war, but there is no evidence to support the idea that Domitian associated the two elements; indeed it is suggested that he waited for some time after the triumph before assuming the title Germanicus. It was a revolutionary concept: Germanicus as a Julio-Claudian family name was perfectly acceptable, but as a permanent reminder of victory, with connotations of supremacy, adoption of the name may have caused some offence, necessitating prudent hesitation before taking such a step.[5]

Preoccupation with the dates of the Chattan war has quite overshadowed discussion as to what actually happened. Evidence is extremely scanty on this point. The reasons for the war and the course it took are not attested in any ancient source. Suetonius maintains that the war was unnecessary, and some modern scholars incline towards the view that it was undertaken merely to satisfy Domitian's lust for glory. This does not quite ring true. Tacitus describes the Chatti at some length, making them sound quite formidable. They were, in Tacitus' opinion, unlike other Germans in many respects, not least in their military organization and ability not only to make plans, but also to execute them. Tacitus' phrase, 'other Germans go to battle, the Chatti make war', sums up their potential threat to Rome. They elected officers and obeyed them, they were trained from earliest youth to kill and were not recognized as full members of the tribe until they had done so. They made plans for daily manoeuvres and built entrenched camps at night. All in all they were not a tribe to be dismissed lightly on the doorstep of Roman territory.[6]

The concentration of finds on the river Eder shows that the Chattan homelands lay around Kassel and Fritzlar, north of the Taunus in modern Hesse. The Romans and the Chatti had already met, or rather clashed, before Domitian's war. In 50 the Chatti overran Mainz, and Pomponius Secundus received triumphal insignia for quelling them. In 69 they attacked Mainz again but to no avail. After the Civil War, Vespasian strengthened the Rhine bridgeheads and occupied the Wetterau, building a line of forts from Mainz-Kastel to Friedberg. It has been suggested that the Chatti were poised for attack when Domitian began his campaign against them, and some scholars have associated signs of destruction at some military sites with the preliminary phases of the war. Such signs of destruction are notoriously difficult to date accurately, and the Chatti may not have been the culprits. Besides, the motive for Roman aggression against the Chatti would not require such a concrete foundation; rumours of unrest would have served just as well. The Roman occupation of the Wetterau may have caused disquiet among the Chatti. There is no real evidence that there had been any violation of Roman territory, but equally it is not possible to state that there was no provocation for the war. The Romans traditionally depicted their wars as just, throwing all the blame for their aggression on to the enemy whether they were guilty or not, thus providing the ideal excuse for annexation. This Chattan war, however, was not one of conquest leading to annexation of territories and expansion of Empire. Domitian stands accused of desiring military successes quickly and cheaply, electing to conduct a campaign in an area which was ripe for war, but which at the same time represented no real danger and was not necessarily valuable to the Empire. If Domitian had indeed entertained such a desire he would probably have adopted the titles Britannicus and Dacicus, spuriously claiming for himself the victories won by his generals at opposite ends of the Empire, but the only title that he insisted upon was Germanicus, which he never dropped for the whole of his reign. Martial describes the honour for the German campaign as 'wholly your own' (*laurea...tota tua est*), indicating that Domitian was fully aware that victories in other areas were owed to his generals. Still, this merely proves that Domitian was proud of his participation in the Chattan war and considered it a worthy achievement; it does not refute the charge that he began hostilities without provocation simply to prove a point. Personal pride, coupled with emulation of Augustus and more likely Tiberius, may have been among his motives, but they were not the only ones. The driving force behind his attack on the Chatti was the establishment and maintainance of security for the territory under Roman control. The way in which he conducted the war, the establishment of the frontier, and the reorganization of the two Germanies after 85 can all be seen as related developments, clearly indicating that Domitian knew what he was doing.[7]

When the war began, it seems that Domitian had at his disposal about 30,000 legionaries and an unknown number of auxiliaries. Strobel estimates the total figure at 50,000 to 60,000 men. The main base for operations was probably Mainz, but during preparations for the offensive the troops may have been gathered elsewhere. It has been suggested that the vexillations at Mirebeau-sur-Bèze near Dijon were destined for the Chattan war. This is highly controversial, and the case for and against the theory must be examined. There are two strands to the argument: the tile stamps from Mirebeau, and the career of Velius Rufus. The evidence from the tile stamps reveals that at an unknown date, vexillations from at least five, possibly nine, legions were assembled at Mirebeau. Intelligently restored, the stamps attest the presence of detachments from the four Upper German legions, *I Adiutrix* and *XIV Gemina, VIII Augusta* and *XI Claudia*, and also, from the Lower German army, *XXI Rapax* from Bonn. Ritterling associated these tile stamps with the eight vexillations attested on the inscription from Baalbek recording the career of C.Velius Rufus, already discussed in the previous chapter. This association, ingenious in its day, is now out of fashion. Strobel assigned this special command to the war against the Marcomanni and Quadi in 89. More recently, Bérard and others re-examined the evidence and concluded that the vexillations of the Mirebeau tiles had nothing to do with Velius Rufus, 'dont les vexillations ne doivent plus être identifiées avec celles de Mirebeau'.[8]

Thus the Mirebeau vexillations and those of Velius Rufus are quite distinct from each other, but the tile stamp evidence must still be examined separately. The troops assembled near Dijon were engaged in some kind of building at the Mirebeau fortress, which leads some scholars to doubt that they were being assembled for Domitian's Chattan war, for instance Strobel, who sifted through the various groups of tile stamps, assigning them to different contexts. He suggested that one group belonged to the years 85–6, and that another group involved in the building work at Mirebeau belonged either to an Antonine phase or possibly even a Severan context. Strobel entirely dismissed the Mirebeau vexillations from his calculations of troop numbers of Domitian's army during the Chattan war. There is an analogy, however, that suggests that despite the building activity which suggests a stay of some permanence, the vexillations may have been destined for an impending war. At the beginning of 1800 when First Consul Bonaparte wished to disguise his intentions towards Austria, he gathered at Dijon, temporarily for a few months, the so-called Army of the Reserve under the command of his Chief of Staff, Major-General Alexandre Berthier on the pretext that this was merely an administrative measure. The deception was successful, and when the attack began in May 1800 it had every advantage of surprise. The distance that these troops had to march to reach their objective was no greater than the Romans would have had to travel to reach theirs at Mainz. The analogy with Domitian's pretended Gallic census is striking.[9]

More controversial is the supposed withdrawal of vexillations of troops from Britain, at a time when the governor Agricola was still campaigning in Scotland. It has been argued in the previous chapter that this was not the case. The most likely context for the withdrawal of vexillations from the legions of Britain would be the period after the abandonment of Scotland, which postdates the Chattan war. Thus Velius Rufus probably played no part whatsoever in the Chattan war. His command was an extraordinary one, and the date of his activities is not necessarily compatible with Domitian's war in Germany. The participation in a German expedition of Roscius Aelianus and the vexillation from *IX Hispana* has been related to Tacitus' statement that when the *legio IX* was subjected to a night attack during the sixth season of Agricola's campaigns in Scotland, it was the weakest of the three separated columns. The idea has gained some acceptance that the legion was under strength because a vexillation of perhaps 1,000 men had been withdrawn from it, but this is not specifically what Tacitus claims. The vexillation presumably fought in some serious engagement, since Roscius received *dona militaria* for his part in the proceedings, but it is imposssible to say where or when.[10]

It seems certain that Domitian employed *XXI Rapax* for the Chattan war and in order to fill the gap at Bonn the new legion *I Minervia* was sent to occupy the fortress. The legion was in existence by 83 or 84; this is borne out by an inscription recording the career of a soldier, L.Magius Dubius, who died during Domitian's reign, having served for 13 years in *I Minervia*. The new troops would need time for training; this they could undertake while fulfilling the functions of guarding the boundaries of Lower Germany, thus releasing *XXI Rapax* for the war. The offensive was most likely northwards from Mainz, but there is little evidence of the army's progress. At Heldenbergen a marching camp is probably a relic of the campaign, but the expected line of camps leading into Chattan territory is not forthcoming, mostly due to lack of dating evidence at the postulated sites. Apart from camps an army on the move leaves little archaeological trace, and it has already been suggested that there would be no large battle sites associated with this war. The only evidence as to where and how the war was conducted is to be found in Frontinus' *Strategemata*, where he refers to the flight of the Chatti into inaccessible places and Domitian's pursuit of them. On one occasion the Emperor pursued them into forests and then made his cavalry fight on foot, so as to overcome the difficulties of the terrain. It sounds as though Domitian was at the scene of the battle, making spontaneous decisions, unless Frontinus has stretched the truth a little. No place-names are given: they would probably not interest Roman audiences. Distances are mentioned in a separate passage, but the precise meaning is disputed. Frontinus states that Domitian advanced *limites* over 120 miles, thus changing the course of the war by laying bare the Chattan refuges. It seemed at one time that this passage referred to the establishment of the Taunus-Wetterau frontier, which just happens to be the required length of about 120 Roman miles (177.5 km). This solution was first suggested by the great German scholar Fabricius, and the concept that literature and archaeology could be so accurately reconciled was exciting. But other scholars have disputed this theory. When Fabricius made his statement, he did not know that the Wetterau was already occupied when Domitian became Emperor, forts having been established there by Vespasian. Furthermore, although the word *limes* (plural *limites*) has given rise to the modern English word limit, it did not originally denote a frontier as such; rather it indicated a road leading across territory or, more pertinently, a road penetrating into enemy territory. Some scholars prefer to interpret Frontinus' description of Domitian's activities not as the establishment of a frontier to watch over the Chatti, but as an invasion of their homelands to root them out of their hiding-places. The only controversy is over the distance mentioned: does it mean that the army covered a total of 120 miles on several separate routes into enemy territory, or that they drove a full 120 miles northwards from Mainz? Such a march would expose the army to flank attacks, but would not be incompatible with other Roman campaigns. It is noteworthy that Kassel in the Chattan heartland lies *c.* 180km = *c.* 120 Roman miles north-east of Mainz. An attack on this location would make sound military sense. Whilst there may have been no cities worthy of the name among the Chatti, many tribes with loose state organization regard certain areas as vital to their economy, or to their spiritual survival. Domitian may have discerned that to strike at the very heart of the Chattan territory would obliterate centralized resistance and disperse the tribe, which could then be dealt with piecemeal. This cannot be resolved on present evidence. It can only be said that Frontinus' *limites* and the establishment of the frontier were two separate concepts, one referring to the course of the war and the other a result of it.[11]

The end of the war is just as problematic as the start. There is no news of a final battle, nor did the triumph of 83 necessarily mark the cessation of hostilities. The victory over Germany is proclaimed on the coinage, beginning with issues of late 84. The majority of coins belong to the early years of 85, and take various forms. The mourning Germany coins of 84, depicting a woman with head bowed, represent the subjugation of the German people. In 85, coins were minted bearing the legends *Germania capta, Victoria Augusti,* and *De Ger(manis)* or *Ger(manis)* (pl. 15). On some coins Domitian is portrayed as victor being crowned; Mars and Jupiter are represented, and peace (*Pax*) is proclaimed. In 85, then, or more likely at the end of 84, Domitian considered his work in Germany completed. The sources cast a derogatory shadow over this achievement, implying that the campaign was worthless to begin with, and once begun it was completely botched. It is suggested that Domitian, simply to satisfy his burning desire for military glory, involved the Roman armies in an unnecessarily extended war – a theme taken up by some modern authors, who represent the war as a prolonged and rather aimless affair that came to an end only because the outbreak of the Dacian war made it imperative to call an inconclusive and unsatisfactory halt. The establishment of the frontier from the Rhine to the Neckar is therefore depicted as something of an accident, not as a considered policy.[12]

The frontier in Domitian's day (Fig. 3) was not like the later frontiers of Hadrian and Antoninus Pius. The concept is anachronistic for the Flavian period, since the mention of frontiers conjures up images of physical barriers, banks and ditches, palisades and walls. The Flavian frontiers were open territories, with the boundaries marked by roads, guarded by watch-towers and forts, probably patrolled and possibly further guarded by means of scouting expeditions in advance of the boundary, though for this there is no direct evidence. Precisely where Domitian erected frontier forts is revealed only by archaeological means. Frontinus relates how Domitian compensated the natives when he laid out *castella*

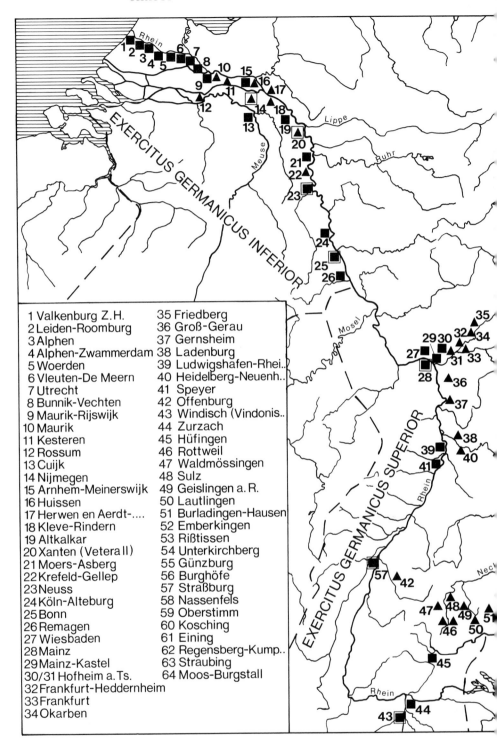

1 Valkenburg Z.H.
2 Leiden-Roomburg
3 Alphen
4 Alphen-Zwammerdam
5 Woerden
6 Vleuten-De Meern
7 Utrecht
8 Bunnik-Vechten
9 Maurik-Rijswijk
10 Maurik
11 Kesteren
12 Rossum
13 Cuijk
14 Nijmegen
15 Arnhem-Meinerswijk
16 Huissen
17 Herwen en Aerdt-....
18 Kleve-Rindern
19 Altkalkar
20 Xanten (Vetera II)
21 Moers-Asberg
22 Krefeld-Gellep
23 Neuss
24 Köln-Alteburg
25 Bonn
26 Remagen
27 Wiesbaden
28 Mainz
29 Mainz-Kastel
30/31 Hofheim a. Ts.
32 Frankfurt-Heddernheim
33 Frankfurt
34 Okarben

35 Friedberg
36 Groß-Gerau
37 Gernsheim
38 Ladenburg
39 Ludwigshafen-Rhei..
40 Heidelberg-Neuenh..
41 Speyer
42 Offenburg
43 Windisch (Vindonis..
44 Zurzach
45 Hüfingen
46 Rottweil
47 Waldmössingen
48 Sulz
49 Geislingen a. R.
50 Lautlingen
51 Burladingen-Hausen
52 Emberkingen
53 Rißtissen
54 Unterkirchberg
55 Günzburg
56 Burghöfe
57 Straßburg
58 Nassenfels
59 Oberstimm
60 Kosching
61 Eining
62 Regensberg-Kump..
63 Straubing
64 Moos-Burgstall

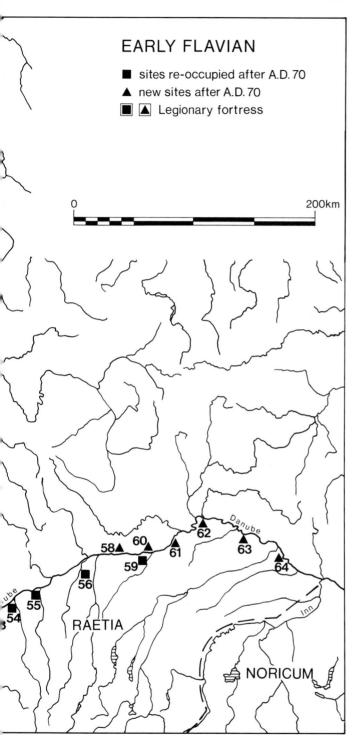

EARLY FLAVIAN

■ sites re-occupied after A.D. 70
▲ new sites after A.D. 70
▣ ▲ Legionary fortress

0   200km

Fig. 3. The German and Raetian frontier in the early Flavian period under Vespasian. (After Schönberger *BRGK* 66 1985, redrawn by Graeme Stobbs)

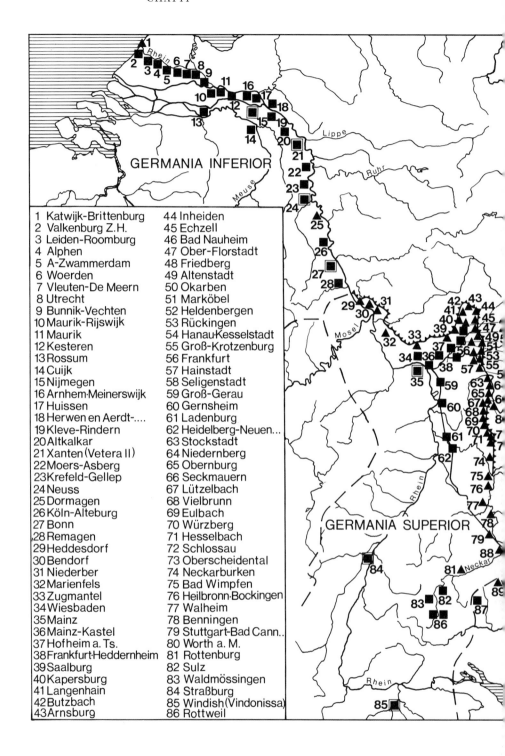

1 Katwijk-Brittenburg
2 Valkenburg Z.H.
3 Leiden-Roomburg
4 Alphen
5 A-Zwammerdam
6 Woerden
7 Vleuten-De Meern
8 Utrecht
9 Bunnik-Vechten
10 Maurik-Rijswijk
11 Maurik
12 Kesteren
13 Rossum
14 Cuijk
15 Nijmegen
16 Arnhem-Meinerswijk
17 Huissen
18 Herwen en Aerdt-....
19 Kleve-Rindern
20 Altkalkar
21 Xanten (Vetera II)
22 Moers-Asberg
23 Krefeld-Gellep
24 Neuss
25 Dormagen
26 Köln-Alteburg
27 Bonn
28 Remagen
29 Heddesdorf
30 Bendorf
31 Niederber
32 Marienfels
33 Zugmantel
34 Wiesbaden
35 Mainz
36 Mainz-Kastel
37 Hofheim a. Ts.
38 Frankfurt-Heddernheim
39 Saalburg
40 Kapersburg
41 Langenhain
42 Butzbach
43 Arnsburg

44 Inheiden
45 Echzell
46 Bad Nauheim
47 Ober-Florstadt
48 Friedberg
49 Altenstadt
50 Okarben
51 Marköbel
52 Heldenbergen
53 Rückingen
54 Hanau-Kesselstadt
55 Groß-Krotzenburg
56 Frankfurt
57 Hainstadt
58 Seligenstadt
59 Groß-Gerau
60 Gernsheim
61 Ladenburg
62 Heidelberg-Neuen...
63 Stockstadt
64 Niedernberg
65 Obernburg
66 Seckmauern
67 Lützelbach
68 Vielbrunn
69 Eulbach
70 Würzberg
71 Hesselbach
72 Schlossau
73 Oberscheidental
74 Neckarburken
75 Bad Wimpfen
76 Heilbronn-Bockingen
77 Walheim
78 Benningen
79 Stuttgart-Bad Cann..
80 Worth a. M.
81 Rottenburg
82 Sulz
83 Waldmössingen
84 Straßburg
85 Windish (Vindonissa)
86 Rottweil

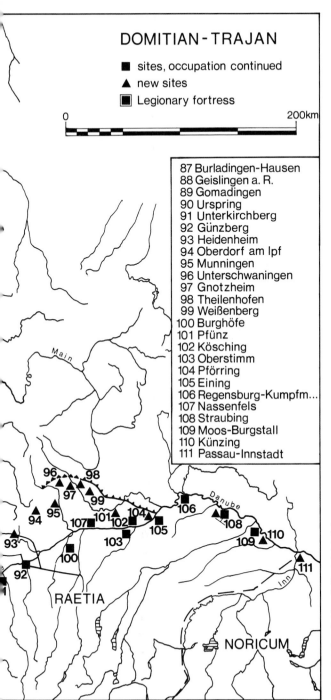

DOMITIAN - TRAJAN

■ sites, occupation continued
▲ new sites
▣ Legionary fortress

0   200km

87 Burladingen-Hausen
88 Geislingen a. R.
89 Gomadingen
90 Urspring
91 Unterkirchberg
92 Günzberg
93 Heidenheim
94 Oberdorf am Ipf
95 Munningen
96 Unterschwaningen
97 Gnotzheim
98 Theilenhofen
99 Weißenberg
100 Burghöfe
101 Pfünz
102 Kösching
103 Oberstimm
104 Pförring
105 Eining
106 Regensburg-Kumpfm...
107 Nassenfels
108 Straubing
109 Moos-Burgstall
110 Künzing
111 Passau-Innstadt

Fig. 4. The German and Raetian frontier under Domitian. The north-facing salient of the Taunus and Wetterau was guarded by forts and watch-towers. The Chattan territories lay to the north of this line. (After Schönberger *BRGK* 66 1985, redrawn by Graeme Stobbs)

over the fields of a tribe called the Cubii, who have not been identified and therefore cannot be located. In any case, it is not absolutely certain that the forts mentioned by Frontinus belonged to the frontier proper or whether they were associated with the campaign, and perhaps occupied only temporarily. With regard to the forts of the frontier line, the date of their foundation cannot be precisely established. Exact dates within a five- to ten-year framework simply cannot be pinpointed using purely archaeological methods. It is not certain whether frontier installations belong to the end of the Chattan war in 85 or to the period after Saturninus' revolt in 89. Sometimes it is not possible to distinguish between Domitianic and Trajanic building activity, but the major part of the work is probably to be credited to Domitian. Strobel suggests that building began when Domitian returned to Rome in 83; there is nothing to prove or disprove this theory. If the major part of the campaign was over and the army had only to root out pockets of resistance during 84, there is no reason why building could not have started at the end of 83. The argument that Domitian did not organize the German frontier until after the suppression of Saturninus' rebellion rests upon the presumption that for four years after the end of the Chattan war the Emperor made no territorial adjustments and no arrangements for security. After a war with a neighbouring tribe, the establishment of the frontier, or at least a protected boundary line, would seem to be a logical procedure, whereas to wait for four years and then to erect frontier forts after an internal rebellion does not display quite such an integrated approach. It could be argued that the systematic establishment of the Taunus-Wetterau line, and the junction of the Wetterau-Neckar sections of the frontier, lends some support to the theory that Domitian had an overall plan for the German frontier, for which the conquest of the Chatti was a major necessity. The forts and towers were constructed in timber, and most of them were replaced in stone during the reigns of Trajan or Hadrian. The demarcation line that Domitian chose was adjusted, though not radically altered, after his reign, indicating that he had found the optimum solution to the problem of Rome versus Free Germany. It was really only the fire-eating literary experts who mourned the abandonment of continuous expansion to the Elbe, or the ends of the earth. Fire-eating generals would soon have enough to do on the Danube and in the east to resent Domitian's halt on the Taunus-Wetterau-Neckar line. The system lasted until 260, and it surely cannot be entirely due to Roman inertia that no one thought of uprooting it entirely and beginning again. This frontier is Domitian's enduring achievement (Fig. 4).[13]

The creation of the two German provinces probably went hand in hand with the reorganization of the frontier, and may have been undertaken soon after the end of the war. Previously, Germany was governed as part of Gallia Belgica, and was divided into two military zones of Upper and Lower Germany, each with its own army. After the winter of 84/5, but before 90, the two Germanies were elevated into separate provinces and detached from Gaul. The victory coins of late 84 and early 85 may have been closely associated with the creation of the two provinces, but it is impossible to be certain, since the earliest attestation of the term province does not appear on an inscription or other document until 90, when the career inscription of Iavolenus Priscus proves that he was in office as *legatus* by October of that year. Prior to this date, lack of epigraphic evidence renders it impossible to be certain whether the individuals known to us were military commanders of the two German armies, or whether they were provincial governors. The most famous are those attested by Dio: L.Antonius Saturninus in Germania Superior, and Aulus Bucius Lappius Maximus in Germania Inferior, two men who entered history through their respective roles in the revolt of 89.[14]

IX

DACIA

The main events of the Dacian war can be set within a broad general chronology, but it is difficult if not impossible to extract accurate dates from the sources. The basic sequence can be quickly enumerated. The Dacians crossed the Danube into Moesia, where the governor Oppius Sabinus was killed. Domitian and the praetorian prefect Cornelius Fuscus hastened to the scene and gained some initial success. Domitian returned to Rome, then disaster struck again. Fuscus was defeated and killed with great loss of troops. After a hiatus of unknown duration, Domitian gathered more troops and, with Tettius Julianus at its head, this army won a victory at Tapae. All this has to be slotted into a timetable somewhere between 84 and 89. For most events not even the exact year can be pinpointed, let alone the exact month, and the search for locations is almost as difficult to resolve as the search for chronological accuracy.

The cause of the war is not established. Jordanes affirms that it began because the Dacians feared Domitian's greed, so they broke the truce that they had observed under other Emperors. This is patently ridiculous, but Jordanes had an axe to grind about the nobility and virtue of the tribes beyond the Danube, and literary tradition had its own axe to grind about Domitian's rapacity. Suetonius remains neutral, but makes it clear that the Dacians struck first. Dio does his best to ennoble Decebalus, the Dacian leader, and manages to imply that Domitian was the aggressor without actually saying so. In reality, the Dacians may have been unsettled by the war against the Chatti, fearing that they themselves were in danger of Roman invasion and conquest. Their attack may have been a demonstration of strength, but that was more likely to provoke retribution, and the Dacians cannot have been ignorant of this fact. It has been suggested that pressure from tribes beyond the Dacians may have precipitated their attack on Moesia, but this is difficult to prove in the absence of reliable source material. The reasons for the initial attack were probably not entirely clear either to the Dacians or to the Romans. Aggression is an emotive term and does not always rest on a foundation of cool, calculated rationality. Settled, sedentary people, including late twentieth-century authors, require a reason for such outbursts of violence, and automatically begin to seek for signs of external pressure, internal instability, grossly unjust treatment, the desire for expansion and conquest, the need for food or new lands in which to settle. Motives for aggression can then be safely ascribed to a nobility of purpose compatible with ethical standards of behaviour. For a proud warrior race, whose ethic demanded prowess in war, fighting and bloodshed for no very lofty reasons, nobility of purpose may have had an altogether different meaning. Value judgements are not innate and universal; they are acquired. Semantic theorizing merely serves to cloud the issue. The past history of the Danube region bears witness to a tradition of raids across the river into Roman territory, and in this respect the Dacians were doing nothing unusual, merely emulating what other tribes had done. Mocsy suggested that the Dacians took advantage of Domitian's preoccupation with his preparations for the coming German war, for which the intended springboard was Pannonia.[1]

Some authors have envisaged a steady escalation of hostility between Romans and tribesmen on either side of the Danube. The movement of peoples and the occasional rise to prominence of one or the other tribe made uncomfortable neighbours for the Romans, who tried to control the natives by various means, including diplomacy, negotiation and the payment of subsidies, and sometimes settlement within the Empire of displaced tribes. One particularly well-documented instance is the settlement in Moesia of 100,000 Transdanubian peoples by the governor Ti.Plautius Silvanus Aelianus in the reign of Nero. This is probably not the only example of such a procedure.[2]

The tribes beyond the Danube were for the most part mobile and potentially troublesome, occasionally launching raids into Roman territory, sometimes causing considerable damage and loss of life. They were difficult to pin down and bring to battle, so the only alternative was to watch for their arrival and try to block their path and, as a preventive measure, to monitor the tribes in their own lands. From the Roman point of view, the balance of power among the northern tribes was notoriously difficult to maintain and needed constant trimming and fine tuning. Agreements made with prominent members of a tribe were not necessarily binding upon all the population, and on the death of the individual concerned, the agreement was null and void. Likewise, the tribesmen considered their obligations at an end when the Emperor with whom they had treated was removed or expired. Diplomacy alone was therefore not sufficient to control the tribes. The Roman Empire needed defences along its borders, and for much of its length the Danube was the natural boundary line. The territories beyond the Danube were vast, and not necessarily easy to patrol and garrison. Absorption and Romanization would take time and effort, if it were possible at all. The choice was therefore between conquering and taking in all the tribes, *sine fine*, or adopting a suitable demarcation line somewhere within these tribes' territories. The latter was merely a half measure. It would solve nothing to take in a few miles of territory beyond the Danube, since that would present Rome with much the same problem in a more northerly location. The only truly secure borders would have been formed by the Baltic and the Urals, which would also have been unrealistically over-ambitious. The Danube was the inevitable frontier.[3]

Tribes facing the Roman provinces of Pannonia and Moesia were the Suebi, comprising the Marcomanni and Quadi, the Sarmatians, divided into two main branches – the Roxolani located to the north of the lower Danube, and the Iazyges east of the Danube bend in the Hungarian plain – and the Dacians, whose territory lay between the two branches of the Sarmatians. Roman troops were mauled by the Roxolani in 67/8, and during the Civil War in 69, the Sarmatians took advantage of the turmoil to attack. Mucianus, hurrying on his way from the east to Rome, detached one legion, *VI Ferrata*, to block the progress of the tribesmen. In the next year, they attacked again, and Fonteius Agrippa, the governor of Moesia, was killed. Vespasian sent Rubrius Gallus to restore order. This appointment and the subsequent building activity was recorded by Josephus, but unfortunately he did not elaborate upon the places where forts may have been added to the existing defences.

He merely says that Gallus stationed garrisons in the area, designed to prevent the natives from crossing the river so easily in the future. Archaeology cannot provide more than a few hints as to where these garrisons may have been established. From the reigns of Tiberius and Claudius the Danube had been progressively fortified, and the strategic locations were identified very early. The legionary bases occupied under Nero were unchanged in Domitian's day, and there was no increase in the legionary garrison, though the legions themselves had been reshuffled by about 81. The whereabouts of *V Alaudae* was for some time a puzzling question, but most authorities now maintain that it had already disappeared by about 70, and therefore did not feature in the build-up to the Dacian wars. There is some evidence to suggest that the number of auxiliary units in Pannonia and Moesia may have been increased. Diplomas for the Pannonian garrison reveal that between 80 and 85 at least four additional units had been added, making a total of six *alae* and fifteen cohorts. In Moesia, three units from Germany had arrived by September 82. A note of caution should be sounded before accepting this evidence at its face value, because it is not absolutely certain that the Pannonian diplomas record the full complement of troops at any one time, and for Moesia it is not possible to discern whether the three units from Germany were definitely additional to the existing establishment. Despite these drawbacks, Wilkes decided that the increase of troops is 'still a valid inference'. If they were indeed extra units, it cannot be said with any certainty where precisely they were placed.[4]

The defence system that Domitian inherited and built upon was based on the usual mixture of legions at communication centres and strategic points, with auxiliary units guarding river crossings, roads and settlements. The number of legions was not large: two in Pannonia, at Carnuntum and Poetovio, one in Dalmatia at Burnum, and three in Moesia at Viminacium, probably Oescus, and Novae. Occupation at other sites is problematic, since it is sometimes difficult to distinguish between the work of Vespasian, Domitian and Trajan. At some sites it is known that occupation began under previous Emperors and continued under Trajan, but irritatingly there is hardly any evidence of Domitianic occupation or activity, and is is even more difficult to identify new foundations which Domitian may have inaugurated. The major contribution that archaeology has made is to provide evidence that the majority of the Danube fortifications belong to the reign of Vespasian, so that the erstwhile conjecture that Domitian established the defence system must be transmuted into the theory that he merely continued and developed it (Fig. 5).[5]

There is slightly more evidence for Domitian's administrative measures. It is known that he divided Moesia into two provinces, called Superior (the western portion) and Inferior (the eastern portion). The date is as elusive as all the other dates for the Domitianic history of the Danube. Most authors represent the measure as an immediate response to the invasion, rather than a considered precaution put into effect before the Dacians crossed the river. The division may have been put into effect in 84/5, or 85/6. Strobel and others date the creation of the two provinces to 86, as part of the reorganization after the disastrous loss of Fuscus and his army but there is no firm dating evidence.[6]

The lower reaches of the Danube do not seem to have been garrisoned in Domitian's reign. Archaeological studies have revealed that the occupation of the Dobrudja was not carried out until the reign of Trajan. This evidence necessitates a revision of the theory that the earthwork defences in this region, the so-called *Trajanswälle*, belong to the period of Domitian's campaigns. It is highly unlikely that there was much activity here during Domitian's reign, except on the part of the fleet, which would take the place of the army in monitoring events in this area. The Moesian fleet had received the title Flavia by 92, but the award may have been made by Vespasian or Titus and need not be indicative of Domitian's specific arrangements for the defence of the Danube. Both the Pannonian and Moesian fleets may have been established before the advent of the Flavians, but there is little evidence. Vespasian may have reorganized the whole system, most likely in connection with the reconstitution of the Danube defences via his legate Rubrius Gallus. The duties of the prefect of the Moesian fleet included defence of the river-banks. Only one inscription attests this, but it is reasonable to suppose that while there were few garrisons in Lower Moesia, the fleet commander guarded the crossing points of the river, and reported upon disturbances.[7]

The growth of Dacian power had been a potential threat to Rome from the days of Augustus, when Burebista exerted some unifying influence upon the tribesmen. Augustus has been accused of magnifying this threat in order to gain personal and political advantage from it, but the centralizing tendencies among the Dacians cannot be ignored. In Domitian's reign, the Dacian leader was Diurpaneus, or Dorpaneus. He is described by Orosius as *Rex Dacorum*. The absolute accuracy of this statement is not certain. It is questionable whether Diurpaneus was king of the whole Dacian state, or just a part of it, either a natural clan division or a breakaway faction with pronounced anti-Roman tendencies which erupted eventually into war. Diurpaneus led the initial attack, and was then perhaps removed by the better-known leader Decebalus. There is some confusion over names, and whether or not Diurpaneus is the same personage as Duras, who according to Dio abdicated in favour of Decebalus because he was the better warrior.[8]

The date of the outbreak of the Dacian war will probably never be satisfactorily resolved. Traditionally, the Dacians crossed the Danube in the winter of 85/6, but various alternative dates have been suggested, ranging from the previous winter of 84/5, via spring or summer 85, to early in 86. Thus there is more than a twelve-month difference in estimations of the commencement of the war. The theory that the Danube crossing took place in winter derives some slight support from Pliny's description of the river bridged over by ice, the best time for the natives and the worst for the Romans because crossing over to the right bank was so easy. The inference is at best tenuous, since Pliny merely stated an obvious fact, and was in any case describing Trajan's preparations, not the outbreak of the Domitianic war. There is no absolute necessity to adhere to the theory that the war broke out in winter. Strobel argues instead for summer 85, and reconstructs a timetable which takes into account Domitian's two Imperial salutations between September 85 when he was still IMP IX and February 86, by which time he was IMP XI. According to Strobel's argument, Diurpaneus crossed the Danube in June 85, Oppius Sabinus mobilized *V Macedonica* from Oescus and *I Italica* from Novae, met the Dacians and defeat simultaneously, and news of the disaster reached Rome in July. Domitian and Fuscus mobilized and pushed the Dacians back by October, resulting in two Imperial salutations at very close intervals in September and October 85. At the same time, Domitian became censor for life.[9]

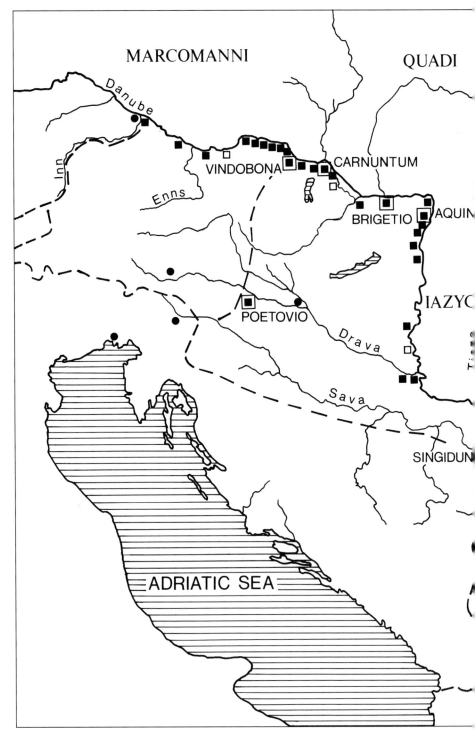

Fig. 5. The Danube frontier at the end of Domitian's reign. The map shows fortresses mentioned in the text. Legionary dispositions were much altered in the late 80s and

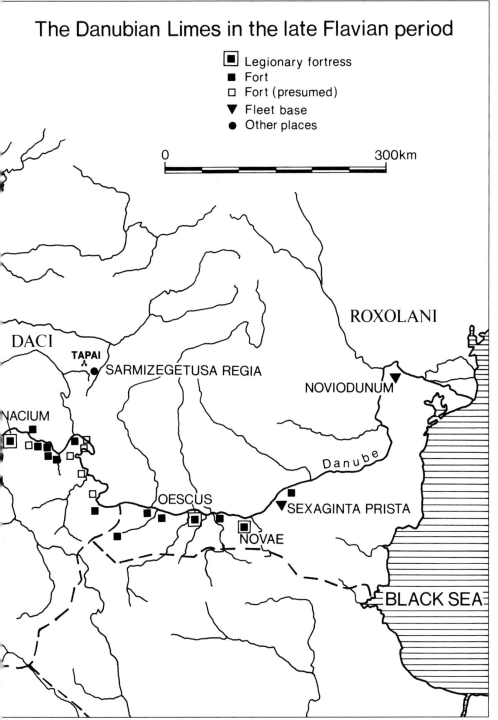

The Danubian Limes in the late Flavian period

■ Legionary fortress
■ Fort
□ Fort (presumed)
▼ Fleet base
● Other places

0   300km

ROXOLANI

DACI

TAPAI

● SARMIZEGETUSA REGIA

NOVIODUNUM ▼

NACIUM

OESCUS

▼ SEXAGINTA PRISTA

NOVAE

BLACK SEA

early 90s, therefore these bases were not all occupied contemporaneously.
(Drawn by Graeme Stobbs)

Between the defeat of Oppius Sabinus and the arrival of Fuscus, the Dacians went on to attack some Roman forts, causing considerable damage. Archaeological traces of this destruction are not forthcoming, so that the route taken by the Dacians is not known, nor the extent of their raid. The location of Oppius Sabinus' defeat, and Fuscus' operations of 85 are likewise unknown. Once the situation was stabilized at the end of 85, Domitian returned to Rome. At the beginning of 86, the Emperor celebrated his Dacian triumph, which some authors dismiss as a figment of the imagination. The total number of Domitian's triumphs is disputed. Gsell insisted that there were only three, while others insist that there were four. Mooney clarified the issue in his commentary on Suetonius, where *duplicem triumphum egit*, referring to the year 89, can be understood in two ways. One school of thought interprets the passage in the sense that in 89 Domitian celebrated a double triumph over the Chatti (a euphemism for victory over Saturninus) and the Dacians. Added to the passage in a later chapter that Domitian changed the names of the months after he had held two triumphs, this gives a total of three, and leaves no room for an extra one in 86. Mooney offers the alternative explanation that Domitian celebrated two triumphs over each of the two tribes of Chatti and Dacians, which makes a total of four. Those who firmly believe that Domitian held a triumph in 86 have no trouble in assigning his twelfth Imperatorial acclamation to the same period. [10]

After the triumph, Domitian held the Capitoline Games in Rome, from mid-May until mid-June 86. Fuscus meanwhile mobilized for an attack on Dacia and crossed the Danube on a bridge of boats, possibly from Oescus, though this is not certain. Then Fortune deserted him. What ought to have been a punitive expedition designed to eradicate opposition among the Dacians turned into a disaster. Fuscus and his army were lost, though it is not known if the disaster was as complete as that of Varus in Germany in the reign of Augustus. The Dacians captured a standard, possibly a Praetorian example, rather than a legionary eagle, which was rescued by the army of Trajan. Attempts to identify this standard with *V Alaudae* must be abandoned in view of the fact that this legion was lost long before Fuscus' downfall. Another theory which has been revised in recent years is that the altar at Adamklissi in Lower Moesia records the names of the men who were killed in Fuscus' expedition. It is now considered that this monument has nothing to do with Domitian's wars, and therefore does not record the defeat either of Oppius Sabinus or Fuscus.[11]

With the demise of Fuscus, which not all scholars would place in 86, the chronological problems arise once again. If it is assumed that Fuscus was wiped out in summer 86, and that Tettius Julianus won his victory at Tapae in summer 88, then some explanation has to be found to elucidate the events of late 86 and all 87. Military activity must be dated to the latter part of 86, since there were no Imperial salutations in 87, whereas between February and September 86 Domitian progressed from IMP XI to IMP XIV. If IMP XII belonged to the triumph in March or April 86, then XIII and XIV must belong to some date before September, and since Imperial salutations are hardly compatible with the defeat of Fuscus they must belong to a restitution of the Danube situation in the late summer and early autumn of 86. It is likely that by July or August Domitian was in Moesia, where he remained until the end of the year. This period of restitution may be the context of Dio's story, in which he accuses Domitian of skulking in one of the Moesian cities, indulging in riotous living, though no dates are specified. Despite the Imperial salutations it seems that there was no heroic campaign, but probably a great deal of unrewarding police work together, possibly, with some skirmishing into Dacia as Moesia was set in order. It can be inferred from Dio that Decebalus made overtures for peace, on condition that Domitian paid a subsidy based on a *per capita* rate of two obols from each Roman citizen. It is not certain whether this suggestion was made before or after Fuscus' campaign, nor is it clear whether Domitian negotiated at all at this time. In a later passage, Dio refers to the treaty which Domitian made with Decebalus in 89 during the campaign against the Marcomanni, informing readers that the Emperor had steadfastly refused to make a treaty before, despite the frequent requests of Decebalus. Perhaps Domitian employed delaying tactics of drawn-out diplomatic wrangling, without coming to any firm conclusion. Whatever the truth or otherwise of this suggestion, Domitian considered that the situation demanded his presence, and Dio's accusation that he did very little is no doubt unfounded. Much of the work may have been administrative. Some scholars date the division of Moesia into two provinces to this period. If this is correct, the existing governor of undivided Moesia, M. Cornelius Nigrinus Curiatius Maternus, became the first governor of Lower Moesia. Alternatively he may already have been governor of the Lower province if the division was made earlier. The governor of Pannonia, Funisulanus Vettonianus was transferred to the post of governor of Upper Moesia. These two men were lavishly rewarded by Domitian, so it may be assumed that they helped to stabilize the position along the Danube. The military activity of late 86 may have been limited to restoring the status quo. More ambitious projects were probably not possible, without large-scale assembly of troops and careful preparation.[12]

Domitian attended to his preparations for the whole of the next year. He patiently collected troops and made no rash punitive assaults across the Danube, though the temptation to do so must have been quite strong, even if only to save face with regard both to the Dacians and to the Roman high command. Troop movements are not securely attested, but highly probable. The evacuation of Scotland surely belongs to this phase, the removal of *II Adiutrix* and possibly some auxiliary units being part of the rearrangements that went with the abandonment. In addition, *IV Flavia* perhaps came up from Dalmatia, and *I Adiutrix* from Germany. *I* and *II Adiutrix* probably shared a base at Sirmium at first. This was one of the important headquarters for the later Roman Emperors during the various Danube crises. Afterwards, *II Adiutrix* went to Aquincum, where a new legionary base was constructed. The important point to note is that the Moesian garrison increased from three to six legions, four in Moesia Superior, and two in Inferior. All this would take time, and Domitian was determined not to hurry. Rashness had probably played a part in Fuscus' disaster, and it would be folly to risk losing a third general complete with his army.[13]

The choice of commander now had to be faced. In 87, Vettonianus was replaced by Tettius Julianus, who had already served in Moesia, and had been instrumental in repulsing an attack of the Roxolani in 69, when he was legate of *VII Claudia*. He thus had relevant experience and some specialist knowledge. What cannot be known is the extent, if any, to which the year 87 was devoted to reconnaissance, nor is there any evidence to illustrate the extent of Domitian's personal intervention. He did not supervise events this time, but remained in Rome. If he did not play any part in the formulation of plans for the campaign, he presumably approved the suggestions of Tettius Julianus and then perhaps gave him a free hand. It is suggested that Julianus based himself at Viminacium when the time came to enter Dacia, since this is the gateway to the heartland, leading to the Dacian stronghold of Sarmizegethusa. This would lead him across the Banat – on the same route that Trajan followed in 101 – leading to Tapae on the south-western edge of Transylvania, where the final battle was fought, a victory for the Romans. Little is known of the details of the preliminaries of the battle, or the troops involved. The Dacians were soundly defeated, but not eradicated. Dio describes how Vezinas, next in rank to Decebalus, pretended to be dead and later escaped. The story continues with the bizarre description of how Decebalus cut down trees and placed armour on the remaining stumps so that the Romans would think they were warriors and withdraw, instead of attacking the royal residence. Nothing more is known of the fighting, save that the decorations won by a centurion of *II Adiutrix* may have been won during the campaign. The battle at Tapae may have been fought too late in the year to pursue the Dacians right into their capital. Domitian had received two further Imperial salutations by September 88, and another by October, reaching a total of 17. Julianus probably thought it prudent to avoid pursuing the campaign in hostile territory in winter and Domitian may have approved or advocated plans for another attack beginning in the following spring. But before the victory could be followed up and the *coup de grâce* delivered, another rather more immediate problem had arisen.[14]

X

AD 89

The victory at Tapae was not followed up by occupation and annexation of Dacian territory. This may never have been part of Domitian's plan, but even if it had been there was a hiatus at this stage of the Danubian wars. It is suggested that preparations were under way at the end of 88 for the continuation of the war in 89, but before the army could take the field, or the Emperor himself could take any action, he had to deal with the revolt of Saturninus in Upper Germany.[1]

The career of L.Antonius Saturninus is obscure. If he had not made a bid for the throne, he would probably have remained completely unknown, shrouded in comfortable anonymity even in his own time. Originally an equestrian adlected to the Senate by Vespasian, he may have been governor of Judaea from about 78 to 81. He was suffect consul in 82, and perhaps governed a consular province before being selected for command in Upper Germany, at an unknown date before 88. It is not certain whether the two provinces of Upper and Lower Germany had been created when he was appointed, so he might have been either governor of the province, or commander of the Upper German army in a territory still administered from Gaul. Whatever his exact status, he was in a responsible position, in command of four legions, *XXI Rapax* and *XIV Gemina* at Mainz, *XI Claudia* at Windisch (Vindonissa) and *VIII Augusta* at Strasbourg. More important, from Upper Germany he had relatively easy and rapid access to Rome, and the precedent set by Vitellius may have encouraged him to imagine that he could succeed where the former general had failed. It is to be expected that Domitian would choose with extreme care the man destined to fill this post, so that when his trust proved to be so totally misplaced, the mental impact would have been quite disturbing.[2]

Domitian hastened to the scene of the action. He left Rome on 12 January 89 with the Praetorian Guard. It is not known at which date he was informed of the plot, nor how long it took to prepare for the journey. The outbreak of the revolt is traditionally dated to 1 January, the twentieth anniversary of the proclamation of Vitellius as Emperor in 69. The time taken for news to travel, by whatever means, from Mainz to Rome has been variously calculated, but as Walser points out, the hazards of winter travel were unpredictable and may have caused delays. The fact that Domitian was ready to leave Rome a mere eleven days after the raising of the revolt presupposes that he had received some prior warning in the final days of 88, but this is not borne out by any of the sources.[3]

The single Spanish legion, *VII Gemina*, was summoned to Domitian's aid with Trajan at its head. Pliny later enlarged this force to legions in the plural. Domitian also collected auxiliaries from the Raetian garrison. He may have intended to go to Vindonissa to ensure the allegiance of *XI Claudia*, but his route is no better known than his intentions. In the event *XI Claudia* did not join Saturninus, nor did *VIII Augusta* at Strasbourg. The two legions at Mainz, *XXI Rapax* and *XIV Gemina*, and perhaps some auxiliary troops constituted the whole of the rebel forces.[4]

Before Domitian reached Mainz, news arrived of the defeat of Saturninus by Aulus Buccius Lappius Maximus, the governor of Lower Germany. Maximus had been legate of *VIII Augusta* under Vespasian and had risen to the suffect consulship with Iavolenus Priscus as his colleague in 86. It is not known how long he had been governor of Lower Germany at the time of the revolt, or commander of the Lower German army if the province had not yet been formed. Likewise nothing is known of the final battle in which Saturninus was killed. It has been suggested that the two armies fought near Remagen or Andernach, but there is no definite evidence, and no details have survived of what actually happened. After the battle, Dio records that Lappius burnt all Saturninus' correspondence, which can be interpreted in either a derogatory or a complimentary light. There may have been nothing but nobility of purpose in Lappius' action; on the other hand he may have been heavily implicated in a rebellion that went wrong or broke out too soon, and so moved quickly against Saturninus and then destroyed the evidence. The latter case is less likely. By the time that Saturninus made his first move, far too many people would have known the facts, and Lappius Maximus could not have hoped to silence them all. Furthermore if there was any suspicion in Domitian's mind on this score, he did not act upon it. Indeed, he rewarded Lappius with a second consulship, much earlier than was usual for such an honour. Other consulars who were promoted by Domitian to their second or third term of office had received their first or second consulships under previous Emperors.[5]

The Epitomator of Aurelius Victor equates Lappius Maximus with Norbanus, and much of the literature on Saturninus still deals with these two individuals as one. Norbanus was procurator of Raetia at the time of the rebellion, and his reward for helping to suppress it was his appointment to the post of praetorian prefect. His role in the fighting is unknown. He may have moved independently against Saturninus from the east as Lappius moved from the west, or they may have acted in collusion. It is possible that after the defeat of the rebels, both Lappius and Norbanus remained at Mainz until Domitian arrived, to prevent the outbreak of further trouble among disillusioned legionaries. [6]

Another source of trouble, apart from Roman soldiers, may have stemmed from the threat of invasion by the Chatti. Suetonius states that the barbarians (he does not specify any particular tribe) were poised on the opposite bank of the frozen Rhine, waiting to cross over to help Saturninus. They were prevented from doing so by a miracle: a sudden thaw set in. This suggests that they were massed at a point where there was no bridge, or if they were near one of the Rhine bridges, then it was held by a Roman force loyal to Domitian, or at least hostile to Saturninus. The whole story may be a complete fabrication invented after Saturninus's death, but some authors have taken it very seriously, and claim that signs of destruction at some Roman sites indicate that the Chatti did cross the river eventually, even if only for hit-and-run raids. If so, Lappius would no doubt have dealt with the problem immediately, rather than wait for instructions from Domitian. The inscription which describes Lappius as *confector belli Germanici* may refer to his activity in this sphere as well as his part in thwarting Saturninus. This episode has earned the name of the second Chattan war, which Strobel labels as ephemeral. There was probably a brief demonstration of strength, not strictly deserving of the label of a war. Some authors have decided that a treaty was arranged with the Chatti, but the facts are obscure. After the suppression of the revolt and the conclusion of the war with the Chatti, Domitian earned two more Imperial salutations, reaching IMP XIX probably by March or April. [7]

Retributions and rewards began when Domitian reached Mainz, possibly in February. The Lower German legions received the honorary title *pia fidelis Domitiana*. After Domitian's murder, they retained only the *pia fidelis*. Suetonius records the lenient treatment of a tribune and a centurion who were of such vile reputation that they could have had no influence over the soldiers. Other conspirators were hunted down, then barbarically tortured and killed. This may not be exaggeration on Suetonius' part, for Domitian would have every right to feel angry. Most of the rank and file were spared, possibly on the grounds that they had been coerced. Outside the army, the extent of the punishments has perhaps been inflated. Xiphilinus is full of praise for Lappius' action in burning Saturninus' papers, then goes on to accuse Domitian of committing murders as a result of his suspicions. Suetonius affirms that Domitian became more cruel after the revolt. For these reasons, the executions of Domitian's last years are sometimes construed as revenge against the senators, either because some of them had been involved in the plot, or because Domitian had by now become so suspicious and mistrustful as a result of the rebellion that he executed anyone on the slightest excuse. Opinion is divided on this matter, and some authors have rejected the Saturninus-revenge theory. Senatorial involvement with Saturninus has been discounted, as has retribution against the Senate, justified or unjustified, as a result of the plot. The rebellion is interpreted as a purely military affair, and the punishments were probably confined to the military sphere, all exacted in Mainz and not extending to the capital.[8]

In the longer term, the aftermath of the revolt was probably not quite so simple. It is true that in 89 the Senate as a body acted correctly, performing the proper ceremonies and sacrificing more than once for the Emperor's safety, victory and return. Dio records the fact that Lusianus Proculus bestirred himself from retirement to rally to Domitian's side. There was without doubt some genuine support for Domitian at this time. But the Senate was a large body, possessed of as many subtle variations of opinions as it had members, to which must be added the fact that words and actions displayed in public are not necessarily representative of private inner thoughts and motives. Those who declare that senators were not involved in the plot and that Domitian did not punish any of them as a result of it, ignore the possible workings of the Emperor's mind after the revolt was put down. There may well have been absolutely no senatorial connection with Saturninus, who could have acted quite independently, if rashly, in raising rebellion. But Domitian could never be sure. He had some relevant experience in this sort of affair, after all, and however dispassionately he evaluated the situation, ultimately he could not fail to make judgements based upon personal experience. If Saturninus intended to usurp the throne, it is almost inconceivable that he had no connections at Rome. To raise revolt with no warning and only afterwards to make an attempt to win over all the senators by marching on Rome with a legion or two would have been the act of a complete madman. A madman Saturninus may have been, but if he was not, if the rebels had a definite goal in view, then preparations and contacts would have been vital. It is quite true, as Syme pointed out, that there were no signs of preparation, from which Syme deduced that the whole episode was accidental and spontaneous. This is, of course, quite possible, but it must also be remembered that preparations for such affairs are by their very nature clandestine, and in this case may have been successfully concealed. In Domitian's mind, the very uncertainty itself would be the most important factor. Speculation augmented by fear would work upon his imagination, probably reaching inordinate proportions. It is this psychological dimension of the affair, not the facts, that would have the greatest effect. Scholars continually establish the 'Truth' of a situation and then express surprise that the original participants did not perceive this glaring 'Truth'. The human mind, however, does not always work with stark reality, but with perceptions and emotions. On rare occasions, these three elements run parallel on the same frequency; more often they run counter to each other.[9]

It has been argued that Domitian did not in fact become more cruel after the rebellion, simply because he was always cruel from the beginning of his reign, if not earlier. It is perfectly true that he was rigidly unbending about the exaction of the proper punishments, in strict accordance with the law, but the change which Suetonius describes was perhaps more subtle. Before 89 Domitian may have considered all aspects of the cases brought before him, and tried to pronounce fair judgement. It is impossible to know how many times he withheld punishments, or how many times he dismissed *delatores* without acting upon the information he had been given – Suetonius says that he did not listen to them at first. After 89 he was perhaps more willing to listen, and meted out death sentences without examining the evidence too closely. The senators who fell victim to him are meticulously recorded, and the pretexts for their removal are flimsy to say the least. The executions of Sallustius Lucullus and C. Vettulenus Civica Cerialis, governors respectively of Britain and Asia, have been linked to the revolt of Saturninus, but it is not known when either of these governors was appointed, nor how long they remained in office, and most important, no dates are provided for either execution. Sallustius Lucullus could have governed Britain at any time between 83 and 96, and although some authors have attempted to find evidence, there is no mention of rebellion of any sort in the sources – Lucullus' crime was to name a lance after himself. Vettulenus Civica Cerialis was executed for reasons unknown. He may have been involved with the rising of the so-called false Nero in the east (one of three rebellions that occurred during the Flavian period, when it was claimed that Nero had never died and had come back to claim his Empire), but there is nothing to prove or disprove this theory. His death may have occurred in 87 or 88, before the rebellion in Upper Germany began. It cannot be said that any of the executions of senators were in any way connected to Saturninus, except in Domitian's long-term memory, biding its time until a suitable excuse arose.[10]

Domitian's suspicions concerning the senators, founded or unfounded, is only one aspect of the aftermath of the revolt. The other important aspect is its military nature. One possible and very important result of the revolt has not been sufficiently stressed with regard to Domitian's later behaviour. He had begun on a very bad footing with the Senate, and any further deterioration would have been merely tantamount to what he or the Senate expected, but alienation from the army must have been an extremely damaging blow to Domitian. He had tried to foster good relations, and was the first Emperor to treat the army as though it mattered and had a part to play in the Empire, for which he strove to reward its services. He probably felt secure in his relationship with the army, and this would bolster him against opposition from other sources. After the revolt, this confidence cannot have failed to waver and diminish. The reiterated common-sense real-ization that the revolt had in the end affected only two legions would not help to eradicate the fear that it might happen again, and it is quite likely that Domitian was no better informed of the reasons for the rebellion than scholars are today. This lack of understand-ing would produce a reaction of near-despair about the unpredictability and uncontrollability of the actions of any sector of the communities of the Empire, of which the most dangerous was the army. Disconnected from the Senate by circumstances, detached from the populace by inclination, uninterested in the provincials, Domitian was now forcibly isolated from any trustworthy support.[11]

At this point it is necessary to discuss Saturninus' possible motives. It is unlikely that he had any connection with the false Nero in the east. This was not an Empire-wide con-spiracy, and events in Upper Germany and the east must be construed as purely coincidental. Saturninus may have been the sole instigator of the rebellion, intent upon gaining the throne for himself, or he may have had the idea thrust upon him. Perhaps he had grievances to air, or perhaps he had been the innocent victim of circumstance, caught up in a sudden flashpoint in a mutiny brought about by officers or men of the two Mainz legions for any number of reasons. If the latter case, then Saturninus ought to have followed the example of Verginius Rufus and politely refused the honour. This judgement is a little unfair: it requires tremendous fortitude to say no to 10,000 determined men with swords.[12]

The possible grievances of the soldiers demand explanation. Pay had been increased and Domitian had made every effort to accommodate the army, short of allowing the men complete licence and leisure. The revolt, if raised by the legions, perhaps had other ori-gins. *XXI Rapax* may have heard of plans to remove it to Moesia, as part of the preparations of 88 for another campaign in 89, designed to round off the Dacian victories. It had already been moved from Bonn, and possibly felt quite unloved. Soldiers, in collo-quial terms, could get quite a little business going with the locals if allowed to remain in one place for long enough; *XXI Rapax* may have seen its potential profit margins rapidly diminishing, and their grievances, fortified by an alcoholic Saturnalia, may then have grown into rebellion. It may, as Syme suggested, be as simple as that. To look for more convoluted and sinister reasons may be unnecessary, though attempts have been made to ascribe the revolt to a sexual scandal, from which the homosexual Saturninus sought to extricate himself by rather drastic, not to say hysterical, means. Allegations of this sort, that Saturninus had never been fit to be a senator in the first place, could easily have been invented, or freshly aired, after the event.[13]

Slight clues as to the course of events can be gleaned from the measures that Domitian took after the rebellion. Saturninus, not having a Mucianus to help finance his aims, had seized all the ready cash at Mainz, consisting of the soldiers' savings and whatever monies the legions required for daily operations. From 89 onwards, Domitian forbade the sol-diers to keep savings of more than 1,000 sesterces in the military chests, which raises the questions of exactly how much a soldier could save during his service, and what he did with the surplus after he had reached the limit in the military strong-room. Did soldiers henceforth arrange their own private banking systems, invest in business or land, or simply drink and whore away the remainder? The hazardous prospect of hordes of veterans dis-charged from the army with only 1,000 sesterces in their pockets must have occurred to

Domitian, who presumably cared deeply about his own welfare even if he did not care about that of the soldiers. It is not known whether the soldiers whose money had been squandered ever retrieved it, or whether they were compensated for their loss.[14]

The next measure, also designed to prevent any future emulation of Saturninus, was to forbid the existence of double legionary fortresses. *XXI Rapax* was moved to Moesia almost immediately; *XIV Gemina* followed some time later, perhaps in 92, though Strobel thinks it was removed in 97. From then onwards, to the end of its career, *XXII Primigenia*, originally from the Lower German army, occupied Mainz. The total complement of legions of Upper Germany was reduced from four to three and Saturninus himself was replaced by a jurist rather than a military man. The new governor of the province of Upper Germany was Iavolenus Priscus. The date of his appointment is unknown, but he was definitely in office by 27 October 90. This date is derived from a military diploma, while the further details of Iavolenus' career are enumerated on his gravestone. He had been legate of two legions, and in his second legionary command was in effect governor of Numidia. Before his appointment as *legatus consularis provinciae* he had served as *iuridicus* in Britain. It is from these two pieces of evidence, the diploma and the career inscription, that it is known that Upper Germany had become a province in its own right by 90. It is quite likely that Iavolenus Priscus was appointed governor immediately after Saturninus was defeated, possibly arriving straight from Rome while Domitian was still in Mainz, in the early spring of 89.[15]

The Rhine now declined in importance as the scene of military action. The major sphere, throughout the rest of Domitian's reign and extending into the reign of Trajan and virtually every Emperor thereafter, would be the Danube. While still in Mainz Domitian heard that the tribes north of Pannonia were stirring and therefore transferred his attention to the new war, coming to terms with the Dacians in order to be able to concentrate on a campaign against the Marcomanni and Quadi. It is unknown whether he was acting in response to definite warlike actions, or whether he struck out to nip potential threats in the bud. Some scholars dispute the fact that he went directly to the Pannonian front from Mainz, but there scarcely seems time for him to have returned to Rome and journeyed outwards again. He may have arrived in Pannonia, perhaps basing himself at Carnuntum, in spring 89, possibly in April or May. The history of Pannonia from this time onwards is one of intermittent but sometimes protracted and serious wars, perhaps the most bitter being those fought under Marcus Aurelius. The wars of Domitian in this region are the least well documented of his reign. Much of the evidence derives from Dio, and most scholars are compelled to mutilate the order of the surviving passages in their efforts to make sense of events.[16]

The exact location of the tribes involved in these wars is not established in minute detail. The wars of the Pannonian frontier are sometimes termed the Suebian-Sarmatian wars, but these names are those of federations of tribes, so that the main antagonists must be more clearly distinguished. The Suebi comprised many peoples. Several tribes recognizable in their own right, such as the Semnones who considered themselves the most important of the Suebi, were part of the federation. The Marcomanni had already emerged as a distinct people by Caesar's day, and shortly afterwards their king Maroboduus extended his rule over a vast area and a number of other tribes. Roman traders knew the Marcomanni well, and according to Tacitus several Romans were settled within the tribal lands. Carnuntum, facing the territory of the Marcomanni, was therefore of considerable military and commercial importance. On the eastern boundary of Pannonia, recently settled between the Danube and the Theiss, were the Iazyges, a branch of the Sarmatians, who came originally from south Russia. The other branch, the Roxolani, settled on the lower Danube, east of Dacia. The fluidity of movement of these peoples and their various fluctuating alliances were to cause Rome even more trouble long after the reign of Domitian.[17]

Traditionally, the reason why Domitian advanced against the Marcomanni and Quadi was their lack of support against the Dacians, which presumably means that they had failed to contribute troops according to the terms of an alliance. The active assistance of the Marcomanni would have secured the western flank of the army marching into Dacia. The sources state that they had given the Romans no help, but that does not necessarily also imply that they had remained passively neutral – they may have antagonized Domitian, but there is no evidence. According to Dio the tribes sent two embassies to ask for peace. Domitian executed the members of the second one. Such a Draconian measure – proclaiming in no uncertain terms that negotiations are at an end – cannot have been undertaken lightly. The date of these embassies is not known. Mocsy places them immediately after Tapae and before the revolt of Saturninus, but it can be argued that Domitian was waiting for the successful outcome of his treaty with the Dacians before showing his hand against the Marcomanni and Quadi.[18]

Strobel dates this treaty to midsummer 89, in June or July. Dio says that Domitian had been defeated before he sent a hasty message to Decebalus. In other words, reduced to a state of panic by his own folly, he was forced to back down from his high-handed attitude and put an end to hostilities with the Dacians. The malignant hyperbole is blatant. The date of the treaty is not attested in any source, but if Strobel's suggestions are correct, Domitian wasted no time at all in arranging a treaty with Decebalus. There may have been more than one campaign, first against the Dacians, resulting in some sort of treaty, and another against different tribes across the Danube. Between April/May and June/July Domitian may have attempted a rapid expedition and met with some reverse. The tribes possibly formed a threatening alliance and forced him to intervene. Providing neither date nor location, Suetonius says that Domitian waged war against the Sarmatians because a legion was lost along with its commander. It is known that *XXI Rapax* disappeared from the record at some time after 89, so some scholars have assigned its demise to this period, but it is more commonly thought that *XXI* arrived from Germany in 89 and survived until 92. Activity across the Danube before the treaty was agreed with the Dacians is by no means certain. It is quite possible that Domitian made no move at all between April and June/July, but held off the Marcomanni by negotiation, finally declaring that he was ready for war by summarily executing the envoys of the Marcomanni and Quadi when the Dacians agreed to allow Roman troops to march through their territory.[19]

The Dacians became a client state of Rome, with all the usual arrangements. The Romans agreed to pay subsidies and render practical assistance to the king. Decebalus decided not to negotiate personally with Domitian, but sent his brother Diegis, who received the crown from Domitian's hands. It is sometimes envisaged that this took place in Rome, but nothing in Martial's sickeningly sycophantic description of the scene suggests that this was the case. Diegis could have met Domitian on the Danube, while the expedition from Pannonia was in the offing. This would certainly have expedited the terms of the treaty and saved considerable time. The fact that Dio goes on to describe the triumph over the Dacians does not mean that it followed instantaneously. Diegis probably came to the Emperor at Carnuntum. There is some evidence that the court was there, probably at this time, and as far as Domitian was concerned, wherever he was present in person, there also was Rome.[20]

Domitian's twentieth Imperial salutation is probably to be associated with the peace treaty with the Dacians. In the sources the treaty is dismissed as unimportant, even shameful, but this can be laid mostly at the door of Trajanic propaganda. The major problem was that Decebalus was still free, and revenge had not been extracted. The payment of subsidies and the lack of territorial gain would seem outrageous to Romans whose conception of the world was *Imperium sine fine.* But in 89 there was very little else that could have been achieved except to fight on two fronts at once, since Decebalus would not have failed to take advantage of the Romans' dilemma, even if he had already suffered serious reverses in the Tapae campaign. The treaty was useful to Romans and Dacians and, as Syme pointed out, it saved face on both sides. According to its terms, the treaty allowed Roman troops to march through Dacia to attack the Marcomanni and Quadi from the flank. This is probably the context of Velius Rufus' expedition, though some authors would prefer to date it to the war of 92. It is clearly attested on Rufus' career inscription that he marched through the kingdom of Decebalus, the king of the Dacians (*per regnum Decebali, regis Dacorum*). Whether or not he did so at the head of his famous eight or nine legionary vexillations is a matter of opinion. The vexillations were drawn from the three legions left in Britain after the withdrawal of *II Adiutrix*, two legions from Upper Germany, and two from Moesia, leaving the two Pannonian legions free to operate probably from Carnuntum. By the time the later war broke out in 92, the Pannonian garrison had been built up and perhaps even trained for another campaign, whereas in 89 there were only two legions in the province, and the fighting against the Dacians and then the turmoil of the civil war would have rendered Domitian relatively unprepared for a campaign across the Danube. There would be greater need for additional vexillations from other provinces in 89 than there would be in 92, and so the assignation of Velius Rufus' special command to this date has much to recommend it. The detachments were probably sent home to their parent units after the campaign of 89.[21]

Details of the fighting and the conclusion of the war are lacking, but the crisis, whatever it was, had been averted, or at least postponed for a few years. At the end of 89, Domitian celebrated a triumph over the Chatti and the Dacians. He gave lavish games and in turn the Senate voted him honours, including the famous equestrian statue, which forms the subject of Statius' poem. He did not assume the title Dacicus, though Martial addresses him unofficially as such in the preface to his eighth book of Epigrams. Domitian made no reference to victory over the Marcomanni, probably because he was painfully aware that the battles were won, but not the war. In the following years he was not blind to the potential danger to the Danube frontier. The number of legions in Pannonia had grown from the original two to four, and Domitian did nothing to diminish that number. This is significant when it is remembered that no other province held more than three legions. *XV Apollinaris* was at Carnuntum, but the locations of other legions are uncertain. *XIII Gemina* perhaps began to build the fortress at Vindobona, which was finished by *XIV*

Gemina. XXI Rapax and *I Adiutrix* were part of the provincial garrison, but it is less certain where they were housed. They may have succeeded each other at Brigetio, where *XXI Rapax* may have been stationed from 89 to 92, and where *I Adiutrix* is attested from 97 onwards.[22]

One more event should be mentioned as significant for Domitian in 89. His niece Julia (pl. 16) died at some time between 87 and 90. She is mentioned in the *vota* of the Arval Brethren for 3 January 87 but she is absent from those of 3 January 90, and she appears as *diva* on coins of 90, during Domitian's fifteenth consulship. The traditional date assigned to her death by most scholars is 89. Domitian was absent from Rome for most of the year, faced with first a revolt, and then another war. If he received news of Julia's death in these circumstances, he could perhaps be forgiven for experiencing a very low moment. He may have remained unaffected by her death, but the sources seem to agree that Julia was one of the few people for whom he ever felt any affection. In the absence of their respective parents, Domitian and Julia may have grown up together. Her death cannot have failed to cause him some pain. The lurid story that Domitian caused the death by forcing Julia to abort his own child can be discounted as one more piece of scandalous fabrication.[23]

XI

THE DARK YEARS

The years between the conclusion of the first Pannonian war in 89 and the eruption of the second in 92 are not greatly illuminated by the sources. Domitian was consul for the fifteenth time in 90; he did not hold the consulship in 89 or 91. His colleagues are not without interest. M.Cocceius Nerva was consul with the Emperor in 90, and in 91 the year opened with M' Acilius Glabrio and M.Ulpius Trajanus as consuls. The year 90 produced a bumper crop of eleven suffect consuls, probably in order to relieve a blockage in promotions, as Syme said, but rewards for loyalty in 89 are not out of the question.[1]

The punishment of Cornelia, the Vestal priestess found guilty of immoral relations with, among others, Valerius Licinianus, marred the year 91. The ancient penalty was live burial, and Domitian insisted upon the application of the law. Pliny reports at length on the affair, long after Licinianus had been exiled and forced to become a teacher of rhetoric. He adds heart-rending detail of Cornelia's nobility of bearing and so on, all of which condemns Domitian yet further for his barbarity. Suetonius provides the additional information that this was Cornelia's second offence, since she had been acquitted the first time she was charged. He also describes how several of her lovers were beaten to death with rods. Only the praetorian Licinianus escaped with his life. The affair is redolent of agony on all sides. Domitian could not afford to allow such crimes to go unpunished, for he had to be seen to be upholding the law, supporting the state religion, rooting out evils and so on. Caesar's Vestals, like Caesar's wife, had to be above suspicion. The exaction of the penalty, however, reveals an insecure reliance upon the law instead of upon personal authority. Vespasian would probably have found some way of showing leniency, while at the same time preserving his authority. On the other hand, if circumstances demanded it, he too could have been just as unbending. It is Domitian's misfortune that there is no more information about this affair which might elucidate why he took such a hard line. It seems that he did not take it light-heartedly, since according to Pliny, when Licinianus confessed, Domitian was delighted, saying that he was justified after all. The execution of Cornelia perhaps cast a slight shadow over the installation in the Forum of the equestrian statue of Domitian, which was voted by the Senate after the wars of 89 and probably unveiled in 91. Statius wrote a long poem about it, noting its position in the Forum but showed no embarrassment about mentioning the temple of Vesta, which lay to the right of the statue. Eusebius and Dio describe the proliferation of statues of Domitian all over the Empire, not without a tinge of disapproval.[2]

On the Danube, ominous movements were fomenting. It is alleged that both the Iazyges and the Suebi were indignant at the help given by Domitian to the Lugii, who were at war with the Suebi. Perhaps in sending 100 cavalry to the aid of the Lugii,

Domitian thought he was being restrained, but he presumably knew how delicate was the balance of power beyond the Danube. Around this time he received at Rome Masyas the king of the Semnones, and the priestess Ganna. The purpose of the visit is unknown, but the link with Pannonian events seems clear. Perhaps Domitian was attempting by diplomacy to isolate the troublesome elements among the tribes, making alliances with those who were useful to him. If so, it may have caused offence. The Sarmatian Iazyges and the Suebi united. Tribesmen crossed the Danube and cut down a legion with its commander, generally agreed to be *XXI Rapax*. Domitian journeyed to Pannonia. Martial says that he was absent for eight months (the moon had not quite completed its eighth orbit), and it is suggested that he was back in Rome in January 93, so it is likely that he left in May of the previous year, probably with a strong sense of *déjà vu*. The damage was repaired, but there is total obscurity about where and how and by whom. The legate of *XIII Gemina*, Caesennius Sospes, received praetorian *dona militaria* in an *expeditio Suebica et Sarmatica*, but this is dated by some scholars to the Trajanic wars. Another inscription attests a military tribune in a *bellum Germa(nicum) et Sarmat(icum)*. The date of the inscription is Trajanic, but the text refers to awards made for exploits in these wars or in wars by previous Emperors. Logically this should refer to both Domitian and Nerva, which implies that the awards were won in the last year of Domitian's reign and the first year of Nerva's, when fighting broke out again on the Danube. But there is a certain coyness in the avoidance of actually naming the Emperors that gives rise to the suspicion that Domitian was the main one concerned in the awards, so there is a marginal possibility that this inscription refers to 92. Though they are undated, the mention on these inscriptions of both Suebi and Sarmatians provides some indication that there may have been a war on two fronts in 92, necessitating Domitian's presence. Bengtson, not usually prone to praising Domitian, portrays him in the background arranging for the army's needs, working hard to facilitate its success. Most importantly he did not let the reins slip from his hands – the victories were rightly his. The groundwork done on the Danube by Domitian contributed significantly to the later successes of Trajan. Indeed, Trajan may have witnessed this war of 92 and played a part in it. He may have been governor of Pannonia in 93, where he could have gained experience that he brought to bear when he embarked on his own campaigns.[3]

Domitian's twenty-second Imperial salutation is to be associated with this war, but this time there was no triumph to mark the end of the fighting in 92 or 93. Martial refers to a 'private triumph', and to the laurels that Domitian dedicated to Jupiter, also attested by Suetonius who associates them specifically with the Sarmatian war. The third *congiarium* was paid to the people after this war, as Martial affirms. Despite the recent successes, Domitian was not convinced that all was over on the Danube front. There is some indication that at his death in September 96, preparations had been made for another war. Some of the troops which featured in Trajan's wars were probably already on the Danube by 96, and Strobel argues that by the late summer of 96 Domitian had already called in Pompeius Longinus as governor of Pannonia, though he is not firmly attested there until the beginning of 98. This war Nerva inherited, and Trajan finished off.[4]

At this point a brief tour of the Empire is instructive. Between the end of the Pannonian war in 92 and Domitian's murder in 96, the Empire was predominantly peaceful. There had been a war in Africa at some indefinite date, perhaps concurrently with the Chattan and Dacian wars, or perhaps later. There are one or two pieces of evidence about the North African war, or wars, which may or may not be related. Possibly in Vespasian's reign, the two provinces of Mauretania Tingitana and Mauretania Caesariensis, normally governed by equestrian procurators, were united under the command of a senator, Sentius Caecilianus. This man was experienced in North African affairs, having been legate of *III Augusta* in Numidia, around 73–5. The date and duration of his Mauretanian command are alike unknown, but the appointment suggests that there was serious trouble, which either subsided and then flared up again, or more likely dragged on interminably as a guerrilla war, for which the terrain is admirably suited. Whichever of these two alternatives is correct, some time later, the tiresomely ubiquitous Velius Rufus, tribune of the *Cohors XIII Urbana* at Carthage, was put in charge of the armies of Africa and Mauretania to bring the tribes to heel, as his career inscription explicity states.[5]

The African wars did not concern Domitian too closely, and did not demand his personal presence. The casual way in which he 'forbade the Nasamones to exist' perhaps illustrates the depth of his interest. Nonetheless the arrangements for the defence of the African provinces ultimately depended upon him. Domitian may have begun the advance towards the Aurès mountains, and it may have been his decision to move *III Augusta* to its new base at Lambaesis in Numidia, much further west than the previous bases at Ammaedara and Theveste. It is unfortunate that Domitian's work cannot be readily distinguished from Trajan's, but this is significant in itself, in that Trajan did not feel compelled to make either radical or retrograde alterations, so that the frontier arrangements can be seen as a continuation of the same policy. Internally the African provinces flourished from this time onwards, and whilst this cannot necessarily be ascribed to Domitian's personal initiative it is at least indicative of the fact that he did nothing detrimental to quell the growing prosperity.[6]

In the east all through Domitian's reign there existed a sort of armed neutrality. Vespasian had rationalized the eastern frontier after the wars of Nero. The number of legions in the eastern provinces was raised from four to six, three stationed in Syria, two in Cappadocia and one in Judaea. The east was defended by means of diplomacy and alliances backed up by armed force. The potential enemy, Parthia, was made up of a conglomeration of vassal states upon which the King of Kings could not always rely. For the Romans, the memory of Crassus, disastrously defeated at Carrhae, lingered long, effectively deterring any overtly aggressive behaviour in the eastern provinces until the reign of Trajan. In Domitian's reign the east was notorious for threats of a different nature, in the appearances of various individuals pretending to be Nero, returned to claim his throne. One Terentius Maximus marched to the Euphrates in Titus' reign, but no war of restitution began. Likewise the false Nero of 88/9 came to nothing in the end, though Civica Cerialis may have been executed because of his association with the abortive rebellion – or because Domitian refused to believe that he was not associated with it. There is some evidence, derived from diplomas, to suggest that Domitian moved extra auxiliary troops into Syria at the time of the false Nero's appearance, and then moved them out again once the crisis was averted. Suggestions that Domitian planned an aggressive eastern war are probably unfounded, being based on eulogistic literature and no solid evidence.[7]

Wars of outright conquest followed by annexation were not a feature of Domitian's reign. The abandonment of Scotland and the reasons for it have already been discussed.

In the Chattan war, Domitian did not annex the tribal territories over which he had campaigned, and he did not return to annex Dacia after the Pannonian wars were concluded in 92. He chose instead to delimit Roman territory and fortify the boundaries facing the potentially hostile peoples. Lower Germany met its free counterpart on the lower reaches of the Rhine, lined with forts and legionary bases. In the Taunus and Wetterau region, Domitian took in the north-facing salient of fertile lands, guarding them by means of towers and forts, with the legionary base in the hinterland at Mainz. The Main-Neckar-Danube link was not improved until the reign of Antoninus Pius, when the whole line was moved roughly 40km (25 miles) eastwards, and re-established more or less as a carbon copy of the old one.[8]

On the Danube, numbers of troops steadily increased while the Rhine faded in importance as the theatre of war. This progressive increase in legions and auxiliary troops was in response to mounting external threat. The least affected of all the Danube provinces in the years of warfare under Domitian and Trajan was Noricum, where contact with Rome had a longer history than in the other Danube lands, resulting in a greater degree of assimilation. Roman ways of life penetrated most settlements, where architecture and art proclaimed a certain prosperity. In Pannonia, though some trading connections had been established during the Republic and early Empire, the military character of most settlements remained unchanged for a long period, and in Moesia assimilation hardly gained a foothold. It was left to Trajan to occupy and garrison the lower Danube, though it is likely that had Domitian survived he would have pursued the same policy. He knew that wars on the Danube were not yet finished, and had wisely decided not to hold a triumph over the Marcomanni, Quadi or Sarmatians. When he was murdered in 96, another war was beginning, or may already have begun, for which he had been granted a four-year reprieve to recruit, equip and train the Danubian armies. It had probably not escaped his notice that armies cannot fight continuously without wearing out, and this is perhaps one reason why he did not embark on offensive wars across the Danube, knowing full well that the time would come soon enough when he would need a properly trained army in that region.[9]

It is doubtful whether the peace and rising prosperity of the provinces behind the frontiers was due in any great part to proactive measures on the part of the Emperor. There was probably a great reliance upon local enterprise, monitored no doubt, and fostered when it emerged, but the principal interest in the provinces and their inhabitants would probably extend only to the extraction of profit and the maintainance of law and order. Beyond that the rule may have been one of *laissez-faire*. Domitian stuck to the rules and followed in his father's tried and tested footsteps. His rule was severe but just. He tried to instil these tenets of government into his governors, but it is not known for certain how far he succeeded. The provincials may have had little to complain of, or it may be that the lack of prosecutions for extortion derived from a feeling of despair that no one would undertake to prosecute the guilty party once he was back in Rome. Counter to that argument, it could be said that Domitian ought to have been pleased to witness a few token prosecutions in order to make his point that no one escaped his notice, and to encourage others to behave in the accepted fashion while they represented Rome abroad. There would surely have been no lack of eager men ready to prove their worth in the courts. At any rate, the trial in 93 of the ex-governor Baebius Massa, accused by

Pliny and Herennius Senecio on behalf of the province of Baetica, was unusual. Pliny's associations with Baetica rendered him susceptible to appeals on behalf of the provincials. Indeed his honour was at stake, though Baebius was a friend and probably an informer of Domitian's, and it must have required great courage to take up the case. Baebius was condemned, but perhaps used his influence to secure the condemnation of Herennius Senecio, who was executed for writing a glowing account of Helvidius Priscus, Vespasian's *bête noire*. No wonder Pliny was worried that he might be next. He claimed that he was on Domitian's list of suspected persons, and in fact he may well have been the subject of rumours and false accusations, but Domitian obtains no credit at all for refusing to act upon such information.[10]

At the same time that Senecio was executed, Arulenus Rusticus met the same fate for writing in praise of Thrasea Paetus, who committed suicide in 66 after being accused of treason. These men, Paetus, Helvidius, Rusticus and Senecio were related by marriage ties and by association to each other and headed the faction known as the Stoic opposition. Domitian had tried to reconcile them, but failed, and in 93 he acted very positively. He exiled the women members of the circle and along with Senecio and Rusticus he also executed Helvidius the younger, on account of his activities as playwright. Helvidius had parodied rather too closely the domestic arrangements of the Imperial household, not in itself a crime worthy of the death penalty, but it may have been the last straw in a veritable cartload of bales. There are people in the twentieth century who never know when to stop, constantly delivering clever gibes, engendering in the recipient a fleeting but intensely pictorial desire for Domitianic powers of retribution. The Helvidius affair placed a stain on the conduct of the Senate of which Tacitus was only too aware, since in accordance with Domitian's wishes, the senators were eager to display their own particular loyalty by physically dragging Helvidius to prison. *Gravitas* must have been forgotten that day in one more demonstration of the corporate servility of the Senate. At the time, there may have been a genuine disgust with Helvidius, not for insulting the Emperor, but for rocking the senatorial boat. In retrospect ,when the tyrant was safely out of the way and everyone could breathe again, courage doubtless returned, along with wishful thinking that at some point someone had stood up to Domitian and pointed out the injustice of the sentences.[11]

The year 93 is considered by some authors, generally following in Eusebius' footsteps, to be a fateful turning point, after which everything was doom, gloom and despondency. This date is manufactured to suit a particular point of view, and more credence should be accorded to Suetonius, whose choice of 89 as the turning point has been disregarded. Syme restated the case for Suetonius, not least because the latter formed his own contemporary judgement and wrote within a very short time after the death of Domitian. Apart from the executions just mentioned the expulsion of the philosophers from Rome and the so-called persecution of the Christians and Jews are also dated to this year. The philosophical opposition had never really been absent since the time of Julius Caesar and Augustus. It was sometimes aimed at the Principate in general rather than the Princeps in person, but since in the 80s and 90s the removal of the Principate in general meant the removal of Domitian in person, this subtle distinction would scarcely carry much weight with him. Augustus found the opposition particularly distressing if Dio is to be believed. He invented a long dialogue for Augustus and Livia about this very topic. Particularly poignant is the passage about friends who must be called friends, even if they are not friends, so that the Emperor is more alone and isolated in company than he is when actually alone. Domitian's preference for solitude can be explained, in part, on these terms; it was easier. The expulsion of the philosophers from Rome removed the necessity of listening to them at close quarters. The practice or study of philosophy for its own sake was harmless, but there was a highly vocal section of those who called themselves philosophers who caused offence by their outspoken criticism. Often it was an excuse for displays of attention-seeking bravado. There was little of practical, reforming use in their ideology, and it is no wonder that Emperors faced with the problems of the real world had no patience with their bleatings. Unfortunately, philosophy often went hand in hand with subversion. What was called for in dealing with it was a superhuman indifference, balance and discriminating judgement. It cannot be ascertained to what degree Domitian possessed these qualities, since we have evidence only of his destructive power.[12]

The evidence for the religious persecutions is slight. Religious differences alone were not the crucial issue. The treatment of the Jews was not classifiable under the heading of anti-semitism; rather, their harassment stemmed from financial motives, pursued with crass insensitivity. The rigorous collection of the tax payments to the *fiscus Judaicus* has been put down to rapaciousness, but it is at least as likely that there was also an element of perfectionism at work, directly attributable to Domitian himself. If there had been any opposition to the actual practice of Judaism, Domitian would have been quite capable of arranging harsher penalties. Judaism and Christianity were seen in a similar light by the Emperors, since intransigence on the part of believers interfered with loyalty to the state and to Roman religious practice. It cannot be said that the Domitianic persecution of Christians was either widespread or long lasting. The chief martyr is Domitilla, wife of T.Flavius Clemens, Domitian's cousin, executed in 95. Domitilla was banished to the island of Pandateria, but she was transmogrified in later sources into a fictitious younger Domitilla banished to a different island. She became the virgin martyr, a condition not easily attributable to the first Domitilla, who was the mother of at least seven children. The sources which condemn Domitian as persecutor are none of them contemporary with him, nor is there any pagan attestation of such persecution, two factors which lend themselves to the suspicion of fabrication. The tales can be dismissed as inventions of Christian martyrology and it should be remembered with what zeal martyrdom was sought and revered – the ultimate validation of faith.[13]

Two senators were dispatched allegedly because of their religious associations, but the facts are obscure. According to Dio, Acilius Glabrio, who was a member of Domitian's *consilium*, was forced to fight in the arena, but the lion was no match for him and so Domitian, seething with jealousy, exiled and later executed him. The charge was impiety, a broad generalization that could mean almost anything, though some authors have attempted to prove that Glabrio was a Christian. T.Flavius Clemens was accused of atheism. Dio associates his death with conversion to Judaism, scarcely distinguishable from Christianity to some of the ancient authors, in which case the atheism in question will have been his repudiation of Roman gods. Suetonius adds that Clemens was lazy and shiftless, and that he was executed on the flimsiest of pretexts. Perhaps the full truth was not known even to contemporaries; in 95 when the execution took place, Domitian had probably reached a point where he considered that there was no reason why he should explain himself. Clemens was a possible source of danger to the Emperor, being the only other surviving member of the Flavian house. The fact that Domitian had adopted Clemens' two young sons, renaming them T.Flavius Vespasianus and T.Flavius Domitianus and clearly marking them out as his successors, may have given Clemens and his wife Domitilla delusions of grandeur, affecting their behaviour in a way intolerable to Domitian. Suetonius uses this execution as the introduction to the death of Domitian himself, as though the removal of his close relative was the final act of tyranny that even the gods could no longer ignore. From the narrative it has been deduced that Domitian survived only another eight months after his cousin, but in fact it was probably rather more than that, and it cannot be stated with any certainty that Clemens was indeed Domitian's last victim.[14]

As far as the other senatorial victims are concerned, the possibility that they may have been guilty of plotting against Domitian is played down in the sources in favour of trivial charges perhaps designed to obscure the truth. The governors Sallustius Lucullus and Civica Cerialis have already been discussed, and may not belong to the so-called post-93 turning-point. Nor perhaps do the executions of Salvius Cocceianus, Aelius Lamia, Mettius Pompusianus and Salvidienus Orfitus. Despite the warning given him by his uncle Otho not to remember too obviously that he was related to an Emperor, Cocceianus made much of his relationship with the former Caesar by celebrating his birthday. Hence it was thought that he must have had designs on the throne. Orfitus was banished after a trial involving Nerva and Apollonius of Tyana, in whose biography Philostratus adds some details to the story. Execution followed sometime later for Orfitus, who may have been guilty of some kind of plot – the execution of his father by Nero may have left sufficient family resentment to induce him to take revenge on the current Emperor. Aelius Lamia seems to have been guilty of very little except acerbic wit. Suspicion and distrust between Domitian and Lamia presumably dated from the earliest times, when Domitian stole his wife. When complimented on his singing voice, Lamia reputedly attributed it to his enforced celibacy, and when Titus urged him to marry again, he asked innocently if Titus was looking for a wife as well. Resentment may have thrown Lamia into the arms of the opposition, but in this case it is more likely that Domitian feared what Lamia might do and looked too earnestly for the evidence, so that he could remove the object of his guilt. Mettius Pompusianus emerges from the pages of Suetonius more as a harmless eccentric than a conspirator. He was executed simply because he carried around a map of the world, and read the speeches of various generals, which is hardly a sound basis for suspicion. Perhaps he was just terminally boring, if not irritating, but most people would be capable of limiting their death-wishes to fantasy.[15]

Suetonius presents a strong case for Domitian's tyrannical cruelty by listing most of the victims together, without dates of execution, or full details of their real or supposed crimes. The impact would have been reduced had the names been distributed throughout a chronological account; 13 senatorial executions in 15 years would not have made such a gripping headline. It has been pointed out that Claudius executed over 200, possibly nearer 300, equestrians, and 35 senators, and yet it is not entirely due to Robert Graves and Derek Jacobi that Claudius emerges as a shrewd and capable, determined but kindly man. If Suetonius' stories are correct, some of Domitian's executions were not tidy affairs. He reputedly had an unnamed spectator, who spoke out loud his opinion of one of the gladiators at the games, thrown into the arena to be rent by the dogs. This is not pre-meditated or considered judgement, but savage bad temper, assertiveness run amok, without even the excuse of fear to alleviate the act. According to Pliny this was not an isolated example, though it may have been the most shocking. Everyone had to toe the line as far as the Emperor's gladiators were concerned, because criticism of them was interpreted as criticism of Domitian himself. No one dared to utter a word, and in this context Pliny's desciption of Domitian as *demens*, literally out of his mind, is probably correct. While Pliny and Suetonius may have exaggerated, they probably did not fabricate the stories entirely, and they are supported in a less sensational way by other authors, principally Tacitus.[16]

There is nothing in the sources which fully illustrates the supposed degeneration of Domitian's character, either after 89 or 93. A bewildered lack of understanding is dis-cernible, which probably leads quite easily to the acceptance of any far-fetched story about Domitian's cruelty. The distance widened between the Emperor and those over whom he had direct influence, with the result that continuity was annihilated, no one knew what was going on, rumours abounded and Domitian's decisions seemed to emanate from nowhere. There was no obvious pattern, which was probably the most upsetting aspect. Most people can play the game according to the rules, and can even adapt to successive changes in the rules, but with Domitian in his later years there were no rules. Present con-duct was perilous in itself, and provided no guarantee that past conduct would not suddenly be reinterpreted in an unfavourable light. Withdrawal from public life was not the answer because it attracted too much attention, and was bound to be considered as silent but pertinent criticism. There was no choice then but to keep on living day by day, trying to avoid trouble and do the right things without a rule book for guidance. The sit-uation was probably as dire as Tacitus says it was, and a few months would be sufficient to wipe out all the years when Domitian was not afflicted. Men would look back and re-eval-uate, finding evidence of this sort of conduct all along, and criticizing themselves for not having recognized it for what it was. Thus history would be rewritten.

Domitian's assassination was inevitable, but perhaps delayed through inertia. There comes a point when shocked surprise no longer has any impact, and only paralysis results. Senators may have talked about the necessity of ridding themselves of the Emperor, but never managed to do anything about it. There may even have been some hope that it would all end, if Suetonius is correct in describing Domitian's early leniency, or that each outburst, if they were sporadic and unpredictable, would be the last. There were probably many days or even months when all went well, beguiling the onlookers into imagining that the future would be brighter. Only when all hope was gone could the true enormity of the situation be realized – the Emperor was beyond reason or rationality and was not going to improve or revert to his former self. It seems that this state should be easily rec-ognizable when recounted in dry words, but in day-to-day life the changes are so subtle, and the recognition so unwelcome, that resolutions to do something about the situation are not usually formed until the situation has deteriorated so far as to make it well-nigh impossible to escape it.

The conspirators were not politicians or even noblemen, though the readiness with which Nerva was proclaimed Emperor presupposes the existence of an acquiescent net-work of influential people probably glad to leave the actual murder to the domestic staff, who were by now beginning to feel nervous about their own survival. It was said that Domitian had drawn up a list of names of those he was about to execute, so an inner circle of domestics decided to pre-empt him. Suetonius and Dio provide the names of some of them. On the day of his death, 18 September 96, Domitian attended a trial in the morning, then went to the bath, but was distracted by his chamberlain Parthenius, telling him that there was an important visitor. The plot had been laid some days before. Stephanus, Domitilla's steward, pretended that he had injured his arm and wrapped it in bandages so that he could conceal a dagger there. He was the important visitor that Parthenius introduced to Domitian. He pretended that he had information about a conspiracy, and presumably gave Domitian some written evidence, because according to Suetonius, Stephanus stabbed him in the groin as he read it. Domitian called for one of the slaves to hand him the dagger that he kept under his pillow, but only the handle was there; Dio says that Parthenius had removed the blade. By this time Clodianus, Maximus, Satur and an unnamed gladiator had attacked the Emperor. Domitian put up a good fight, trying to wrest the dagger from Stephanus and to gouge out his eyes as they grappled. He clearly wanted to cling to life, despite its difficulties. He was forty-five years old.[17]

There are two mysteries which have never been adequately explained about the plot. Suetonius makes no mention of the two praetorian prefects, Petronius Secundus and Norbanus. Dio says that they were aware of the plot, but it is not until Eutropius' account in the fourth century that there is any suggestion that one of them was involved in the killing. It would have been dangerous to attempt to murder the Emperor without the complicity or purchased silence and inactivity of the Praetorians. Another puzzle is why there was no immediate revenge for Domitian's death; that came later, when Nerva was forced to hand over Parthenius for brutal elimination. Perhaps the Praetorians had been promised something that never materialized. The second problem is the position of Domitian's wife. Dio insists that Domitia was fully aware of the plot to kill her husband, and as the object of his hatred she lived in fear of her life in the Imperial palace. If there had been an estrangement, perhaps after the death of Julia, there was no public scandal. The sources would surely have seized upon such news had it been available. The political situation may have been her only concern, if indeed she was aware of the plot. It had probably reached the point where there was no other solution except to remove Domitian, talk and advice being long since rejected. She played no active part in her husband's murder, but on the other hand she was probably not present at the funeral arranged by Domitian's nurse, Phyllis. No one can tell where she went or what happened to her on the day of the murder or immediately afterwards. She survived her husband, and did nothing to eradicate his memory, calling herself Domitian's wife on brick stamps issued from her factory, perhaps in defiance of the wishes of the Senate. *Damnatio memoriae* was proclaimed throughout the Empire, and all trace of Domitian was supposedly removed. The wonder is that so much does survive.[18]

XII
THE PSYCHOLOGY
OF SUSPICION

It is time, then, for the final summing up and an attempt to understand. Those who believe that the tenets of modern psychology can find no place in a historical work are advised to ignore this chapter. On the other hand there are those who do think that psychology has a place in history, who probably also share the view that human evolution has not yet progressed much further than necessary to provide for the efficient functioning of a tribe of hunter-gatherers. In this biological, evolutionary respect we are close to the Romans, in that there are certain human mental processes which transcend social customs and acquired responses.

K.H.Waters assessed Domitian's character favourably while admitting that it was that very character which helped to bring about the breakdown in relations between Emperor and subjects. Waters accepted the theory of a gradual change in Domitian's character, as Suetonius describes. Dio has no good word for Domitian, but reflects the developed tradition of the tyrant; it is Suetonius who depicts something of the real man, of whom there are revealing glimpses among the defamatory remarks. Chapter 9 of Suetonius' life of Domitian is wholly favourable, setting out the Emperor's admirable qualities perhaps so that they could be followed by a negation of them all in Chapter 10. The admirable qualities presumably had some basis in fact, just as did the tyrannical ones, however much both may have been distorted. According to Suetonius, Domitian was at first kind, generous and conscientious about the welfare of his subjects.[1]

In person, Domitian was tall and reasonably handsome, with a ruddy complexion which suggested either the blush of modest countenance, or to Tacitus, an effective mask for everything for which he ought to have blushed with shame. A tradition has arisen from Suetonius' description that Domitian was sensitive about his appearance, especially about his encroaching baldness. The Emperor wrote a pamphlet called *The Care of the Hair*, in which he quoted from the *Iliad* and commented on the short-lived quality of beauty. These are the words of a reasonably well-educated realist. Suetonius makes much of the supposed sensitivity, implying that no one could mention baldness even in someone else. On the other hand, Martial could write a poem addressed to a certain Labienus, whom he mistook for three separate people because he had luxurious hair on either side of his head and none at all in the middle. The book of poems was dedicated to Domitian – if he did not read the poem himself, there would surely be many a helpful soul willing to point it out to him. Thus the fact that Martial was not invited to go and live somewhere a long way from Rome indicates that Domitian could accept the change in his appearance with resignation and some humour. A son of Vespasian perhaps could not fail to inherit or acquire a sense of humour. Suetonius reports that Domitian once remarked, 'I wish

I were as handsome as Maecius thinks he is,' which denotes a certain shrewdness, and also a tolerance of pretentiousness. His recorded opinion of Maecius would otherwise have been a little more savage.[2]

Domitian's sense of humour could, however, take a macabre turn, not amusing at all to those on the receiving end. Dio reports at 'shock-horror' length the banquet that Domitian gave for eminent equestrians and senators. He had prepared a room in which décor and fittings were black, and insisted that the guests should arrive at night, unattended by servants. The food was based on the ingredients of a funeral banquet, all served on black dishes, and the places were marked for each guest by a slab shaped like a gravestone, each with a lamp like those hung in tombs for illumination. Domitian sent all his guests home accompanied by one of his own servants, unknown to each potential victim. After waiting a few moments, he sent the place-markers, which turned out to be solid silver, as gifts. Significantly the context of this scenario in Dio's narrative is 89, presumably just after Saturninus' revolt. If so, it was a lesson in insecurity, no doubt extremely effective, but the victims would not identify in any way with Domitian's own insecurity. Perhaps he gained enormous satisfaction from planning and executing the banquet. It was a reminder of his potential power as well as a lesson in living with the fear of death. He probably realized that he had outlived sympathy.[3]

An examination of Domitian's character must begin with his childhood. It is a commonplace theory that events occurring in childhood can determine the later attitudes, both conscious and unconscious, of the adult. A reconstruction of Domitian's attitudes and their possible origins necessarily involves much speculation, but there are interesting parallels in modern psychological literature which may be brought to bear. It is known that Domitian's mother died at some time before 69, but it is not known how old Domitian was at the time of her death. It can be postulated that he was quite young, perhaps old enough to have developed some sort of relationship with her, but still too young to understand death and the sudden removal of the person with whom he perhaps felt secure. There need not have been continual, day-long contact to provide the emotional ties and experience of security. In many cases the early death of the mother is seen as some sort of betrayal. Even in later years when the nature of death comes to be fully understood, there is still a residue of great insecurity, usually unexplained because it is felt emotionally rather than understood intellectually, and unexpressed because the insecurity was felt most keenly at an age before the child could verbalize his feelings. Whilst the effects are by no means universally deleterious, the loss of the mother at a crucial age can damage later development. According to a modern study 'if a child enjoys a particularly close relationship with the mother which is suddenly terminated before he is old enough to understand any possible reasons for such a betrayal, he is likely to mistrust all other human beings whom he later encounters, and only be gradually persuaded that anyone at all is trustworthy'. This was the fate of Isaac Newton, who was deprived of his mother at the age of three. At Oxford he was described by one of his contemporaries as 'of the most fearful, cautious, and suspicious temper that I ever knew'. He was extremely unwilling to face criticism, inclined to be fiercely solitary, and heartily disliked, all of which attributes can be applied to Domitian. Thus far the ancient authors may have been correct in their assumption that these particular aspects of Domitian's character were always in evidence, from childhood onwards. The charges of cruelty and avarice are more difficult to sustain

PLATE 1. Portrait of Vespasian, depicting him with uncompromising realism, in his sixties
and balding. The sculptor has captured shrewdness, determination and humour in the expression,
described by Suetonius as 'always straining' (*Vespasian* 10: *vultu veluti nitentis*).
(Courtesy Ny Carlsberg Glyptotek, Copenhagen)

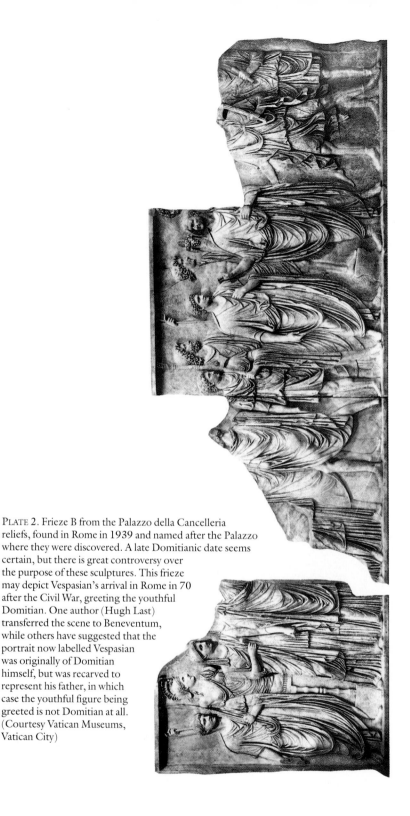

PLATE 2. Frieze B from the Palazzo della Cancelleria reliefs, found in Rome in 1939 and named after the Palazzo where they were discovered. A late Domitianic date seems certain, but there is great controversy over the purpose of these sculptures. This frieze may depict Vespasian's arrival in Rome in 70 after the Civil War, greeting the youthful Domitian. One author (Hugh Last) transferred the scene to Beneventum, while others have suggested that the portrait now labelled Vespasian was originally of Domitian himself, but was recarved to represent his father, in which case the youthful figure being greeted is not Domitian at all. (Courtesy Vatican Museums, Vatican City)

PLATES 3 and 4. Two views of the head of Domitian from Frieze B of the Palazzo della Cancelleria reliefs. It is disputed whether this is in fact Domitian (see caption to pl. 2), but the hair-style, the expression, and the slightly protruding upper lip argue for identification with him. (Courtesy Vatican Museums, Vatican City)

PLATE 5. Titus as magistrate or law-giver. This portrait may have stood in a niche or against a wall, since it is not properly finished at the rear. It was found in a garden near the Lateran in Rome. It has been suggested that the original statue portrayed Domitian, but that after the *damnatio memoriae* the head was recarved, in which case this is not a contemporary likeness of Titus. Nevertheless the family resemblance to Vespasian is unmistakable. (Courtesy Vatican Museums, Vatican City)

PLATE 6. Bust of Domitian as a young man, probably dating to Vespasian's reign. (Courtesy Museum of Fine Arts, Boston)

PLATE 7. Cuirassed statue of Domitian, possibly dating to the reign of Titus.
(Courtesy Vatican Museums, Vatican City)

PLATE 8. Bronze coin, undated. Obverse: Domitia Longina, with elaborate Flavian hairstyle. Legend: DOMITIAE AUG IMP CAES DIVI F DOMITIAN AUG. Reverse: *Divus Caesar* Domitian's infant son, with his mother. Legend: DIVI CAESAR MATRI. SC. BMC II 413 no. 501. (Copyright British Museum)

PLATE 9. Bronze bust of Domitian, found in the Tiber in Rome in 1891, perhaps a casualty of the *damnatio memoriae*. It probably dates from the earliest years of his reign. (Courtesy Ny Carlsberg Glyptotek, Copenhagen)

PLATE 10. Larger than life-size head of Domitia Longina, Domitian's wife, as a young woman. The date is probably 79–81. (Courtesy Hermitage Museum, St Petersburg)

PLATE 11. A very fine marble bust of Domitian showing him as Emperor, older and more mature. The hair-style is probably a product of artistic licence, since Domitian had a tendency to baldness like his father. (Courtesy Toledo Museum of Art, Ohio)

PLATE 12. Aureus AD 82. Obverse: Domitian wearing a laurel and bearded. Legend: IMP CAES DOMITIANUS AUG P M. Reverse: helmeted Minerva showing breast and shoulders. Legend: TR POT IMP II COS VIII DES IX PP. BMC II 304, no. 33. (Copyright British Museum)

PLATE 13. Silver coin of AD 85 (8 denarii?). Obverse: Domitian with laurel wreath and bearded. Legend: IMP CAES DOMIT AUG GERM P M TR POT V. Reverse: Seated figure of Minerva, helmeted, holding victory in her right hand. Legend: IMP VIIII COS XI CENS POT PP. BMC II 316 no. 83. (Copyright British Museum)

PLATE 14. Frieze A from the Palazzo della Cancelleria reliefs, found in 1937. This scene is thought to represent the *profectio* of Domitian to the wars, either against the Chatti in 82/3, or against the Sarmatians in 92/3. He is led by his patron deity Minerva, and the god Mars. The head was later recarved to represent Nerva, with the result that it now seems too small for the body. (Courtesy Vatican Museums, Vatican City)

PLATE 15. Bronze coin showing *Germania capta* after the Chattan war. Obverse: Domitian wearing laurel and bearded. Legend: IMP CAES DOMIT AUG GERM COS XI CENS POT PP. Reverse: German woman on left, seated on the ground, trophies in centre, German standing on the right. Legend: GERMANIA CAPTA. SC. BMC II 369 no. 325. (Copyright British Museum)

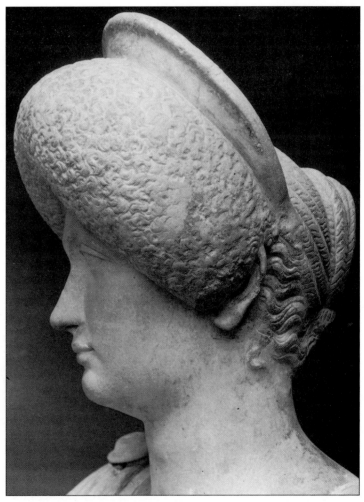

PLATE 16. Julia, daughter of Titus. As children, Julia and Domitian may have been brought up together. It was said that Domitian entertained an inordinate passion for her, taking her to live with him in the Imperial palace after the execution of her husband, Flavius Sabinus. She died probably in 89. After Domitian was murdered, his nurse Phyllis mingled his ashes with those of Julia, so they would not be disturbed. (Courtesy Vatican Museums, Vatican City)

PLATE 17. Head of Domitia Longina (the bust is modern). She is portrayed as a mature and rather determined matron, similar to the depictions of her on the later Domitianic coinage. This portrait may date from the Trajanic period, some years after Domitian's death. (Courtesy Hermitage Museum, St Petersburg)

PLATE 18. The Piazza Navona, Rome. The outline of Domitian's stadium is preserved almost intact. Remains of the curving northern end are still visible under modern buildings. The Piazza is laid out symmetrically, but in Roman times the southern end was straight. The obelisk is one of many still visible in Rome. This example may have come originally from the Temple of Isis and Serapis. Domitian is mentioned by name on the inscription, but since it is in hieroglyphics it survived the *damnatio memoriae*. (Photo: Dr J.C.N. Coulston)

PLATE 19. View of the Forum Transitorium, also called the Forum of Nerva, since it was dedicated by him in 97. The work is Domitianic, providing a link between the Subura and the Forum Romanum. The Forum enclosed a temple of Minerva, of which nothing is now visible except the scant remains of the podium. (Photo: Dr J.C.N. Coulston)

PLATE 20. Remains of the south perimeter wall of the Forum Transitorium. The sculptured frieze depicts the story of Ariadne, with a relief of Minerva above. (Photo: Dr J.C.N. Coulston)

PLATE 21. Domus Augustana on the Palatine, seen from across the Circus Maximus. Spectators at the Circus could hardly have been presented with a more robust demonstration of power. (Photo: Dr J.C.N. Coulston)

PLATE 22. Circus façade of the Domus Augustana from the south-east. The Circus Maximus is on the left of the photo. (Photo: Dr J.C.N. Coulston)

PLATE 23. The sunken peristyle of the Domus Augustana. (Photo: Dr J.C.N. Coulston)

PLATE 24. The so-called stadium or hippodrome of the Domus Augustana. It is best interpreted as a private garden rather than a real hippodrome, since it is too small to hold races in the enclosed space. This type of public/private building and landscaping is paralleled at Domitian's Alban villa. (Photo: Dr J.C.N. Coulston)

as a result of the childhood trauma of loss of a mother. Newton was not cruel or greedy, being absorbed in his studies, but who can say how he would have behaved after 15 years as an Emperor of Rome?[4]

Domitian's claims that he was the son of Minerva would nowadays elicit derisory disbelief, and would perhaps be interpreted as manipulative showmanship in order to play the monarch with the support of a deity to give added weight. Perhaps that was all it was. On a deeper level, however, it is reminiscent of the orphaned child's fantasy that he or she is really the descendant of some fabulous prince or princess. This is not only a sad attempt at creating a mother-substitute, but elevates the child above mundane and sometimes insupportable normality. It is impossible to know when Domitian's attachment to Minerva began, nor the reasons behind it. The process probably began while he was a child, becoming deeply engrained as he grew up – just how deep was his conviction of descent from the goddess cannot be gauged. He can probably be forgiven the play-acting if that was what it was, but total belief indicates either an unhinged personality or a pitiable lost soul seeking comfort.[5]

Devotion to a deity of some kind is a very common attribute of people who have faced death and survived. People in this situation usually experience a change in their ways of thinking and life-styles. 'In the short term, we are debilitated by our vulnerability... We may feel less self-directed as a result and sense that other factors beyond our control have had a hand in our being. This is why many survivors turn to some sort of god...' Domitian's experience on the Capitol, too readily dismissed in most modern accounts, may have given impetus to his veneration of Minerva. It was Jupiter Custos whom he publicly thanked, but the two deities worked together for his preservation. Suetonius relates that Domitian had a dream just before his murder, in which Minerva appeared to him to explain that she could no longer protect him because Jupiter had disarmed her. The story is told along with the account of the natural disasters, storms and manifestations that presaged Domitian's end. Even if there is no truth in the tale of the dream, it is at least indicative of accepted contemporary opinion about Domitian's regard for Minerva.[6]

Was Domitian capable of giving and receiving affection? His relationship to Domitia (pl. 17) is said to have been passionate, at least at first, though this may refer only to sexual passion. Enduring affection is sometimes a separate matter. Throughout his life Domitian seems to have been emotionally independent and fond of solitude, but this need not mean that he was devoid of affection. Though their relationships cannot be fully depicted, Domitia and Julia were probably the only people that Domitian loved, in any sense of the word. He may have found it difficult to express affection, possibly hampered by fear of rejection, and he may have refused to receive it through fear of eventual loss. Such a crippling outlook is not uncommon. Perhaps Domitia and Julia saw through the façade, relying for sustenance on the rare glimpses of the real personality underneath. If Domitia was sufficiently self-reliant and mature enough to understand, then the marriage may have proceeded along a tolerable course, except for the upheaval of about 83. Her acquiescence, if such it was, in her husband's murder may have derived from despair, if the disintegration of his personality had reached an irreversible point. If he was not open to reason or to any restorative process, then death would have seemed the only alternative. Afterwards, when she had no compelling reason to advertise her relationship to him, Domitia described herself publicly as Domitian's wife, perhaps remembering him as a youth and a young Emperor. Here is some support, then, for the theory that he was not wholly evil, that he had begun well but finished badly.[7]

Towards his father Domitian may have been unable to express any affection. While Vespasian was banished from court, father and son may have been closely associated. This would have been the only opportunity where they could be anything other than near strangers to each other. The evidence is slight, but it is possible that Vespasian both overawed and overwhelmed his younger son. This may not have been wholly detrimental, since there may have been some element of respect and admiration in Domitian's continuation of his father's policies. It could be that he was unimaginatively and unquestioningly convinced of the perfection of his father's measures, but with his passion for exactitude in administration, it may be postulated that he would have rooted out anomalies and corrected them, even if only for the sake of being right.[8]

Domitian's strong inclination for solitude could have arisen from one of two opposite sentiments. Solitude is a necessity for some temperaments to thrive or to produce anything. This is the positive, confident aspect of solitude. The fearful, withdrawn kind of solitude, the negative type, arises from a fear of persecution and criticism. The tragedy is that some people who withdraw for these negative reasons do not have the capacity to be alone; they are therefore maladjusted in any and all situations. For those who do have the capacity to be alone, solitude can be beneficial, especially for those who find constant company burdensome because of the restrictions imposed on freedom of thought and action. Complete relaxation is possible only in solitude for such people, of whom Domitian may have been one. In modern parlance, solitude provides the space and time in which to recharge the batteries. This need not be indicative of selfishness; on the contrary, indulging in periodic solitude is a means of achieving a balance, of facing obligations and fulfilling public duties. Perhaps for these positive reasons, for periodic regeneration and contemplation, Domitian seemed to make strict divisions between his private and public life. He did not convene the Senate in his Imperial residence, and seems to have required a filter system for visitors. Domitian's mistake was his failure to recognize that private life was a concept unfamiliar to the Romans and quite unbecoming for the head of state. Medieval monarchs were in the company of courtiers or servants almost all their lives; it was a necessary part of their existence that even the most private functions, by today's standards, were undertaken with at least one other person in attendance. One can almost sense Domitian shuddering with horror. Accessibility on a permanent basis was not in his make-up. Transported into the twentieth century, he would have banned mobile phones and chiming doorbells, and executed their salesmen with grim zeal.[9]

It is the view of modern scholars that Domitian was a perfectionist in his approach to administration. This is quite consistent with his solitary habits, since psychologists have noted 'the tendency of the perfectionist to be comparatively independent of other people'. He had an obsessional passion for administrative efficiency, but did not noticeably deal tactfully with subordinates, even if they were obedient and successful. He displayed 'the obsessional person's typical impatience and intolerance of matters which he cannot himself immediately control'.[10]

This search for absolute control entailed rigid adherence to the rules, or at least to established precedent. It has been pointed out that Domitian's legislation emphasized the proper way of doing things. Barbara Levick describes him as conventional to the extreme and not in the least bit innovative. He squashed innovation in others too, insisting that all officials kept to the existing regulations. All this is supported by his own decrees. Adherence to regulations gave legitimacy to his regime. 'Legitimacy in the political system is the strict analogue of confidence in the monetary system; legitimacy is therefore to be considered an *essential* aspect of the possession of social power.' These are sentiments which Domitian would have entirely endorsed, since his passion for legitimacy and confidence in the monetary system went hand in hand.[11]

The unknown quantity is the extent to which Domitian's behaviour was innate and pre-ordained and how much of it was a product of experiences during his early years and throughout his reign. Since his life, like everyone else's, took only one course, suggested alternatives are purely academic, but it is reasonable to ask if any part of the tragedy could have been avoided. If other circumstances had obtained at any time in his life, or even if events had occurred in a different sequence, it is possible that some of the direst consequences could have been averted although he was at a serious disadvantage to start with, if he was already mistrustful of most people. Mistrust and its attendant alienation seem to have been built into his character from the earliest times, so that even the smallest event that apparently reinforced his attitude would assume the greatest importance for him, while positve events that had the potential to reverse the trend would have been ignored, if indeed they had even been noticed in the first place. Mistrust is not converted by one or two acts of generosity; the mistrustful person merely waits for the proof that he or she is justified, and when this proof is found, as it always is, either genuine or imagined, then all other benevolent acts are negated. It gives a whole new meaning to the command, 'Seek and ye shall find.' People read into occurrences only those aspects with which they are most familiar. Indeed they can do no otherwise, unless they are continually guided by superhuman introspective analysis.[12]

In psychological terms, the authoritarian personality has little experience of self or of others because he has to put all his energies into maintaining a precarious order and safety. 'He confronts with a façade of spurious strength a world in which rigidly stereotyped categories are substituted for affectionate and individualized experience.' This accords well with Domitian's insistence on his titles to underline his power and legitimate authority. The authoritarian sees people as merely a means to an end, and 'his judgements are governed by a punitive conventional moralism; his conventionality has a heavy investment in maintaining the status quo'. Any challenges to the proper order of things are seen as extremely threatening. 'If such persons feel *personally* vulnerable to attack...their authoritarian aggression might especially rise.' Suetonius would have agreed with this judgement; he recognized that fear made Domitian cruel, and his cruelty increased after the suppression of the revolt of Saturninus. It has been claimed that the revolt was purely military, with no senatorial involvement in this plot, and that therefore Domitian's treatment of the senators did not change as a result of it. But what may have happened was probably more subtle. Rationality would not enter into the matter. Absence of senatorial support for Saturninus would not make Domitian feel any more secure. He could not be certain that there would never be another attempt, next time *with* senatorial support. But much more important was the fact that he now had the added and quite unexpected fear that he did not enjoy the complete support of the army, support which he had tried to foster by various means. He had hitherto been fairly confident of the army's loyalty; now he was alone. His fear and suspicion would naturally increase, and by its very nature suspicion creates fear and reciprocal suspicion in others, leading to attempts at pre-emptive strikes on either side. It is a cycle which escalates very easily, impossible to halt without the elimination of the chief protagonists. The fact that Domitian was assassinated by his domestic staff does not preclude any direct senatorial interest in his removal.[13]

There is a humorous expression which sums up the situation: 'Just because I'm paranoid it doesn't mean that they aren't out to get me.' Paranoia as a cause of Domitian's behaviour and how he was perceived by others deserves consideration. By modern definition, paranoia leads to sensitiveness to slights, rigid adherence to rules, social isolation, over-criticism of others, self-righteousness and overt delusions of persecution and grandiosity. The paranoid person thinks that others are trying to destroy him; he is certain that any sign of weakness will lead to destruction. The reason why everyone seeks his downfall is that they are jealous of him, which implies that he must be important. This in turn leads to delusions of grandeur. Constantly on the alert for attacks, he often misinterprets purely fortuitous events and reads into them personal meaning. But it is important to note that the individual can still function in everyday life, his intelligence is preserved, and to all intents and purpose he is normal; he fails only in his incorrect interpretation of some areas of reality. 'Paranoid reactions are essentially disturbing behaviours with few if any other indications of abnormality,' and this is the real tragedy of the condition.[14]

The problem can develop very slowly, 'logically elaborated after a false interpretation of an actual occurrence'. Most important is that the behaviour of the paranoid person may increase the threat that he perceives as emanating from others. If he confides in anyone, he will interpret their disagreement as proof that they do not understand and do not really care, or worse still he will imagine that the disbeliever is in fact a member of one of the conspiracy groups all around him. One of Domitian's sayings was that no one believes in the existence of plots until the victim is dead. The increasing isolation of the paranoid person leads to an inexorable progression in the deterioration of his behaviour. The study of paranoia was taken an important stage further when in 1962 a psychologist insisted that the paranoid individual does not exist in a vacuum, and it is just as important to study the activities and attitudes of the people around him. The situation is composed of a series of escalating responses and increasing tensions, where the people with whom the paranoid person has to deal are not always without blame. Modern psychological and psychiatric labelling tends to throw all the blame on to the maladjusted individual, exonerating his contemporaries once the patient has been pronounced abnormal. Even in the present day, where such problems are recognized, the application of scientific names for behavioural oddities tells only half the story. The novelist Wiliam Faulkner knew this, when he made one of his characters say, 'It's like it ain't so much what a fellow does, but it's the way the majority of folks is lookin' at him when he does it.' Paranoia is an ancient word for a condition recognized only recently. In the Roman world there would be no such recognition of the condition.[15]

Whilst the predisposition to paranoid tendencies may be present at birth, in optimum circumstances there need be no development of anything more than an irritating over-sensitivity. In adverse circumstances, paranoid tendencies can manifest themselves after a change in environment, such as loss of position, death of relatives or friends, or simply after physiological and psychological changes while growing older. Precisely what had gone wrong between the Senate and Domitian, and when it happened, cannot be established. Possibly the contemporaries of Domitian could not have explained it. The necessary execution of Flavius Sabinus may have provided the trigger for Domitian's gradually increasing paranoia, which would be fuelled by the opposition of the philosophers and one or two senators, and fanned by the military revolt of Saturninus. If the change in Domitian had occurred suddenly, completed overnight and producing a visibly different Emperor the next morning, then the Senate, the people and the army would have been unanimous in their recognition of the symptoms for what they were. But a gradual onset of a progressively worsening disorder, that moreover displayed no overt traces of abnormality, would have left everyone confused and fearful of actions and reactions that they did not understand. The situation would be compounded by previous knowledge of the Emperor before his attitudes and behaviour deteriorated; the older conceptual map that each person absorbed from their dealings with him would be their guide to handling the present situation, but they would not know why or how their in-built rules and regulations were so woefully inappropriate and out of date. In the ordinary spheres of life, the friends and family of a paranoid individual would be able to cover up and make excuses for their problematic associate, and probably prevent him or her from causing any harm. The aid of the state could be sought to help restrain him if necessary, and the world need hear no more of him. When the paranoid individual is himself the embodiment of the state, with unrestricted access to supreme power, supported by compliant intelligence services composed of a network of informers telling him what they thought he wanted to hear, this is clearly a recipe for disaster. Such a situation would be impossible to deal with, as the history of Domitian's last years tragically demonstrates.

DOMITIAN AS BUILDER

Domitian has been justly described as one of the great builders of the Empire, so no biography would be complete without a description of the most important monuments founded or restored by him. It is not known how much direct interest Domitian took in the planning and construction of individual buildings, but given that he displayed minute interest in all other aspects of Imperial administration, it is permissible to believe that he srutinized plans and discussed, constantly and intensely, all the details of his new buildings and his restoration work. It is probable that under the Flavians, when large works were planned, consultations were held with the members of the government department (*opera Caesaris*) that was responsible for all public buildings. Domitian's chief architect was Rabirius, specifically named by Martial as the builder of the Imperial palace on the Palatine (*Epigrams* 7.56.2; see also 10.71). It is likely that the same man also designed and built the Alban villa. Of the lesser architects and builders there is no trace.

In the city of Rome, Domitian inherited various incomplete building programmes from his father and brother, as well as a recent catastrophe when a large part of the city was consumed by fire in 80. According to Dio (66.24.1–3) all the buildings between the Pantheon and the Capitol were destroyed or damaged. At the time, Titus was absent in Campania assessing the damage caused by the eruption of Vesuvius. It must have been a very low moment. With regard to Rome, it is not known how far clearance of the damage had progressed by September 81, but the reconstruction work can be safely attributed to Domitian, and it is likely that he restored all the buildings that had been destroyed.

Evidence of his work is not always easy to identify. Some of his buildings have disappeared altogether, and others have been restored so heavily at later dates that all trace of Domitianic work has been obliterated. The Baths of Titus, for instance, were completed by Domitian, but the building has almost wholly disappeared. The Colosseum, or Flavian amphitheatre, probably owes its fourth storey and most of the interior to Domitian, but the work of all three Flavians merges so successfully that it is impossible, metaphorically speaking, to see the joins. The Arch of Titus and the temple of Vespasian, situated at opposite ends of the Forum Romanum, were probably completed during Domitian's reign, but opinion differs as to how much of these structures should be attributed to him. Literary sources provide evidence for much of Domitian's building activity, but not all the structures listed can be identified. The most important document is the list of the Chronographer of 354, who affirms that Domitian built 'seven *atria*, two *horrea*, a temple of Castor and Minerva, and the Porta Capena; temples of the Flavian *gens*, the *Divorum*, Isis and Serapis, and Minervia Chalcidia; the Odeum [rendered as

'Odium' in the text; perhaps a psychological slip on the part of the copyist?], the porticus Minucia Vetus, the stadium, the baths of Titus and Trajan, an amphitheatre, the temple of Vespasian and Titus, the Capitol, the Senate, four *ludi*, the Palatine, the Meta Sudans and the Pantheon.'

Some of the buildings included in this list were not new foundations of Domitian's. The Flavian amphitheatre and the temple of Vespasian, minus the dedication to Titus, were already under construction when Domitian became Emperor. Buildings destroyed in the fires of 64 and 80, such as the Senate, the Pantheon, and the buildings on the Capitol, would require repair, possibly quite extensive, but perhaps not from the foundations. Reading between the lines of Suetonius (*Dom.* 5) there is an implication that Domitian claimed the restored buildings as his own, because even though he was usually careful to make it clear that he had restored an existing building, he neglected to name the original builder. This may be a ploy on Suetonius' part to curry favour with Hadrian, whose goodwill he seems to have lost whilst writing the *Lives of the Caesars*. Perhaps he hoped to reinstate himself by alluding to the fact that in completely rebuilding the Pantheon, Hadrian had acknowledged only Agrippa as the builder, with no mention of himself.

Of the rest of the buildings in the Chronographer's list, next to nothing is known of the seven *atria* and the porticus Minucia Vetus. The *horrea Vespasiani* are completely unknown, while the *horrea Piperataria* may have preceded the Basilica of Maxentius, or Constantine, as it is sometimes known. Brickwork found underneath this structure has been labelled Domitianic, but without the positive evidence of brick stamps. The mention of the Porta Capena in the old Servian walls is a mystery, because it had ceased to serve as a gateway by Domitian's day.

More positive is the identification of the Odeum in the Campus Martius, of which a few scant remains have been found. This was a building devoted to the arts, designed for the performance of musical entertainments, and was still extant in the fourth century, when Ammianus Marcellinus described it (16.10.14) The Meta Sudans was a conical fountain, depicted on Domitian's coins with the Colosseum in the background, and identified with the circular structure outside the amphitheatre, demolished in the 1930s, and excavated in the 1980s. Of the temples, that of Castor and Minerva poses unanswerable questions. It is not known whether this was a single structure dedicated to two deities, or whether the buildings referred to were shrines near the Imperial palace. The temple of the Flavian *gens* has already been mentioned (see above p.126). It was built on the Quirinal on the site of Vespasian's house and is known from literary references, but no actual remains have been discovered. The *templum Divorum* was situated in the Campus Martius, and may have been the building to which the Cancelleria reliefs (pls. 2–4) originally belonged. It may have been the starting-point of the triumphs of Vespasian and Titus, and of Domitian himself.

The original temples of Isis and Serapis were destroyed by fire, and Domitian rebuilt them as one entity. The building is depicted on the Severan marble plan of Rome, and its monumental entrance is displayed on the sculptures of the Tomb of the Haterii, clearly labelled *Arcus ad Isis*. If Domitian really did escape from the Capitol in 69 disguised as a priest of Isis, he would perhaps have felt a great veneration for this goddess, just as he did for Jupiter and for Minerva, his joint protectors. No archaeological evidence has come to light for the temple of Minverva Chalcidia, but this building is known from the Severan plan, and was sited not far from the temple of Isis and Serapis.

It was in the Campus Martius that much of Domitian's building activity was concentrated. The area was devoted to entertainments on the grand scale. Suetonius (*Dom.* 5) lists the stadium, the Odeum and the Naumachia in this area. The Odeum has already been mentioned. The Naumachia was built on the banks of the Tiber to facilitate naval displays, but has not been discovered; it is not even certain on which bank it lay. The stadium was a circus without the usual *spina*, and it is marked out almost exactly by the modern Piazza Navona. It was about 250m (275yd) long, with a squared southern end and rounded northern end. Some of the original Roman masonry of the northern end can still be seen in the basement of houses west of the via Agonale. The stadium was restored by Severus Alexander in the third century and for some time it was known as his work, until Domitian's contribution was fully recognized in the nineteenth century.

Eusebius omits some of the buildings listed by the Chronographer, but adds more details. He attributes to Domitian the Forum Transitorium, the Forum of Trajan, and an otherwise unknown structure called the *mica aurea*, whose location, size, shape and purpose elude investigators. The Forum Transitorium was inserted into the long, narrow space between the Forum of Augustus and Vespasian's Forum of Peace. Domitian's new Forum was not dedicated until 97, after his murder, and was therefore officially known as the Forum of Nerva. Its alternative name, Forum Transitorium, derives from the positioning of the structure. It joined the Subura to the Forum Romanum, acting as a passage between the two. A temple of Minerva was built in this Forum. It was still standing in the sixteenth century, but nothing is now visible except the scant remains of the podium. Development of the area later occupied by the Forum of Trajan may have been one of Domitian's intended projects, for the ground was cleared during his reign, but it cannot be ascertained precisely what he planned to build here. The whole complex was not dedicated until 112, which means that if Domitian was the founder, as Eusebius implies, then there was at least a 16- to 20-year gap between commencement of the work and dedication of the finished product, which is wholly Trajan's in concept and execution.

The most imposing and most important architectural work of Domitian's reign is the building of the Imperial residence on the Palatine. Tiberius had already founded an Imperial house in this area, but the state of the Domus Tiberiana after the fire of 80 is not known, nor is the condition of the rest of the Palatine when Domitian commenced work. He took in the Domus Tiberiana and laid out a far more extensive palace covering most of the hilltop. The Imperial residence was built on two different levels. The later alterations, for instance under Severus, have obliterated some of the first-century work, so it is difficult to ascertain the original appearance of the Domitianic building. The palace, popularly called the Palatium, and officially entitled Domus Augustana, was divided into two sections (Fig. 6). The public and state apartments were accessible from the road running from the Forum to the Palatine, the Clivus Palatinus; the private apartments faced the Circus Maximus. Complications arise because some authors have restricted the name Domus Augustana to the private sectors of the residence while others have attempted to remedy this confusion by labelling the public apartments the Domus Flavia, and the private sectors the Domus Domitiana. Thus there are three names for what is essentially the same building.

0   150m

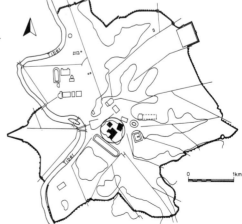

Fig. 6. Plan of the Domus Augustana on the Palatine in Rome. The palace was as daring as it was grandiose, covering most of the Palatine Hill and incorporating the earlier Domus Tiberiana. Since the imperial residence was occupied by successive Emperors who made alterations to the buildings, it is difficult to ascertain the original appearance of Domitian's palace. (After Ward-Perkins, redrawn by Graeme Stobbs)

The architect responsible for the Imperial residence was Rabirius, and it is generally agreed that his work was innovative, daring and grandiose. In one area he was too daring. By Hadrian's reign, one of the walls of the Domus Flavia required extra strengthening to support the barrel vault roof. The public areas contained a large reception area (*aula regia*), sometimes translated as Throne Room, a banqueting hall, basilica and peristyle, as well as numerous other rooms and corridors. The private apartments were connected to the public areas by adjoining peristyle courtyards, but the main entrance was on the lower level, away from the public gaze. The sunken garden, known as the hippodrome or stadium, was a later addition, after the main areas of the complex were finished in 92. This was a long, enclosed garden with a covered, colonnaded walk all around it to provide privacy and shade. It is probable that there were further buildings beyond the stadium which belonged to Domitian's vast residence, perhaps left unfinished at his death.

Little can be said about how the household functioned. Somewhere all the family members would be accommodated, along with hosts of slaves. Domitia Longina would require apartments of her own, as would Julia when she took up residence on the Palatine. It is possible to identify rooms intended for general use, but the intimate details are obscure. The opprobrium which Domitian incurred through his desire for solitude and his later harshness to all who were deemed his enemies, led to suspicions that his activities were dastardly and unmentionable. He had deliberately avoided any association with the Golden House of Nero for these very reasons, and superseded it with a residence that was probably even more imposing and grandiose than ever Nero's had been. During Domitian's lifetime, the Domus Augustana was described in suitably laudatory terms, but after the removal of the tyrant opinion changed, and descriptions tended towards the derogatory, using words such as 'haughty' and 'arrogant'. Presumably the building functioned smoothly enough and satisfied most Imperial wants, since no one subsequently felt a compelling need to tear the whole edifice down and start all over again. One can only admire the stoicism of later Emperors who overcame their distaste, and forced themselves to live in it, surrounded by such awesome grandeur.

Domitian owned and used several villas outside Rome, among them Circeo, Tusculum and Antium. These Imperial residences were accompanied by other smaller villas owned or used by members of the Imperial entourage. Literary references to the Alban villa, perhaps the first which Domitian acquired, where he pursued his illicit affair with Domitia, give the impression that it was his personal favourite and the most commonly used of all his houses (Fig. 7). It was close to Rome, well within a day's journey from the capital, and situated in a very pleasant area, one of the main attractions being that it was cooler than the capital.

The original villa at Albano had belonged to Pompey, and Domitian lived in the older house while the new one was being constructed. Rabirius is not named in any ancient source as the architect, but there are similarities of construction with the Domus Augustana, so it is generally assumed that he was responsible for the design and execution of the building.

Unfortunately, little is known of the Alban villa, except that it was very large, incorporating in its grounds several smaller villas which were swept away to accommodate the whole complex. The main residential part of the villa was laid out on a terraced slope facing the sea, and may have been three storeys high. It was as palatial as the Domus

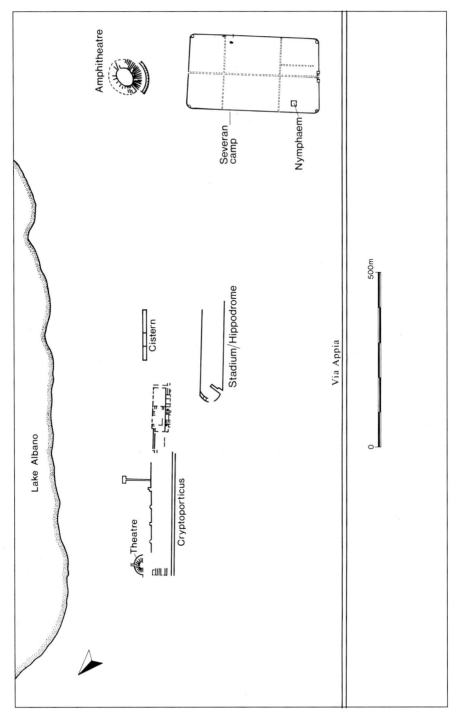

Fig. 7. Plan of the Alban villa, showing the known remains. The villa extended over a large area, part of which is now occupied by Castel Gandolfo, one of the Papal summer residences. (After *Coarelli Guide Archeologiche Laterza* redrawn by Graeme Stobbs)

Augustana in Rome, and surrounded by smaller buildings, such as a theatre, a stadium, ornamental fountains and colonnaded walks. Juvenal's Fourth Satire depicts Domitian and the Imperial courtiers at the villa. The architectural features of the villa influenced later buildings, principally Hadrian's villa at Tivoli, and at the end of the second century, Albano figured largely in the military arrangements of Septimius Severus. Since the property was part of the Imperial domain, Severus was able to put it to use when he needed a headquarters for his newly raised legion, which he kept close by the city of Rome at Albano, causing some disquiet to contemporary Romans and much debate among modern archaeologists as to his real or pretended purpose.

Further reading

Domitian's buildings in Rome are discussed under individual headings, with further references, by E. Nash *Pictorial Dictionary of Ancient Rome*. New York 1981, reprint of 1961–2 edition, and by S.B. Platner and T. Ashby *Topographical Dictionary of Ancient Rome*. Oxford 1929. For general studies of architecture in Rome and Italy under Domitian, see: M.E. Blake *Roman Construction in Italy from Tiberius through the Antonines*. Washington 1959, 89–115; B.W. Jones *The Emperor Domitian*. London 1992, 79–98; W.L. Macdonald *The Architecture of the Roman Empire* I: *An Introductory Study*. Yale rev. edn 1982; J.B. Ward-Perkins *Roman Imperial Architecture*. Harmondsworth 2nd edn 1981, 73–95; J.B. Ward-Perkins *Roman Architecture*. London 1988, 79–98. The sculptures of the Forum Transitorium have been the subject of a recent study by E. D'Ambra *Private Lives, Imperial Virtues: The Frieze of the Forum Transitorium in Rome*. Princeton 1993. The Alban villa: F. Coarelli *Dintorni di Roma. Guide Archeologiche Laterza*. Rome 1981, 72–94.

NOTES

The notes relate to each individual paragraph. References which are cited only once are given in full within the notes, whereas those used several times are cited in Harvard style (author's surname, date of publication and relevant page number(s)). Full details can be found in the Bibliography.

I Early Years *pp.1–12*

1. Josephus was Vespasian's mouthpiece, and since his subject was the war in Judaea, he had no need to take notice of Domitian's youth. His statements about Domitian's conduct in 69 presumably represent what Vespasian and Titus were prepared to endorse.

2. Waters 1964, 51 refutes the idea that Statius, Martial and Silius Italicus provided outlets for official pronouncements, but nonetheless all authors publishing works in Domitian's reign larded their writings with references to the Emperor, which quite naturally were all complimentary. 'Monster': Pliny *Pan.* 48.3, '*immanissima belua*'. He depicts Domitian as 'lapping the blood of his murdered relatives' in this same passage. Hysterical hyperbole of this sort affords a glimpse of the depth of feeling about Domitian in his last years.

3. Hearsay: Suet. *Dom.* 1.1: '*satisque constat*' and '*nec defuerunt qui affirmarent*'. '*Simulavit*': *Dom.* 2.2. Waters 1964, 52 draws attention to the parallel with Tiberius, who was reluctant to accept the throne, but since towards the end of his reign he refused to share power with the Senate, his earlier reluctance must have been feigned. Any saving graces Domitian may have possessed are all negated because of his last years. The 'future paragon': Baldwin 1983, 297. Mooney 1930, 508 sedately affirms that there is no evidence to sustain the charge against Nerva; Syme 1958, 628: 'which genre of erotic poetry knew Nerva as an expert is not a theme to linger on'.

4. *Cursus honorum*: before embarking on any career it was essential to hold one of the 20 junior magistracies of the vigintivirate, all of which were in the gift of the Emperor. After holding one of these administrative posts, a young man could be appointed military tribune. Although it was not essential for the furtherance of a career, *novi homines* tended to serve as tribunes more often than not (Talbert 1984, 13–14). Since Vespasian and Titus had done so, it is likely that Domitian followed suit.

5. Suffect consulship: Suet. *Vesp.* 4.2; *Dom.* 1.1. Flavius Petro: *Vesp.* 1.2. Vespasian's brother Sabinus was governor of Moesia for seven years (Tacitus *Hist.* 3.75) possibly from 53 to 60 (*PIR2* F 352) or from 50 to 56 (Nicols 1978, 29).

6. Civil wars: Syme 1939, 352–4 describes how equestrian families could rise to senatorial status in two or three generations, after Augustus' reign. Military service became a recognized step to promotion, and equestrians rose in importance in the army, in administration and finance, since they were banned from politics (ibid. 355). See also Syme 1958, 585–624; Waters 1964, 52 n.7.

7. *Imagines*: Suet. *Vesp.* 1.1; Mooney 1930, 373. Poverty a myth: Jones 1992, 1–3. Marriages: *Vesp.* 1.3; Jones 1992, 2. Statues: *Vesp.* 1.2; Mooney 1930, 376.

8. Dio 65.10; Sejanus: Bengtson 1979, 15; Caligula and Nero: Jones 1992, 2.

9. Reluctance to become a senator (*diu adversatus est*): Suet. *Vesp.* 2.2. Client of Sabinus: *anteambulationem fratris appellat*, literally the man who walked before his patron to clear his path. Sabinus superior to Vespasian in influence and fortune: Tacitus *Hist.* 3.65. Vespasian's early career: Suet. *Vesp.* 2.2 – 4.6; *PIR2* F 398; Bengtson 1979, 12–24; Nicols 1978, 1–11, where he redates some of the offices that Vespasian held. *II Augusta*: Suet. *Vesp.* 4.1; Tacitus *Hist.* 3.44. Britain: Eichholz 1972, 149–63.

10. Patronage: Saller 1980; 1982; Townend 1961.

11. Marriage: Suet. *Vesp.* 1.3; 3. Caenis: *Vesp.* 3; Dio 65.14; *CIL* VI 12037. Narcissus: *PIR2* N 23; Suet. *Vesp.* 4.1.

12. Four families: Birley 1981, 38f, 227f; Jones 1992, 3–5. Titus educated at court and taught by the same masters as Britannicus: Suet. *Titus* 2.

13. Agrippina: Suet. *Vesp.* 4.2. Disfavour not extreme: Jones 1992, 9. Proconsulship of Africa: *Vesp.* 4.3; Thomasson 1960, II 42; 1984, 376; Vogel-Weidemann 1982, 205–14 on Vespasian in general: it is still not possible to be more precise about the date than 63–4. See also Nicols 1978, 10; Bengtson 1979, 22.

14. Retirement: Suet. *Vesp.* 4.2. Nicols 1978, 22 says Vespasian did not withdraw from public life, only from court. Denied access to Nero's court: *Vesp.* 14. Domitian brought up in poverty: Suet. *Dom.* 1.1. Mortgage: Suet. *Vesp.* 4.3; Tacitus *Hist.* 3.65. Ejection from Senate: Talbert 1984, 12.

15. Trade: Suet. *Vesp.* 4.3. Mules: Mooney 1930, 391 says that Reate was famous for its asses, which were much prized for breeding mules, according to Varro *De Re Rustica* 2.1.14. Slaves: Bengtson 1979, 23. Sharp practice: Suet. *Vesp.* 4.3 uses the term mango, derived from the Greek, meaning charm, and applied to slave-traders, cattle dealers and vendors in general who tried to make their goods seem more valauble than they really were.

16. Silver plate: Suet. *Dom.* 1.1. Even the poorest families possessed silver plate for the purpose of sacrificing to the household gods (Mooney 1930, 507). Domitian deserved the penalty he paid for *cupiditas et saevitia*: *Vesp.* 1.1.

17. Falacrina and Cosa: Suet. *Vesp.* 2.1. Aquae Cutiliae: *Vesp.* 24. Mortgage: *Vesp.* 4.3; Tacitus *Hist.* 3.65. Alban villa: Suet. *Dom.* 19; Tacitus *Agr.* 45; Juvenal 4.145; Dio 67.1.2. Flies: Suet. *Dom.* 3.1; Dio 65.9.4.

18. Revolt of Saturninus: Suet. *Dom.* 6.2; 7.4. Increased cruelty after civil war, i.e. suppression of revolt: *Dom.* 10.5. Deceitfulness: *Dom.* 2.2; Dio 67.1.

19. Domitian's conduct in 69: Suet. *Dom.* 1.3; Tacitus *Hist.* 4.2; Dio 65.2.3; 3.4; 9.3. Tacitus says that Vespasian returned to Rome as a result of Domitian's behaviour *Hist.* 4.51.2. Hugh Last (1948, 12) in analysis of the Cancelleria

reliefs, dismissed the rumours that Vespasian was displeased with Domitian in 69/70.

20. Titus was born 30 December 39. Suet. *Titus* 1.1 wrongly ascribes his birth to 41, when Caligula was assassinated, but he notes Titus' correct age at death (Mooney 1930, 467). Description of Titus: Suet. *Titus* 3. Military service and marriages: *Titus* 4. Domitian's jealousy and plotting: *Dom.* 2.3. Stirring up troops: *Titus* 9.3. Titus advises Vespasian to be lenient with Domitian: Tacitus *Hist.* 4.51.2. His own leniency towards his brother: Suet. *Titus* 9.3. Caecina: *Titus* 6.2. Jewish prisoners: Josephus *BJ* 7.37. Associates at court: Dio 67.2. Julius Bassus: Pliny *Ep.* 4.9.

21. Tacitus *Hist.* 3.75 says that Sabinus served Rome for 35 years, governing Moesia for seven years and serving for a total of 12 years as *praefectus urbi*. Nicols 1978, 26–30 outlines the difficulties caused by acceptance of this chronology and summarizes the main arguments. The 35 years is perhaps not to be understood as continuous service, but the number of years in total in which Sabinus held office, both in the civil and military spheres. Proof is lacking for exactly which offices he held during those years. The post of city prefect was important in that it entailed command of the urban cohorts and involved policing of the city. Tacitus *Annals* 6.10–11 outlines the history of the post. Sabinus' role in Rome is played down by Wallace (1987) who maintains that he was totally ineffective and even cowardly. In emphasizing his concern for self-preservation, she perhaps underestimates the difficulties and dangers that Sabinus faced.

22. On the status of Flavia Domitilla, Vespasian's wife: Ritter 1972; *PIR2* F 416; Suet. *Vesp.* 3. Statius *Silvae* 1.1.94f depicts Domitian's father, brother, sister and son descending from heaven to admire a new statue of the Emperor (Hardie 1983, 190). Coins: *memoriae Domitillae*: *RIC2* 134, 135. Flavia Domitilla, Vespasian's daughter: *PIR2* F 417. Townend 1961, 58 suggested that Flavia Domitilla may have been married to Q. Petillius Cerialis. He assumed that she was born in the long chronological gap between Titus and Domitian, but Nicols 1978, 9 disagreed, arguing that Suetonius listed the children of Vespasian in the correct chronological order, and that Domitilla was therefore the youngest of the three. Domitian and Cerialis: Birley 1973, 186–7, followed by Jones 1975, 456–7, suggested that Q. Petillius Rufus, *cos. ord.* in 83, was Cerialis himself, and not his son as was previously thought. There are some difficulties over the number of his consulships, but if Cerialis was consul in 83 it indicates that Domitian chose to honour him quite early in his reign, and that their relations were good.

23. Minerva: Girard 1981; according to Philostratus (*Vita Apoll.* 7.24) an official of Tarentum was prosecuted because he forgot to add, while sacrificing, that Domitian was the son of Minerva. Caenis: Suet. *Vesp.* 3; 21; *Dom.* 12.3; Mooney 1930, 386. Phyllis: Suet. *Dom.* 17.3; Dio 67.18; Mooney 1930, 593.

24. Julia's birthday: Suet. *Titus* 5.2. Marcia Furnilla's daughter: Mooney 1930, 475. Arrecina Tertulla's daughter: Castritius 1969, 493 points out that Arrecina's mother was a Julia; Jones 1992, 38. Domitian refuses her in marriage: Suet. *Dom.* 22.

25. Jones 1979, 8. Statius' father: Hardie 1983, 11. *Condiscipulus*: Suet. *Dom.* 1.2.

26. In Senate: Tacitus *Hist.* 4.40. Domitian spoke briefly and modestly, referring the question of hounding down informers to the Emperor.

27. Feigned interest in poetry: Suet. *Dom.* 2.2; Tacitus *Hist.* 4.86. On Domitian's own poetry: Jones 1992, 12 collects all references, pointing out that before 96 all references are naturally laudatory and after 96 entirely derogatory. Lack of interest in literature: Millar 1967, 19. Politically motivated: Suet. *Dom.* 20.

28. Physical description of Domitian: Suet. *Dom.* 18. Suetonius uses almost the same words in describing both Caligula (*Cal.* 50.1) and his father Germanicus (*Cal.* 3.1), and Nero (*Nero* 51).

ɪɪ *Bellum Jovis* pp.13–23

1. Conspiracy of Piso: Nicols 1978, 21, 30, 88; Tacitus *Annals* 12.42; 15.48–74. Vinicianus: Warmington 1959, 156; Nicols 1978, 88, 118.

2. Opposition to Nero: *CAH* 10, 37; Rudich 1993. Death of Corbulo, and the Scribonii: Dio 62.17.

3. Flavian dissociation from Gaius and Nero: Jones 1992, 11–12.

4. Helius: Suet. *Nero* 22–4; Dio 63.8–19; Rudich 1993, 187, 207.

5. Nero and Vindex/Galba: Dio 63.26–7. It has been suggested that Vindex was attempting to create a separatist Gallic state, but this is probably not the case. Tacitus gives no hint that he considered the revolt a nationalist movement: Chilver 1957, 29; Rudich 1993, 211.

6. Galba arrived in Rome possibly in October 68: Nicols 1978, 59. Titus to Rome: Nicols 1978, 93–4.

7. Sabinus reinstated: Tacitus *Hist.* 1.46. Links with Nero: Wellesley 1989, 27. Vespasian planning: Wellesley 1989, 44–5; Nicols 1978, 93–4.

8. Vitellius voted all honours: Tacitus *Hist.* 2.55.

9. Sabinus in Rome: Tacitus *Hist.* 2.55; Vitellius enters Rome: *Hist.* 2.89.

10. Acclamation of Vespasian in Egypt and Judaea: Tacitus *Hist.* 2.79; in Syria: 2.81. *III Gallica*: Nicols 1978, 114–15.

11. Titus at Corinth; Tacitus *Hist.* 2.1. Titus the motivating force: Wellesley 1989, 44–5; Nicols 1978, 93–4.

12. Josephus *BJ* 4.585–604. Tacitus *Hist.* 2.6–7, 74–80. Nicols 1978, 63, 71, says that Josephus altered his dates to fit Flavian propaganda. Chilver 1957, 34 points out that the clockwork precision of the acclamation on 1 July presupposes long-term planning on the part of Mucianus and Vespasian, probably beginning long before Vitellius left Germany. He also remarks on the thoroughness of Vespasian's agents in penetrating most of the higher commands in the Empire.

13. Aponius Saturninus: Tacitus *Hist.* 2.96. Domitian could have escaped: *Hist.* 3.59. Sabinus negotiating with Vitellius: Tacitus *Hist.* 3.65 says that Sabinus and Vitellius negotiated frequently in private. Wellesley 1989, 136 thinks that Sabinus would have been kept informed of Vespasian's plans.

14. Vespasian's original plan for blockade of Italy: Wellesley 1989, 125. Antonius Primus through the Alps: Tacitus *Hist.* 3.2; Wellesley 1989, 130–1.

15. Arrest of Caecina: Tacitus *Hist.* 3.14, 36, Nicols 1978, 80. Second Cremona and sack: Wellesley 1989, 149–53; Tacitus *Hist.* 3.15–34. Vitellius willing to abdicate but unable to control his followers: Tacitus *Hist.* 3.66; Wellesley 1989, 165–6; Nicols 1978, 83.

16. Vitellians versus Flavians: Tacitus *Hist.* 3.64–9; Wellesley 1989, 188–91.
17. Siege of Capitol: Tacitus *Hist.* 3.70–75; Wellesley 1989, 192–4; Wiseman 1978.
18. Suet. *Dom.* 1. Flavius Sabinus Domitian's cousin escaped with him: Dio 64.17.4; Tacitus *Hist.* 3.74; Briessman 1955, 69–83; Wellesley 1955, 211–14; but Jones 1992, 14 prefers the interpretation of Wiseman 1978.
19. Jupiter Conservator/Custos: Nash 1981, 518; Platner and Ashby 1929, 292. No leader: Tacitus *Hist.* 3.71. Domitian's poem: Martial 5.5.7. Court poets: Silius Italicus 3.609; Statius *Thebaid* 1.21; Martial 9.101.13 '*pro Iove bella*'.
20. The literary reaction: Briessman 1955, 77.
21. Domitian presents himself to the troops: Suet. *Dom.* 1.3; Tacitus *Hist.* 3.86. Mucianus brings Domitian to the people: Josephus *BJ* 4.654; to the soldiers: Dio 64.22.2.
22. Antonius Primus: Wellesley 1989, 195–8. Disorder in Rome: Tacitus *Hist.* 4.1. Mucianus arrives: *Hist.* 4.11; Josephus *BJ* 4.654.
23. Senate's attitude to Mucianus: Tacitus *Hist.* 4.4. Populace turn to Mucianus: *Hist.* 4.11. Domitian urban praetor: Suet. *Dom.* 1.3; Tactus *Hist.* 4.3. Frontinus resigns post: *Hist.* 4.39. Mooney 1930 comments that the appointment was unprecedented, and Domitian held none of the judicial powers attendant upon the post, which he held in name only (*titulo tenus*). Domitian in the Senate: Tacitus *Hist.* 4.39. Restores Galba's memory and refuses to open records on *delatores*: *Hist.* 4.40. Proposes to forget the past; addresses troops: *Hist.* 4.44; 46. Powers of Mucianus: Dio 65.2.1–4.
24. Mucianus eliminates rivals: Tacitus *Hist.* 4.11; Wellesley 1989, 213–14. Prevents Antonius from approaching Domitian: *Hist.* 4.80. Martial on Antonius in retirement: 10.23.5–8.
25. Domitian during revolt of Civilis: Tacitus *Hist.* 4.68, 85–6; Josephus *BJ* 7.85; Suet. *Dom.* 2.1. Civilis before the revolt: Wellesley 1989, 169–88. Domitian writes to Cerialis: Tacitus *Hist.* 4.86. Afraid of Vespasian: Dio 64.3.4; 65.9.3.
26. Fly stabbing: Dio 65.9.3, 10.1. Vespasian thanks Domitian for not replacing him: Suet. *Dom.* 1.3; Dio 65.2. Vespasian returns to Rome: Tacitus *Hist.* 4.51.
27. Vespasian concerned about Mucianus: Jones 1992, 16; Crook 1951, 164–5. Titus' plea for leniency for Domitian: Tacitus *Hist.* 4.52; Jones 1984, 88–9.
28. Cancelleria reliefs: Last 1948.

iii *Augusti Filius* pp.24–33

1. Dio 65.10.1; Suet. *Dom.* 2.1. Dynasty: Jones 1984, 77–8.
2. Triumph: Suet. *Vesp.* 8.1; *Titus* 6.1; *Dom.* 2.1; Josephus *BJ* 7.152. Mooney 1930, 512 recounts how Tiberius and Marcellus rode in Augustus' triumph after Actium. The white horse Domitian rode would match the horses drawing Vespasian and Titus.
3. Suet. Titus 6.1 '*receptaque ad se prope omnium officiorum cura*'. Brunt 1977, 102 and 107 on *lex de imp. Vesp.*: confers usual powers and not designed to limit them. No one but Vespasian in charge: Jones 1984, 100.
4. Succession by sons: Suet. *Vesp.* 25. Mooney 1930, 464 remarks that it makes more sense if Vespasian did say this towards the end of his life, having survived various

conspiracies, as Suetonius implies. Dio 65.12 reads as though something is missing; at best it is a strange *non sequitur.*

5. Titus second in command: Jones 1984, 86–8, 100. Titus' powers: Suet. *Titus* 6.1; Jones 1984, 80–4; Mooney 1930, 481–2.
6. Consulships of Domitian kept pace with Vespasian and Titus: Jones 1984, 119; 1992, 19. Titus reads speeches in Senate: Suet. *Titus* 6.1. Both sons read speeches: Dio 65.10.6.
7. Idleness: Gsell 1894, 39, questioned by Waters 1964, 63 n.33. Importance and duties of consuls: Talbert 1984, 21–2. Mucianus exceptional: Townend 1961, 54; Jones 1992, 19. Titus steps aside for Domitian: Suet. *Dom.* 2.1. Domitian *cos. suff.* March to June 71: *CIL* XVI 14–17; V 7239; *cos. II ord.* 73: *CIL* VI 1877; *cos. III suff.* 74: *CIL* IV 5526; *cos. IIII suff.* 76: *CIL* VIII 10116; *cos. V suff.* 77: *CIL* III 6993; *cos. VI suff.* 79: *CIL* III 12218. Senatorial colleagues: Waters 1964, 61. Domitian forms alliances in Senate: Jones 1992, 19.
8. *Trib. pot.:* Talbert 1984, 165, 187; Jones 1960, 9–12; Grant 1946, 446–50; Mooney 1930, 428–9, 482. Senatorial recognition: Jones 1984, 80.
9. *Consors successorque:* Suet. *Titus* 9.3. Domitian *cos. ord.* 80: *CIL* II 4803= *ILS* 5833. Coinage: Waters 1964, 62 n.31; *RIC* 2 1926 41–4, 66–7, 89, 95–100, 108, 112. Vespasian's will altered: Suet. *Dom.* 2.3; Titus a forger: Suet. *Titus* 3.2; Mooney 1930, 515. Titus may have intended to share power later: Jones 1984, 119–21.
10. Domitian expected to share power: Suet. *Dom.* 2.3; Mooney 1930, 515. Tiberius: Levick 1976, 221 compares Domitian and Tiberius.
11. Marriage to Domitia Longina: Suet. *Dom.* 1.3; Dio 65.3.4. Jones 1992, 33 says Vespasian first tried to make Domitian marry Julia, as recounted in Suet. *Dom.* 22. Nicols 1978, 119–20 suggests the political purpose behind the marriage to attract Corbulo's followers. Berenice: Crook 1951; Rogers 1980.
12. Son born in second consulship: Suet. *Dom.* 3.1. Discussion of alternative dates: Mooney 1930, 518. Scott 1936, 71–5 suggests that the child died in 74, rejecting the idea that a daughter was born then. Coins: Mattingly *BMC* 2, 311, nos. 61 and 63. Statius *Silvae* 1.1.97; Silius Italicus 3.629; Martial and snow: 4.3.
13. Martial 6.3: *'nascere, magne puer'.* Scott 1936, 75 says the supposed pregnancy is only a wish. Jones 1992, 37 endorses this, adding that from Martial 9.86 it is inferred that Domitian only ever lost one child.
14. Vologaeses: Suet. *Dom.* 2.2; Dio 65.15.3; Jones 1992, 19. 40,000 troops: Tacitus *Hist.* 4.51. Gold crown: Josephus *BJ* 7.5. Harmozica inscription: *Année Philologique* 31, 423. Tiridates: Mooney 1930, 515.
15. Philosophers and astrologers: Suet. *Vesp.* 13. Helvidius Priscus: Tacitus *Hist.* 4.5–9; Dio 65.12. Helvidius was at least consistent, being exiled in 66 by Nero and opposing Vitellius in the Senate: Dio 64.7.2. Bengtson 1979, 230 wonders why Vespasian put up with him for so long.
16. Continuous plotting (*'assiduas in se coniurationes'*): Suet. *Vesp.* 25. Removal of suspects by Titus: Suet. *Titus* 6.1. Caecina: *PIR*2 C 99; Suet. *Titus* 6.2; Mooney 1930, 433. Dio 65.16. Second Nero: Suet. *Titus* 7.1. Aurelius Victor *Epit. de Caes.* 10.4 connects the downfall of Caecina with Titus' mistress Berenice.

17. Caecina had revolutionary designs and had prepared the soldiers to help him: Dio 65.16.3. Marcellus an unlikely associate of Caecina: Jones 1984, 91–3; 109–10, n. 86–8. Fear of succession of Titus: Jones 1984, 92. Crook 1951, 170–1 says there was no plot; Jones 1984, 109 n. 87 says the evidence of Suetonius and Dio makes it very likely. No ancient author seems to have attempted to implicate Domitian in the plot, even though Suet. *Titus* 9.3 affirms that he was always plotting the overthrow of Titus.

18. Marcellus (*PIR2* E 84) in the senate: Tacitus *Hist.* 2.53, 4.6–8. Helvidius attacks him and at next session Domitian proposes cessation of hostilities: *Hist.* 4.43–4. Jones 1984, 91–3, 108–10 n. 86–90. Dio 65.16.

19. Death of Vespasian: Suet. *Vesp.* 24, from too free use of the cold springs. Mooney 1930, 463 on the springs at Cutiliae. Hadrian: Dio 66.17. Succession: Jones 1984, 115, 120–1. Tiberius: Shotter 1992, 24–8; Levick 1976, 68–81.

20. Titus' reign unexpectedly benign: Suet. *Titus* 7.1; Jones 1984, 114–80. Dismissal of Berenice and favourites: Suet. *Titus* 7.2. Independence from Vespasian's system: Jones 1984, 122. Titus and Domitia Longina: Suet. *Titus* 10.2, but Suetonius discounts the story because Domitia would have boasted of it. Promotion of Aelius Lamia: Suet. *Dom.* 1.3; Jones 1984, 117–18.

21. Domitian killed Titus: Mooney 1930, 503–4 outlines all the various versions of Titus' death, discussed by Jones 1984, 154–5. Philostratus *Vit. Apoll.* 6.32 says very specifically that Domitian poisoned Titus, even naming the fish that he mixed with Titus' food. It just happens to be the same fish with which Nero always poisoned unwanted associates. Domitian ordered attendants to leave Titus: Suet. *Dom.* 2.3. Dio 66.26.2–3 says that Domitian packed his brother in ice, then rode for the camp and distributed donatives. Flavius Sabinus' prominence: Jones 1992, 45, 206 n.100. Townend 1961, 54–6 deduces that Sabinus *PIR2* F 355, listed as the son of Vespasian's brother Sabinus *PIR2* F 352, must be the latter's grandson. Another Flavius Sabinus *PIR2* F 354, consul in 69, not previously considered as part of the family, is most likely the son of *PIR2* F 352 and the father of *PIR2* F 355. Attendants in white: Suet. *Dom.* 12; Mooney 1930, 569 says Imperial attendants (*aulici ministri*) wore white tunics with gold borders. Sabinus the husband of Julia: Philostratus *Vit. Apoll.* 7.7. Consul in 82: Jones 1992, 45–6. Execution: Suet. *Dom.* 10.4 where he says Domitian executed his cousin (*patruelis*), but Townend 1961, 55–6 thinks this is used in the very widest sense. Julia taken to live with Domitian: Suet. *Dom.* 22; Dio 67.3.2.

22. No honours save deification: Scott 1936, 62–3 disagrees, listing the honours Domitian rendered to his brother. Deification very soon after Titus' death: Jones 1984, 155–6. Vespasian's deification late: Scott 1936, 40; Jones 1984, 152. Senators assemble: Suet. *Titus* 11. Date of confirmation of Domitian's powers: Jones 1992, 19, 202 n.74.

IV Domitian *Imperator* pp.34–44

1. The surviving epigraphy is of importance in a study of Domitian's administration, but does not elucidate the events described by the ancient authors. Britain and Germany: the controversy over the dates of the campaigns of Agricola and the ending of wars

against the Britons and the Chatti has produced a quantity of literature (see notes to Chapters 7 and 8).

2. Dio's account (Book 67) of Domitian's reign survives as an amalgam of sections by the Epitomator Xiphilinus, together with some passages by Zonaras. Though Dio adopted the annalistic approach it is not possible to be certain that the order of events has been preserved in the surviving sections.

3. Eutropius 7.23.4; Aurelius Victor *De Caes.* 11; *Epit.* 11.2. Domitian became greedy through need and cruel through fear: Suet. *Dom.* 3.2; not cruel at first: *Dom.* 9.1; after Saturninus: *Dom.* 10.5.

4. Troops hail Domitian Imperator: Dio 66.26. Imperial acclamations Vespasian, Titus, Claudius: Campbell 1984, 124.

5. Tiberius: Talbert 1984, 187.

6. Domitian's *Trib. pot.* years: *PIR2* F 259, p150. Titles: *ILS* 1995; Germanicus and *censor perpetuus: ILS* 269. 17 consulships: Suet. *Dom.* 13.3. Statius *Silvae* 4.1 on the seventeenth consulship. Pliny: *Pan.* 65.3. After the Chattan war the Senate voted Domitian a ten-year consulship: Dio 67.4.3; Mooney 1930, 573.

7. Domitia Augusta: Suet. *Dom.* 3.1; Mooney 1930, 519; *CIL* VI 2060. Agrippina: Tacitus *Annals* 12.26.

8. *Dominus et deus*: Suet. *Dom.* 13.2; Martial 5.8.1; Mooney 1930, 571 quoting Eusebius *Chron.* p.161, Schoene edn, dates this title between 1 Oct. 85 and 30 Sept. 86.

9. Titus never put to death any senator: Dio 66.19; does not punish plotters: Suet. *Titus* 9.1. Emperors who do not have to punish are only lucky: Dio 67.2.3. Titus not popular if he had lived longer: Dio 66.18.

10. Fire in Rome: Dio 66.24.1–3. Fourth-century Chronicle: Mommsen *Chron. Min.* I 146; Anderson 1983. Restoration of Capitol: Suet. *Dom.* 5.1. Domitian restored most of the buildings destroyed in the fire of 80: Blake 1959, 100. Baths of Titus and Colosseum: Blake 1959, 99. Jupiter Capitolinus: Platner and Ashby 1929, 300; Martial refers to a god building the temple; 13.74.2. Statius *Silvae* 1.6.102 and 4.3.16 on the restoration of the Capitol. Jupiter Custos: Blake 1959, 101; Platner and Ashby 1929, 292; Nash 1981, I, 518–20, pls. 638–40 shows remains of podium before destruction in 1896. Tacitus *Hist.* 3.74 describes this temple as huge (*ingens*). Scott Ryberg *The Panel Reliefs of Marcus Aurelius*, New York 1967, 19 and fig. 9a, discusses and doubts the identification of Domitian's temple on the later sculpture. The panels are now in the Musei dei Conservatori, Rome.

11. Titus without Divus: *CIL* VI 2060. Arch of Titus begun by Titus and finished by Domitian: Blake 1959, 111–12. Dedication and deification associated: Pfanner 1983, 91. Jones 1992, 93 rejects idea that Nerva or Trajan dedicated the arch. Pliny on Domitian wanting to be the brother of a god: *Pan.* 11.1.

12. *Templum gentis Flaviae*: Platner and Ashby 1929, 247; Blake 1959, 114. It was struck by lightning in 96: Suet. *Dom.* 15. Martial refers to the house site: 9.20.1. *Templum Divorum*: Blake 1959, 113; Platner and Ashby 1929, 152–3.

13. Gifts and privileges: Dio 67.2; Titus the first to issue one edict covering all gifts: Suet. *Titus* 8. Confiscations: Dio 67.4.5; Jones 1992, 77, dates the first confiscations to 85.

14. Eunuchs: Suet. *Dom.* 7.1. Earinus: Dio 67.2. On the benefits of Domitian's ban on castration: Martial 9.5 and 9.7. Aversion to bloodshed: Suet. *Dom.* 9.1.

15. Vendetta: Dio 67.2. *Amici* not fixed appointments: Jones 1992, 50; co-opted occasionally: Jones 1975, 454. *Equites, liberti*: Devreker 1977, 224.

16. Trajan's *bon mot*: *SHA* Alex. 65.5. Suet. *Titus* 7.2.

17. Continuity of advisers: Crook 1955, 48; Waters 1964, 64. Juvenal *Satires* 4; Devreker 1977, 227–37 on Domitian's *amici*. Jones 1974, 461 suggests a break with tradition under Titus; Devreker 1977, 234 disagrees.

18. Jones 1992, 36 refutes idea of plot formed by followers of Titus.

19. Domitia and Paris: Suet. *Dom.*3; Mooney 1930, 519; Dio 67.3. Juvenal 7.88 on the influence of Paris at court. Paris' pupil: Suet. *Dom.* 3. Martial on Paris' tomb: 11.13.

20. People demand return of Domitia: Suet. *Dom.* 3. Coins of 83: Castritius 1969, 497. Mooney 1930, 519 says she was banished from court between 82 and 84. Ursus: Mooney 1930, 519 says he is Flavius Ursus of Statius *Silvae* 2.6, but Jones 1992, 40–2 more plausibly says he is L. Julius Ursus, possibly a distant relative of the Flavii.

21. Titus and Domitia: Suet. *Titus* 10.2. Vinson 1989 investigates the literary themes in the traditional story and reinstates Domitia. Castritius 1969, 497 assumes she needed consolation for an empty marriage.

22. Julia Titi: Suet. *Dom.* 22; Dio 67.3. Philostratus *Vit. Apoll.* 7.7.

23. Sabinus *cos. ord.* 82, Domitian's own choice; Jones 1975, 456; 1992, 46. Consular elections: Suet. *Dom.* 10.4. Gsell 1894, 248 presumes there was a second consulship. Links with Saturninus: Waters 1964, 72. The list of executions: Suet. *Dom.* 10. Eusebius *Chron Canonum* A Abr 2099; Jones 1992, 47. Dio of Prusa: *Or.* 13.1. Von Arnim 1898, 228–31 considers the identity of Dio's friend, and decides 230–1 that he must be Sabinus. Jones 1992, 47 places the execution of Sabinus before the Chattan war.

24. The possibility of a plot involving both Sabinus and Dio of Prusa as adherents of Titus: von Arnim 1898, 231. Philosophers: MacMullen 1992, 69–71. Dio of Prusa annoyed Trajan as well as Domitian: Campbell 1984, 337 n.63; Pliny *Ep.* 10.81 and 82.

▼ Imperial Rule *pp. 45–59*

1. *Auctoritas/potestas*: Pleket 1961, 300–1. *Dominus et deus*: between 1 October 85 and 30 September 86 according to Eusebius, quoted in Mooney 1930, 571. Martial does not mention the title until 89: 5.8.1. Pliny/Trajan: Bengtson 1979, 185; Henderson 1927, 29. Pliny *Pan.* 2 praises Trajan for not making any claim to divinity. Obeisance: Pliny *Pan.* 24.2; Epictetus 4.1.17; Talbert 1984, 164.

2. Gold statues: Suet. *Dom.* 13. September/October: Suet. *Dom.* 13.3; Dio 67.4.4 mentions only October, which was changed to Domitianus in honour of the month of the Emperor's birth. The *Acta Arvalia* for 87 (*CIL* VI 2065) retain the old names of the months, therefore the date of the change was probably post-87: Mooney 1930, 575.

3. Imperial cult: Scott 1936, 79–82 for epigraphic references to priests from all parts of the Empire. Domitilla: *ILS* 6692; Julia: *ILS* 6487.

4. Vespasian made use of Emperor-worship: Waters 1969, 397. Temples: Domitian included a temple of Minerva in the Forum Transitorium, rebuilt the *templum Castorum et Minervae*, founded the temple of Minerva Chalcidia: Jones 1992, 100. Festivals: *Quinquatria* celebrated in March at the Alban villa, with poetry contests and plays, as well as animal shows: Suet. *Dom.* 4.4; Dio 67.1.2. Domitian identified himself with the state: Scott 1936, 129. Tiberius holding a wolf by the ears: Suet. *Tiberius* 25.11. Absolute control: Levick 1982, 51.

5. Trajan the autocrat: Waters 1969, 385–6; Brunt 1983, 65. Nothing sordid: Suet. *Dom.* 8.2, 9.2. Aristotle: Trans. J.K.Thompson, Penguin edn 1988, 150–1.

6. Imperial palace: Blake 1959, 115–22. Gypsum: Suet. *Dom.* 14.4.

7. Tacitus *Hist.* 1.84. Rebuilding Senate House: Talbert 1984, 115; *Chronography* of 354, ed. Mommsen 1842, 142. Exclusion of senators: Talbert 1984, 118; Suet. *Dom.* 20; Tacitus *Annals* 15.39; Dio 62.18.2.

8. Domitian and the Senate: Jones 1979; Epictetus 4.1.140; Pliny *Pan.* 54.4. Opposition: Brunt 1983, 65.

9. Domitian co-operated with the Senate at first: Jones 1979, 21, 29, 39–42.

10. Censor: Jones 1973b, 276–7. Emperors exercising censorial powers without the title: Talbert 1984, 16. Dismissal of *pantomimus*: Suet. *Dom.* 8.3; Dio 67.13.1. Palfurius Sura: Suet. *Dom.* 13.1. Orientals: Jones 1979. 28; Levick 1982, 62.

11. *Senatus Consulta*: Talbert 1984, 357–8. Domitian tried to eliminate the Senate as governing body: Pleket 1961, 299. Domitian to proconsul of Cyrene: Talbert 1984, 402; *AE* 1954, 188.

12. *Ab actis*: Tacitus *Annals* 5.4; Talbert 1984, 310, 334–7. Neratius Marcellus: *PIR2* N 55; Talbert 1984, 334; Birley 1981, 87–91.

13. Equestrian careers: Millar 1963, 195 reviewing Pflaum 1961, questions the existence of a career structure; see also Saller 1980, 46; Brunt 1983. Rivalry between the two orders not apparent: Brunt 1983, 66.

14. Letter to Laberius Maximus: *P. Berlin.* 8334, accessible in Lewis and Rheinhold 1966, 129; Sherk 1988, 140–1. Patronage: Saller 1980, 56–7; Brunt 1983, 51. Loyalty of equestrians: Brunt 1983, 63–6. Special skills not necessary: Brunt 1975; 1983, 47. Equites capable and willing: Dio 56.26.2. Some tasks repugnant to senators: Brunt 1983, 43.

15. L. Julius Ursus: Syme 1958, 635–6 reconstructed Ursus' career from several sources. Dio 67.3.1, 4.2 attests the Ursus involved in the divorce of Domitia and the intercession of Julia, but the epigraphic evidence may refer to more than one man; *AE* 1939, 60 attests a Julius Ursus as prefect of the *annona* and of Egypt; the *Fasti Ostienses* attest the consul [U]rsus in 84; the letter to Laberius Maximus attests the promotion of a Julius to the Senate. Fuscus: Suet. *Dom.* 6.1; Jones 1992, 179 says the appointment was an innovation. C. Minicius Italus: *PIR2* M 614; *ILS* 1374= *CIL* V 875; Talbert 1984, 397; Gsell 1894, 57.

16. Imperial administration: Duff 1958, 221–8 for a list of freedmen and equites in central administration posts.

17. Vitellius: Duff 1958, 225; *ILS* 1447=*CIL* XI 5028. *Equites* and *liberti*: Suet. *Dom.* 7.2.

18. Dismissal of *a rationibus*: Evans 1978, 112. Weary old age and fortune deserted: Statius *Silvae* 3.3.156–7. Duties of *a rationibus:* ibid. 85–110. In charge of both public and private expenses: Brunt 1966, 89–90.

19. Dismissal of second in command: Statius *Silvae* 3.3.160–2; Weaver 1972, 290. Classicus: Jones 1992, 64; *AE* 1972, 574. Atticus: Jones 1992, 63; Weaver 1972, 32.

20. Abascantus/Capito: Pflaum 1961, 143–5; Jones 1992, 63. *A cognitionibus:* Weaver 1972, 261. Duties of *ab epistulis: Silvae* 5.1.76–107; Millar 1967, 14–19. Dictation: ibid. 13.

21. Bucolas: *ILS* 1567; Jones 1992, 62; Weaver 1972, 274.

22. Parthenius: Suet. *Dom.*16 and 17; Mooney 1930, 587. Right to wear a dagger: Dio 67.15. Martial to Parthenius to bring poems to Domitian's attention: 5.6, 11.1, 12.11. Aurelius Victor *Epit.* 12.8 for account of Parthenius' death. Stephanus and Maximus: Suet. *Dom.* 17.

23. Dio 67.2.1–3.

24. Suet. *Dom.* 8.2. Domitian 'guards every quarter of the earth with well-chosen servants' Statius *Silvae* 5.1.79. Trial of Baebius Massa: Pliny *Ep.* 3.4, 7.33. Baebius: *PIR2* B 26. Political orientation: Levick 1982, 64.

25. Compensation not always granted: Brunt 1961, 205. Exploitation should be intelligent: ibid. 190 n.2.

26. Pride in legislation: Levick 1982, 64. Filtered information, Vietnam War: K. Boulding *Three Faces of Power*. London 1990, 43, 134.

27. Antistius Rusticus: *AE* 1925, 126; McCrum and Woodhead 1966, no. 464; Pleket 1961, 307; Levick 1982, 57–8.

28. Acmonia: McCrum and Woodhead 1966, no. 500; Pleket 1961, 307; Levick 1982, 55. Claudius Athenodorus: McCrum and Woodhead 1966, no. 466; Sherk 1988, no. 95. Pleket 1961, 304–5; Levick 1982, 51–3.

29. Spanish *municipia*: McCrum and Woodhead 1966, nos. 453, 454; Levick 1985, 25–30; Lewis and Rheinhold 1966, 321–6; Salpensa: Sherk 1988, 97. *Lex Irnitana: AE* 1986, 333; H. Galstener *'Municipium Flavium Irnitanium'*, *JRS* 78, 1988, 78–90; J.L. Mourges 'The so–called letter of Domitian at the end of the *lex Irnitanium'*, *JRS* 77,1987, 78–87.

30. Vine edict: Suet. *Dom.* 7.2, 14.2; Levick 1982, 69–72; Jones 1992, 7–9. *Concilium* of Asia: Philostratus *Vit. Soph.* 1.21.6.

31. Nasamones: Dio 67.4. There is no sign of disapproval in Tacitus' account of Ostorius Scapula's assertion that the Silures should be wiped out, just as the Sugambri had been extinguished (*Annals* 12.39). Impossible to ensure good government over whole Empire: Brunt 1961, 221–2.

32. Reaction of people to Domitian's death: Suet. *Dom.* 23.1. Bread and circuses: Juvenal *Satires* 10.77. Domitian ignores the people: Pliny *Ep.* 1.8; *Pan.* 26. *Congiaria*: Suet. *Dom.* 4.5; Mooney 1930, 528 computes the total at each *congiarium* as 60,000,000 sesterces; Jones 1992, 74 gives a figure of *HS* 135,000,000 for all three hand-outs. Dates: Jones 1992, 74; Martial 8.15.4 describes the 'third round of gifts after the Pannonian war' which dates to 93. *Naumachia*: Suet. *Dom.* 4.2.

vi The Cost of Empire *pp.60–67*

1. *Fiscus/aerarium*: Carradice 1983, 157; Brunt 1966, 77–8. Nerva/Trajan restore some control to people: Carradice 1983, 154–5.

2. Statius on *a rationibus: Silvae* 3.3.86–105. Coinage/finance link: Carradice 1983, 157. Dates of new issues: Jones 1992, 75. Minerva reverse types: Carradice 1983, 142; no bronze 82 to 84: ibid. 142. Critical disdain: Sutherland 1974, 198.

3. Domitian's character reflected in the care and attention to coinage: Carradice 1983, 148. Suetonius declares that Domitian at first refused inheritances, but later began to seize them: *Dom.* 9 and 21; but he descended into cruelty before greed: *Dom.* 10.1. Corellius Rufus: Pliny *Ep.* 1.12.7–8. Confiscations: Jones 1992, 77 dates the first of these to 85; Rogers 1984, 75 assigns the confiscations to the period when Suetonius describes Domitian's worsening cruelty, i.e. after Saturninus. Gsell 1894, 264 groups confiscations, executions, persecutions in the years 93 to 96. Suetonius as adolescent/*fiscus Judaicus: Dom.* 12.2; Jones 1992, 76 interprets this as the beginning of the more stringent tax collections, in 85.

4. Dacian war: Jones 1992, 226 n.7 lists all the alternative dates; Strobel 1989, 40, 42 n.30 argues for mid-year 85; see also Strobel in *ZPE* 64, 1986, 265–86. Date of devaluation: Carradice 1983, 28; also 143 where the debasement is described as sudden. Credit: Rogers 1984, 74–5. Frontinus *Strategemata* 2.11.7 on payment for crops. Coinage output and problems of estimating using statistics from hoards: Casey 1986, 122–4 and fig. 18.

5. Refusal to devalue leading to financial difficulties: Carradice 1983, 165–6. Rogers 1984, 75, 77 takes the view that there was never an insurmountable problem in Domitian's reign, but that in the 90s he had to find money to pay the bills run up in the 80s.

6. The treasury empty/full on Domitian's death: Gsell 1894, 333–4 said that it was bankrupt. Syme 1930, 55–70 (esp. 68) stressed Domitian's intelligence and capabilities, arguing that there was sufficient for Nerva to squander. Sutherland 1935, 150–62 restated the case for financial disaster at the end of Domitian's reign. Garzetti 1974, 281–4 stressed Domitian's efficient revenue collection, which yielded more than enough for him to spend on his various projects. Rogers 1984, 77 concluded that the treasury was not full when Nerva took over, but that Domitian had settled all accounts.

7. Vespasian: Suet. *Vesp.* 16.3; Rogers 1984, 61. Agrippa: Dio 52.6. Vespasian doubled taxes: Suet. *Vesp.* 16.1.

8. Suetonius on Domitian and taxes: *Dom.* 12.2. Revolt of Nasamones: Dio 67.4.6. Gifts to Domitian: Dio 67.1.3. Water revenues: Frontinus *De Aquis* 2.116–18; Carradice 1983, 154–5.

9. Domitian spends more than income: Suet. *Dom.* 3.2, 12. Confiscations: Syme 1930, 66 argues for political motives; Carradice 1983, 165 stresses the moral and legal aspects. Rogers 1984, 62, 71, 76 n.63 thinks there was both a financial and political motive, suggesting that the confiscations provided considerable income, and that Domitian used the money so raised for public necessities in Rome. Domitian possessed more than he required: Pliny *Pan.* 50.5. New owners of estates: *Pan.* 50.4. Jealousy: *Pan.* 50.5.

10. Finance in Suetonius: *Dom.* 3.2, 7.3, 9.2–3, 10.1, 12.1–2. Army pay-rise: Suet. *Dom.* 7.3, 12.1; Dio 67.3. Dio's figures are in drachmae, but they corroborate those given by Suetonius.

11. Gilding: Rogers 1984, 68 n.36, quoting Plutarch's figures, *Publ.* 15.3–5. Martial on glory of contributing: 5.25.12; also 10.4.5, 4.67.5.

12. Caesar doubles pay: Suet. *Divus Julius* 26.3. Mutiny of 14: Tacitus *Annals* 1.17. Number of pay-days (*stipendia*): Suet. *Dom.* 7.3; Mooney 1930, 542 says that the number of pay-days remained at three, as implied by Zonaras 11.19=Dio 67.3.5. Speidel 1973, 141 thinks there were four *stipendia* all through Domitian's reign, reverting to three after his death. Output of aurei: Carradice 1983, 161–2; army pay reckoned in aurei: Alston 1994, 114.

13. *V Alaudae* and *XXI Rapax*: Syme 1928, 45–7, 54. *I Minervia*: Jones 1992, 130. Rogers' figures for legionary pay: 1984, 66 n.26.

14. Little difference between legionary/auxiliary pay: Speidel 1973, 146. No difference: Alston 1994, 122. Subsidies to Decebalus: Dio 67.7.4; Rogers 1984, 67. Army costs half of state expenditure: Campbell 1984, 164–5. Expansionist wars: Birley 1974, 16.

15. Edict on privileges granted to veterans: *FIRA2* 1 no.76; Campbell 1984, 210, 443. Soldiers avenge Domitian: Dio 68.3.3

VII *Perdomita Britannia* *pp.68–78*

1. *Perdomita Britannia et statim missa*: Tacitus *Histories* 1.2. Tacitus' life of Agricola was probably his first published work, written when he was aged about forty. R.M. Ogilvie and I.A. Richmond *Cornelii Taciti De Vita Agricolae*, Oxford 1967 is still the most detailed commentary, but the archaeological information has undergone some revision. Carlisle founded in the early Flavian period: D. Charlesworth 'Roman Carlisle', *Archaeological Journal* 135, 1978, 115–37, esp. 137; D.C.A. Shotter 'The evidence of coin loss and the Roman occupation of north–west England', in N.J. Higham (ed.) *The Changing Past: Some Recent Work in the Archaeology of Northern England*, Manchester 1979, 1–13, esp. 9; W.S. Hanson and D.B. Campbell in *Britannia* 17, 1986, 73–89, esp. 88. Dendrochronology: *Britannia* 21, 1990, 320. On Agricola and his successors see also: D.J. Breeze *Northern Frontiers of Roman Britain*, London 1982. W.S. Hanson *Agricola and the Conquest of the North*, London 1987; W.S. Hanson and G.S. Maxwell *Rome's North West Frontier*, Edinburgh 1983; G.S. Maxwell *The Romans in Scotland*, Edinburgh 1989.

2. Agricola's career: Hanson op.cit. n.1. above; Birley 1981, 73–81; 1975, 139–54. Last two seasons under Domitian: A.R. Birley in *Liverpool Classical Monthly* 1.2, Feb. 1976, 11–14, esp. 13.

3. Agricola's consulship: the problem is discussed by D.B. Campbell in *ZPE* 63, 1986, 197–200, esp. 199–200 where he argues for the consulship in 76; see also Birley 1981, 77 n.34. For 77: *PIR2* J 126; Jones 1992, 131–3. For 78: Ogilvie and Richmond op. cit. n.1 above, 318; Syme 1958, 22 n.6. On the seven seasons divided into summers and winters: J.G.F. Hind in *Northern History* 21, 1985, 1–18.

4. M.-T. Raepsaet-Charlier discussed the evidence for the date of Agricola's term of office in Britain and concluded that 77–83 are the most acceptable dates: *ANRW* II,

33.3, 1807–1857, esp. 1842 and 1857. Third season: Tacitus *Agricola* 22. Fourth season: *Agricola* 23. Barochan and Elginhaugh, and reasons for halt: Hanson and Maxwell op.cit. n.1 above, 39–40. Number of place-names in Tacitus, 'Five tribes, three islands, three rivers, one hill, and a port': A.R. Burn in T.A. Dorey (ed.) *Tacitus*, London 1969, 35–61.

5. Fifth season: Tacitus *Agricola* 24. The sea crossing was the Clyde, 'that is unambiguous': Birley 1981, 80.

6. Sixth season and attack on *legio IX*: Tacitus *Agricola* 26.

7. C.Velius Rufus: *ILS* 9200, discussed by D. Kennedy in *Britannia* 14, 1983, 183–96. Expedition in wars against Marcomanni and Quadi: K. Strobel 'Zur Rekonstruktion der Laufbahn des C. Velius Rufus', *ZPE* 64, 1986, 265–86, esp. 277–9.

8. Roscius Aelianus: *ILS* 1025. In reply to Kennedy's suggestion (op. cit. n.7 above) that Roscius and the vexillation of *IX Hispana* fought in Germany in 89, Strobel points out that Roscius was suffect consul in 100: *ZPE* 64, 1986, 266 n.6; K. Strobel 'Nochmals zur Datierung der Schlacht am Mons Graupius', *Historia* 36, 1987, 198–212, esp. 205 n.36. *IX Hispana* may have left troops to guard communications: Birley 1976 op. cit. n. 2 above, 14; at York to keep watch over Brigantia: Birley 1981, 81 n.53.

9. Edward I, the invader starves before the natives: J.E. Morris *The Welsh Wars of Edward I*. Oxford 1901, 293–4. Necessary to control the Highlands, 'a military truth which Cromwell was the first to realize': R.L.G. Ritchie *The Normans in Scotland*, Edinburgh 1954.

10. Glen forts founded by Agricola or his successor: D.J. Breeze in *Scottish Archaeological Forum* 12, 1981, 14–24, esp. 22 argues that Agricola could not have built forts while he was campaigning; Hanson and Maxwell op. cit. n.1 above, 43 and refs. also place the glen forts in a later phase after Agricola's campaigns. Ptolemy's *Geography* compiled from information gathered during Agricola's campaigns: A.L.F. Rivet and C. Smith *The Place-Names of Roman Britain*, London 1974, 114.

11. Mons Graupius: Tacitus *Agricola* 35–8. Location discussed by G.S. Maxwell *A Battle Lost*, Edinburgh 1990. Date: Birley 1981, 77–8 summarizes the evidence; K. Strobel in *Historia* 36, 1987, 198–212, esp. 210 is probably the latest to argue for the battle fought in 84. Honours to Agricola: Tacitus *Agricola* 40. Lack of promotion: *Agricola* 42.

12. Coin evidence for abandonment of Scotland: A.S. Hobley 'Numismatic Evidence for the Post-Agricolan Abandonment of the Roman Frontier in Scotland', *Britannia* 20, 1989, 69–74. Inchtuthil: L. Pitts and J.K. St.Joseph *Inchtuthil: Legionary Fortress Excavations* 1952–1965, London 1985.

13. Coins at Wroxeter: Hobley op. cit. n. 11 above, 71–2. Abandonment of Inchtuthil and northern Scotland in winter 86/7: Strobel 1989, 58. *II Adiutrix* in Moesia Superior by 87: Strobel 1989, 72, n.12 and Appendix I. A. 2; Jones 1992, 132 says that it was transferred between 87 and 88; it is not attested on the Danube until 92. *Cohors II Batavorum*: A. Poulter 'The Lower Moesian limes and the Dacian wars of Trajan', *Studien zu den Militärgrenzen Roms* III: *Vorträge der Internationalen Limeskongresses, Aalen 1983*, 1986, 519–28, esp. 527 n.35. Lack of central authority: M. Millett *The Romanization of Britain*, Cambridge 1990, 100.

14. Phased withdrawal: Breeze op. cit. n.1 above, 61; Hanson op.cit. n.1 above, 153; Hanson and Maxwell op. cit. n.1 above, 43–5, and refs. Mortarium rim from Gask House and pottery from Westerton: A.S. Robertson in *Transactions of the Perthshire Society of Natural Science*, Special Issue, 1974, 14–29, esp. 20–1; Hanson op. cit. n.1 above, 153. The towers may belong to the sixth season: M. Todd *Roman Britain 55 BC to AD 400*, London 1981, 114; S.S. Frere and J.J. Wilkes *Strageath: Excavations Within the Roman Fort 1973–86*, Britannia Monograph no. 9, London 1989, 12–13. Tacitus and Domitian: Briessman 1955; Nesselhauf 1952, 234, points out that Agricola had received the very highest recognition for his achievements in Britain, but this did not diminish Tacitus' polemic. Birley 1975, 141–2 says that such prejudice would be expected in the *Agricola* but it also extends into the *Histories* where more sober judgement should be evident.

15. Newstead and Dalswinton: Hanson and Maxwell op. cit. n.1 above, 45–6.

16. Enemy action: Hanson and Maxwell op.cit. n.1 above, 46–7.

17. Sallustius Lucullus: Suet. *Dom.* 10.3; rebellion: Birley 1981, 82–3. Karus: *AE* 1951 88; he was prefect of *Cohors II Asturum* which was in the Lower German army in 89, and was awarded the title *pia fidelis Domitiana* for loyalty to Domitian during Saturninus' rebellion. The unit was in Britain by 105: *CIL* XVI 51; V. Maxfield *The Military Decorations of the Roman Army*, London 1981, 165 considers Karus' awards unparalleled. *Singulares Britannici/Britanniciani*: Jones 1992, 134, 226 n.57.

VIII Chatti *pp.79–91*

1. The account in Dio 67.3 is reconstructed from different sources, where the ordering of events cannot be verified. The affair of the Vestals is followed by Domitian's arrival in Gaul, then by the army pay rise, then by the war in Germany. Eusebius and Hieronymus: Scott 1936, 187 n.1; Gsell 1894, 80 n.4. Chatti *in armis*: Frontinus *Strategemata* 1.1.8; Henderson 1927, 99. War in 82: Jones 1992, 129–30, summarizing and emending his own arguments put forward in *Historia* 22, 1973, 79–90, where it is suggested that the Chatti attacked at the end of 81. On dating the war see also: Evans in *Historia* 24, 1975, 121–4; Jones in *Latomus* 41, 1982, 329–35. Discharge of veterans September 82 and three auxiliary units in Moesia: *ILS* 1995.

2. Strobel 1987, 427 dates the beginning of the campaign to spring 83. Triumph laughable: Tacitus *Agricola* 39; Pliny *Pan.* 16.3 on the Capitol witnessing Domitian's 'masquerade of a triumph'. Dio 67.4.1 says that Domitian never saw any fighting.

3. Frontinus *Strategemata* 1.1.8. Dio splits his account into two parts: 67.3.5, Domitian set out for Gaul, and plundered some tribes beyond the Rhine; 67.4.1 he made an attack on Germany.

4. No pitched battles: this may be why Dio sneers that Domitian saw no fighting; a war without such events would probably be considered null and void. Triumph of Vespasian and Titus: Kneissl 1969, 48–9; Jones 1992, 129.

5. IMP I–VII: Jones 1992, 128–9; Buttrey 1980, 30–1. Syme in *CAH* XI 1936, 164 n.2 points out that fighting in Britain and Mauretania could have given rise to some of the acclamations. Germanicus: Braunert in *Bonner Jahrbuch* 153, 1953, 98 n.11; Kneissl 1969, 44 nn. 12–15. Jones in *Historia* 22, 1973, 79–90, esp. 80, 85 argued

that the war was over by 83, because Domitian would never have adopted the title unless there had been a decisive victory. First attested evidence of title: Braunert in *Bonner Jahrbuch* 153, 1953, 98f, citing *RIC* 2.39; *IGR* 1.1138; *Pap. Flor.* 3.361 and *Pap. Oxy.* 2.331. Kneissl 1969, 46–7 and Strobel 1987, 433–4 on the coin; Kneissl 1969, 4–6 on the papyri and inscription; on the papyri see also Martin in *Historia* 36, 1987, 73–82. Kneissl 1969, 48, and Perl 1981, 571–2 date both title and triumph to late 83 or early 84. Strobel dates triumph to autumn 83: 1987, 434.

6. Suetonius on unnecessary war: *Dom.* 6.1. Chatti in Tacitus: *Germania* 30.

7. Chattan homelands and previous attacks: Filtzinger 1986, 52; Cüppers 1990, 70–1; Baatz and Herrmann 1982, 71–3. Chatti poised for attack, based on Frontinus 1.1.8: Henderson 1927, 99. Occupation of Wetterau: Strobel 1987, 424–5. *Bellum justum*: Strobel 1987, 428–9. Domitian did not adopt titles Britannicus and Dacicus: Kneissl 1969, 49–50. Gsell 1894, 229, tried to read into Martial 9.93 an unofficial Sarmaticus. Martial *laurea* 2.2; 14.170 on the Rhine giving a true name to Domitian.

8. Numbers of men: Strobel 1987, 441. Mirebeau tiles: *ILS* 2285; E. Ritterling *JÖAI* 7, 1904, 23–38, esp. 25. Velius Rufus: *ILS* 9200. Syme 1928, 42–3 endorsed Ritterling's association of the tiles from Mirebeau with Velius Rufus, and speculated that the vexillations were gathered to meet Domitian when he entered Gaul, ready for a sudden assault on the Chatti. Bérard et al. divorce the Mirebeau tiles from Velius Rufus, 'Le camp militaire romain de Mirebeau', in H. Vetters and M. Kandler (eds) *Akten des 14 Internationalen Limeskongresses 1986 in Carnuntum*, Vienna 1990, 311–17, esp. 315.

9. Strobel on Mirebeau vexillations: 'Zu den Vexillationsziegelstempeln von Mirebeau', *ZPE* 64, 1986, 257–64. Dijon 1800: J. Tranié and J.-C. Carmigniani *Napoléon Bonaparte: La Deuxième Campagne d'Italie 1800*, Paris 1991, 109–32.

10. Velius Rufus: *ILS* 9200, discussed by D. Kennedy in *Britannia* 14, 1983, 183–96, esp. 189–91; K. Strobel 'Zur Rekonstruktion der Laufbahn des C. Velius Rufus', *ZPE* 64, 1986, 265–86, esp. 276–7. Roscius Aelianus: *ILS* 1025. Vexillation from *IX Hispana*: Kennedy in *Britannia* 14, 1983, 196 prefers to date this expedition to 89; Strobel disagrees: *ZPE* 64, 1986, 266 n.6; *Historia* 36, 1987, 205 n.36. Tacitus on *legio IX* being weakest of three columns in the sixth season: *Agricola* 26.

11. *I Minervia*: *CIL* XIII 8071 recording the career of L. Magius Dubius. Northwards offensive and Heldenbergen marching camp: Schönberger in *BRGK* 66, 1985, 374; Strobel 1987, 430. Flight of Chatti: Frontinus *Strategemata* 2.3.23. *Limites*: Frontinus *Strategemata* 1.3.10. Fabricius in *ORL* A Strecke 3, 43–5 first suggested that the 120-mile frontier was the Taunus-Wetterau line, having changed his mind about his earlier opinion that Frontinus referred to roads into Chattan territory, propounded in RE 3. 573 and 586; Schönberger 1985, 370–1.

12. Mourning Germany coins of 84: Carradice 1983, 24; Strobel 1987, 435–7; legends: *Germania capta*: *RIC* 2.252; *Victoria Augusti*: *RIC* 2.268; *De Germanis*: *RIC* 2.255.

13. German frontier under Domitian: Filtzinger 1986, 52–4; Baatz and Herrmann 1982, 71–6; Schönberger 1985, 383; Tacitus *Germania* 29. Frontinus on *castella* in territory of Cubii: *Strategemata* 2.3.23. Literary experts: Tacitus complained that the complete conquest of Germany was taking a long time: *Germania* 37.2.

14. Creation of German provinces: Filtzinger 1986, 54; Baatz and Herrmann 1982, 76–80. Issue of coins 84/5 associated with the creation of provinces: Strobel 1987, 437–8. Iavolenus Priscus first attested governor of Upper Germany: diploma of 27 October 90, *CIL* XVI 36= *ILS* 1998. Dio 67.11.1 on Saturninus and Bucius Lappius Maximus; W. Eck '*Die Statthalter der Germanischen Provinzen von 1–3 Jahrhundert*', *Epigraphische Studien* 14, 1985, 44–5, 149–51.

ɪx Dacia *pp.92–100*

1. Jordanes *Getica* 13.17; Suet. *Dom.* 6.1; Dio 67.6. Dacians took advantage of preparations for German war: A. Mocsy *Pannonia and Upper Moesia*, London 1974, 83.
2. Uncomfortable neighbours: Wilkes 1983, 259. Ti. Plautius Silvanus Aelianus and settlement of natives: *ILS* 986.
3. Problems of annexation: Wilkes 1983, 263; Jones 1992, 136.
4. Roxolani 67/8: Syme 1936, 68. Mucianus: Tacitus *Histories* 3.46. Fonteius Agrippa and Rubrius Gallus: Josephus *BJ* 7.4.3. *V Alaudae:* Wilkes 1983, 279 n. 42, 283 n. 68; Jones 1992, 138–9. Pannonian diplomas: *CIL* XVI 26, 30, 31; units from Germany to Moesian garrison: *CIL* XVI 28= *ILS* 1995. Valid inference: Wilkes 1983, 279 n. 43.
5. Danube fortified under Vespasian: Wilkes 1983, 266, 279–80 n. 46. Strobel 1989, 1–24 enumerates the archaeological evidence for Domitian's fortifications on the Danube.
6. Two provinces: in 84/5: Evans 1978, 119; Wilkes 1983, 268; in 86 after Fuscus' disaster: Bengtson 1979, 201; Strobel 1989, 66.
7. No garrison on Lower Danube/Dobrudja: A. Poulter, 'The Lower Moesian limes and the Dacian wars of Trajan', *Studien zu den Militärgrenzen Roms* III: *Vorträge des Internationalen Limeskongresses, Aalen 1983*, 1986, 519–28, esp. 520–1. Earthworks in Dobrudja: Syme 1936, 169–70; dismissed by Wilkes 1983, 280 n. 53. Fleet: title Flavia awarded before 92: *CIL* XVI 37; *praefectus classis Moesicae et ripae Danuvii: AE* 1969/70, 572; E. Dorutiu-Boila in *Studien zu den Militärgrenzen Roms* II 1977, 289–96; Wilkes 1983, 281 nn.54–60.
8. Burebista and Augustus: Wilkes 1983, 258–9. *Rex Dacorum*: Orosius (following lost section of Tacitus' work) *Histories* 7.10.4. Duras: Dio 67.6.1; Syme 1936, 168 n.2. Stein *PIR* D 110 says that Diurpaneus was distinct from Duras, ruling only a section of the Dacians, but Duras and Decebalus ruled the whole state.
9. War broke out winter 84/5: Jones 1992, 138, 226 n.77. Summary of sources: Wilkes 1983, 282 n.64. Early in 85: H. Halfmann in *Chiron* 3, 1973, 356. In the course of 85: Syme 1936, 168, and in *JRS* 35, 1945, 110. Diurpaneus crossed Danube midsummer 85, and course of events: Strobel 1989, 35–42. War began in 86: A. Stein *Die Legaten von Moesien*, Budapest 1940, 38. Frozen Danube: Pliny *Pan.* 12.3–4.
10. Destruction by Dacians: Jordanes *Getica* 13.76. *Duplicem triumphum egit*: Suet. *Dom.* 6.1; total of four triumphs: Mooney 1930, 535–6. Total of three triumphs: Gsell 1894, 198–200, 216, 223. IMP XII associated with the triumph of 86: Jones 1992, 139.

11. Fuscus and bridge of boats: Jordanes *Getica* 13.77. Crossing point at Oescus: Strobel 1989, 54. Wilkes 1983, 283 n.68 disagrees with the theory that Fuscus crossed from Oescus, preferring to place the advance in the west across the Banat. Lost standard: Dio 68.9.3. Probably praetorian: Wilkes 1983, 279 n.42; Jones 1992, 139. Adamklissi altar not Domitianic: Poulter op. cit. above n. 7, 523–6; Wilkes 1983, 279 n.42; Jones 1992, 139.

12. IMP XI to XIV: Carradice 1983, 29–30; IMP XII between 17 March 86 and 13 May 86: *CIL* XVI 32, 33. Domitian indulging in riotous living: Dio 67.6.3. Decebalus' overtures for peace: Dio 67.6.5. Domitian makes treaty in 89, though he had refused before: Dio 67.7.2. All this is discussed in more detail by Strobel 1989, 62–6. M.Cornelius Nigrinus may have been the last governor of undivided Moesia: H. Halfmann in *Chiron* 3, 1973, 356. Rewards to Nigrinus: V. Maxfield *The Military Decorations of the Roman Army*, London 1981, 151. Funisulanus Vettonianus: *ILS* 1005; Evans 1978, 119; Wilkes 1983, 283 n.69.

13. Troop movements in 87: Jones 1992, 141–2; Strobel 1989, 69–73.

14. Viminacium as base: Strobel 1989, 74. Route: Wilkes 1983, 269, 283 n.71. Battle: Dio 67.10.1–3. On preparations for renewed campaign in 89: Strobel 1989, 76–8.

x AD 89 *pp.101–109*

1. No source states whether Domitian formed long-term plans to annex Dacian territory: Strobel 1989, 81. Possible preparations for another campaign in 89: ibid. 77.

2. L. Antonius Saturninus: *PIR2* A 874. Procurator of Judaea: Syme 1978, 13, 15. Consular province before Germany: ibid. 16. Suet. *Dom.* 6.1 uses the term *praeses* to describe Saturninus, which is not specific enough to discern whether Upper Germany was yet a province. Saturninus suffect consul 82: *CIL* IX 5420. Jones 1992, 145–6 questions whether Saturninus originally had command of *I Adiutrix* as well as the four other legions, but this depends on the date of his appointment; *I Adiutrix* was moved from Germany in 86.

3. Domitian leaves Rome 12 January: *Acta Fratrum Arvalium* of 88–9 in McCrum and Woodhead 1962, no. 15. Time taken for news to reach Rome: Walser 1989, 454–5, esp. n. 28. Rebellion on 1 January: the reasoning is set out by E. Ritterling in *Westdeutsche Zeitschrift* 12, 1893, 266, followed by Syme 1936, 172; 1978, 13; Murison 1985, 31; Walser 1989, 453. Jones 1974, 529 n. 5 discusses the alternative dates and lists the arguments for the outbreak of revolt at the end of 88.

4. Trajan and 'legions': Pliny *Pan.* 14.5. Domitian's route to Mainz unknown: Walser 1989, 454 n. 29. Murison 1985, 44 sees no reason to stop at Vindonissa.

5. Lappius Maximus: *PIR2* L 84. Domaszewski rendered the name as Lappius; see Henderson 1927, 111 n. 2. In Dio 67.11.1 the name is given as Lucius Appius. Burning correspondence: Dio-Xiphilinus 67.11; Waters 1964, 73 n. 55 doubts the entire story. Lappius rewarded with two consulships: Jones 1974, 532.

6. *Epit. de Caes.* 11.10 equates Lappius with Norbanus. Procurator of Raetia and praetorian prefect: *PIR2* N 162 for references. Martial addressed a poem (9.84) to Norbanus, praising his loyalty to Domitian (*sancta fides*).

7. Barbarians waiting to cross the Rhine: Suet. *Dom.* 6.2. *Confector belli Germanici*: *ILS* 1006. Second Chattan war; Strobel 1986, 204–7; 1989, 78, 83. Treaty: Syme 1936, 174–5; Statius *Silvae* 3.3.168 *'victis parcentia foedera Chattis'*; see also 1.1.22. IMP XVIII, XIX: Strobel 1986, 219.

8. Domitian arrives at Mainz in February: Walser 1989, 455, draws up a timetable for the events of late 88 to autumn 89. Dio-Xiphilinus 67.11.2 on executions following revolt. No senatorial involvement: Jones 1974, passim. Punishments confined to Mainz: Syme 1978, 20.

9. Senate sacrificing for Domitian's safe return: *Acta Fratrum Arvalium* of 88–9 in McCrum and Woodhead 1966, 27 no. 15, lines 13, 20, 26; Talbert 1984, 390 n. 44. Lusianus Proculus: Dio 67.11.5; Talbert 1984, 154. No signs of preparation: Syme 1978, 19–20.

10. Domitian felt himself surrounded by enemies after 89, and stopped listening to his advisers: Bengtson 1979, 208. He also took more notice of *delatores*: Charlesworth 1936, 26. False Neros: Jones 1992, 157.

11. Jones 1974, 530 and 1992, 147 argues that the revolt was purely military in origin and did not influence Domitian's attitude towards senators.

12. Saturninus' motives discussed by Syme 1978, 19–21.

13. Plans to move *XXI Rapax* for a new campaign in 89: Strobel 1989, 77. Saturninus not fit to be a senator: Syme 1978, 20; Talbert 1984, 86 n. 44 says this may be fabricated. Homosexuality: Eck *'Die Statthalter der Germanischen Provinzen vom 1–2 Jahrhundert'*, *Epigraphische Studien* 14, 1985, 41, considers the story not without some foundation.

14. Soldiers' savings: Suet. *Dom.* 7.3; Mooney 1930, 541–2 refers to Grenfell, Hunt and Hogarth *The Fayum Towns and Their Papyri* 252, for accounts of soldiers' savings dated to *c*.180.

15. Double fortresses: Suet. *Dom.* 7.3. *XIV Gemina* in Pannonia after destruction of *XXI Rapax* in 92: Jones 1992, 149; Wilkes 1983, 284–5 n.83; on Danube from 97 onwards: Strobel 1989, 100 n.63. Iavolenus Priscus in office by 27 October 90: *CIL* XVI 36=*ILS* 1998; career inscription: *CIL* III 9960=*ILS* 1015. Eck op. cit. n. 13 above, 42–3 says it is almost certain that Iavolenus Priscus succeeded Saturninus immediately after the rebellion.

16. Campaign against the Marcomanni and Quadi in 89: Jones 1992, 151–2; Strobel 1989, 83–99.

17. Suebi: *CAH* XI 1936, 54: Tacitus *Germania* 2; 45, where he calls the Baltic *Suebicum mare*. Marcomanni in Caesar's day: *Gallic War* 1.51. Traders in territory of Marcomanni: Tacitus *Annals* 2.62.

18. Lack of support for Romans in Dacian war: Dio 67.7.1. Protection for western flank of army in Dacia: Strobel 1989, 85. Execution of envoys: Dio 67.7.1. Embassies after Tapae and before Saturninus: A. Mocsy *Pannonia and Upper Moesia*, London 1974, 84.

19. Treaty midsummer 89: Strobel 1989, 93–5; Syme 1928, 50. Loss of *XXI Rapax* attributed to 89: L. Barzoczi in A. Lengyel and G.T.B. Radan *Archaeology of Roman Pannonia*, Budapest 1980, 93, 480.

20. Client state: Strobel 1989, 95. Diegis: Dio 67.7.2–3. Martial on Diegis meeting with the god Domitian: 5.3. Court at Carnuntum: *CIL* II 4497 records the death of one of the Emperor's readers, which Strobel 1989, 101 assigns to the campaign of 92.

21. Treaty saved face; Syme 1936, 176. Wilkes 1983, 269 points out the merits of the treaty. Velius Rufus: *ILS* 9200; the expedition to be dated to 89: Strobel 1989, 96–8; *ZPE* 64, 1986, 280. Other authors assign the expedition to 92: Jones 1992, 152; Wilkes 1983, 270, 284 n.80.

22. Triumph: Dio 67.7.4; Suet. *Dom.* 6.2. Games: Martial 4.19.3. No province held more than three legions: Syme 1983, 139. Brigetio: Strobel 1989, 100 and n.63. Laurels to Jupiter: Suet. *Dom.* 6.1.

23. Julia in *vota* of Arval Brethren: *CIL* VI 2065; but absent from VI 2067. Her death: Suet. *Dom.* 22; Jones 1992, 39 rightly labels the story of the abortion 'a farrago of nonsense'.

xi The Dark Years *pp.110–118*

1. Nerva as consul: *CIL* VI 621=*ILS* 3532. Trajan: *CIL* VI 2067. Blockage in promotions: Syme 1983, 127; Jones in *Historia* 25, 1965, 499–500.

2. Cornelia: Eusebius (Hieronymus) A. Abr 2107=October 90 to September 91; Suet. *Dom* 8.4; Pliny *Ep.* 4.11. Equestrian statue: Statius *Silvae* 1.1.35–6 makes reference to the temple of Vesta.

3. Assistance to the Lugii and visit of Masyas and Ganna: Dio 67.5.2; Wilkes 1983, 270, 284 n. 79. Loss of a legion: Suet. *Dom.* 6.1. Absent from Rome eight months: Martial 9.31.3; Strobel 1989, 101. Back in Rome by January 93: Gsell 1894, 227, followed by Jones 1992, 152. A. Mocsy *Pannonia and Upper Moesia,* London 1974, dates the war to either 92 or 93. Caesennius Sospes: *CIL* III 291=6818=*ILS* 1017, discussed by Syme in *JRS* 67, 1977, 38–49; Jones 1992, 152. Military tribune: *CIL* XI 5992. War on two fronts: Strobel 1989, 99. Domitian did all that was possible: Bengtson 1979, 205–6. Trajan may have been governor of Pannonia in 93: Jones 1992, 152; *AE* 1985, 722.

4. IMP XXII after the conclusion of the fighting: Strobel 1989, 102; Wilkes 1983, 284 n.81. No triumph, except personal ones: Martial 8.15.5. Laurels to Jupiter: Suet. *Dom.* 6.1. Statius *Silvae* 3.3.171. *Congiarium*: Martial 8.15. Troops assembled for another Danube war: Jones 1992, 153–4; Strobel 1989, 106 and n.3. Pompeius Longinus: Strobel 1989, 104, 106; *CIL* XVI 42.

5. War in Africa: Syme 1936, 149–50; Jones 1992, 139–41. Sentius Caecilianus: *ILS* 8969. Velius Rufus: *ILS* 9200; his command of the African armies may have been in 85–6, Rufus having been tribune of *Cohors XIII Urbana* in 83–5. The cohort may have been transferred to the Danube in 85–6: Syme 1936, 149.

6. Nasamones: Dio 67.4.6. Lambaesis: Jones 1992, 140, 227–8 n.99; *AE* 1954, 137 attests a detachment of the legion at Lambaesis by about 80, but it is uncertain whether the whole legion followed soon after. S. Raven *Rome in Africa*, 3rd edn, London 1993, 68–9 assigns the fortress at Lambaesis to Trajan. Africa prosperous from mid-first century and especially famed for its grain production: Raven op. cit. xxi, 89.

7. The east: Syme 1936, 137–44; Jones 1992, 155–9. Civica Cerialis: Tacitus *Agricola* 42; *ILS* 1374. Terentius Maximus: Dio 66.19.3. Troops into and out of Syria: Jones 1992, 158–9; *CIL* XVI 35; *RMD* 1978, 32–4, nos 3, 4. Plan for war in the east based on literary references: Jones 1992, 159, 232 n.75. Statius *Silvae* 4.4; Hardie 1983, 164–71.

8. On frontiers generally: Syme 1936, 137–87 is still useful though the archaeological evidence has accumulated and been reinterpreted since he wrote. On the German frontier: Schönberger *BRGK* 66, 1985, 370–83.

9. Noricum: G.Alföldy *Noricum*, London 1974, 106–42; frontier: 145–52. Pannonia and Moesia: A. Mocsy *Pannonia and Upper Moesia*, London 1974, 80–91.

10. Baebius Massa: Pliny *Ep.* 3.4.4, 6.29.8, 7.33. Herennius Senecio: Pliny *Ep.* 3.11; Dio 67.13.2; R. MacMullen 1992, 51. Suetonius attributes the panegyric on Helvidius Priscus to Arulenus Rusticus, but Tacitus *Agricola* 2, Dio 67.13 and Pliny *Ep.* 7.19 all agree that the author was Senecio: Mooney 1930, 559. Pliny in danger: *Pan.* 95; *Ep.* 7.27.14; Henderson 1927, 13.

11. Arulenus Rusticus: Suet. *Dom.* 10.3; Pliny *Ep.* 1.14, 2.18, 3.11; Dio 67.13.2. Women of the group exiled: Pliny *Ep.* 3.11. On family relationship between members of the Stoic opposition: MacMullen 1992, 43. Helvidius the younger: Tacitus *Agricola* 45; Suet. *Dom.* 10.4.

12. Eusebius on persecution of Christians in 93: *Historia Ecclesiastica* 3.15–20. On turning-point in 89 rather than 93: Syme 1983, 121–7. Expulsion of philosophers, Suetonius provides no dates: *Dom.* 10.3. Eusebius dates removal of philosophers to 93 (October 92 to September 93), but Hieronymus puts the event a year later: Mooney 1930, 560; MacMullen 1992, 62, 308 n.18. Dio 67.13.3 says that the philosophers were banished again from Rome, referring possibly to the earlier expulsion by Vespasian; Mooney conjectured that there may have been some similar event after the revolt of Saturninus in 89, which may account for Dio's duplication of the banishment; Jones 1992, 119–21. Plots against Augustus: Suet. *Divus Augustus* 19; Dio on Augustus and Livia 55.14, esp. 14.3. Philosophy and subversion: MacMullen 1992, 53. Even 'the judicious Quintilian discovered pretence as well as pretension in the grim visages and heavy beards': Syme 1983, 126.

13. Religious persecution: Jones 1992, 114–19. Domitilla(e): Eusebius *Historia Ecclesiastica* 3.18; Suet. *Dom.* 15.1; Dio 67.14; Mooney 1930, 581, 589.

14. Acilius Glabrio: Dio 67.14. Member of *consilium*: Juvenal *Satires* 4.94; Mooney 1930, 556–7; Jones 1992, 184. T. Flavius Clemens: Suet. *Dom.* 15.1; Dio 67.14.1; Jones 1992, 187.

15. Senatorial victims: Suet. *Dom.* 10; Jones 1992, 182–8; Dio 67.11.3. Orfitus: Philostratus *Vit.Apoll.* 7.8, 7.33, 8.7.10. Lamia: Suet. *Dom.* 1.3, 10.2. Mettius Pompusianus: Dio 67.12.2; Suet. *Dom.* 10.3.

16. Suetonius groups victims together: *Dom.* 10, 15.1. Spectator thrown to the dogs: Suet. *Dom.* 10.1. No one dared to show dislike of Domitian's gladiators, and the Emperor *demens*: Pliny *Pan.* 33.3–4.

17. Murder of Domitian: Suet. *Dom.* 16, 17; Dio 67.15. Domestic staff: Dio 67.15.3. Parthenius: Mooney 1930, 587. Philostratus *Vit. Apoll.* 8.25 relates how Apollonius announced the murder as it was happening, crying out the name of Stephanus.

The murder was pre-planned, but no senatorial involvement: Jones 1992, 193, 196.

18. Praetorian prefects: Dio 67.15.2. Petronius Secundus as one of the murderers: Eutropius 8.1; Jones 1992, 194–5. Domitia: Dio 67.15.2. Brick stamps: 'From the Sulpician brickyards of Domitia, wife of Domitian', *CIL* XV 548a – 549d. The date is 123, many years after Domitian's death when Domitia could have legitimately and conveniently forgotten about him and ensured that no such legend appeared on bricks from her factory.

XII The Psychology of Suspicion *pp.119–125*

1. The character of Domitian: Waters 1964.
2. Domitian's complexion: Suet. *Dom.* 18.1. Blushing: Tacitus *Agricola* 45; Mooney 1930, 595. Martial on Labienus' baldness: 5.49. Maecius: Suet. *Dom.* 20.
3. The black banquet: Dio 67.9.1–5.
4. Child deprived of mother: Anthony Storr *The School of Genius*, London 1988, 165. Isaac Newton: described by Whiston, quoted in J.M. Keynes, 'Newton the Man', *Essays in Biography,* London 1951, 311.
5. Minerva: Girard 1981 is the most comprehensive study.
6. Domitian's dream: Suet. *Dom.*15.3. Survivors of near-death experience: Dr Graham Powell, Director of Clinical Psychology, University of Surrey in an interview.
7. Dio 67.1.3: 'there was no human being for whom he felt any genuine affection except for a few women'. Domitia involved in plot to assassinate Domitian: Suet. *Dom.* 14.1; Dio 67.15.2–4 is more cautious, as Jones 1992, 37, points out. Domitia called herself the wife of Domitian in inscriptions on brick stamps: 'from the Sulpician brickyards of Domitia, wife of Domitian', *CIL* XV 548a 549d: Jones 1992, 37.
8. Domitian would not reinstate Palfurius Sura, who had been exiled by Vespasian, either because he considered him dangerous or because he was unwilling to reverse his father's decisions: Talbert 1984, 29; Suet. *Dom.* 13. He referred to his father's measures and insisted that existing regulations should be obeyed in his instructions to the procurator in Syria: Levick 1982, 51–2.
9. On the capacity to be alone: Donald Winnicott *The Maturational Process and the Facilitating Environment*, London 1969, 29; Anthony Storr *Solitude*, London 1988, 18. Filter system: Talbert 1984, 69, 118; Pliny *Pan.* 79.6.
10. Perfectionist: Karen Horney *New Ways in Psychoanalysis*, New York 1959, 215–17. Obsession with efficiency: Talbert 1984, 311–12. Obsessional characteristics: Anthony Storr *The School of Genius*, London 1988, 156.
11. Domitian's conventionality; Levick 1982, 52. Legitimacy: B. Barnes *The Nature of Power*, Cambridge 1988, 15–16.
12. Pleket 1961, 297 points out that most accounts of Domitian's reign do not allow for a slow psychological change over a number of years.
13. The authoritarian personality: B. Altemayer *Enemies of Freedom* London 1988, xii, 124. Suetonius on Domitian's fear: *Dom.* 3.2, 14.3–4, 16.1. Lack of senatorial involvement in Saturninus' revolt: Jones 1974, 535; 1979, 34.

14. Paranoid behaviour: L. Ullman and L. Krasner *A Psychological Approach to Abnormal Behaviour*, New Jersey 1969, 429–33. Lack of other indications of abnormality: ibid. 443.

15. 1962 study of paranoia: E.M. Lemert 'Paranoia and the dynamics of exclusion', *Sociometry* 1962, 2–25. William Faulkner *As I Lay Dying*, New York 1946, 510.

SELECT BIBLIOGRAPHY

Abbreviations

AE	*L'Année épigraphique*
AJPh	*American Journal of Philology*
ANRW	*Aufstieg und Niedergang der Römischen Welt*
BAR	*British Archaeological Reports*
BJ	*Bonner Jahrbücher*
BMC	*Coins of the Roman Empire in the British Museum*
BRGK	*Bericht der Römisch-Germanisch Kommission*
CAH	*Cambridge Ancient History*
CIL	*Corpus Inscriptionum Latinarum*
CJ	*Classical Journal*
CQ	*Classical Quarterly*
FIRA	*Fontes Iuris Romani Antejustiniani*
IGR	*Inscriptiones ad Res Romanas Pertinentes* Paris 1911–1927
ILS	*Inscriptiones Latinae Selectae*
JÖAI	*Jahreshefte des Österreichischen Archäologischen Instituts in Wien*
JRS	*Journal of Roman Studies*
ORL	*Obergermanische-Raetische Limes der Römerreiches*
Pap. Flor.	*Papiri Fiorentini* Milan 1906–1905
Pap. Oxy.	*Oxyrhynchus Papiri* London 1898–
PIR	*Prosopographia Imperii Romani*
RE	*Real-Encyclopaedie der Classischen Altertumswissenschaft*
RIC	*Roman Imperial Coinage*
RMD	*Roman Military Diplomas 1954–1977; 1978–1984.* ed. M. Roxan, London, 1978; 1985.
SHA	*Scriptores Historiae Augusta*
ZPE	*Zeitschrift ür Papyrologie und Epigrafik*

Ancient sources

AURELIUS VICTOR	*De Caesaribus*
AURELIUS VICTOR	*Epitome de Caesaribus*
CAESAR	*Gallic War*
DIO	*Roman History*
EPICTETUS	*Discourses*
EUSEBIUS	*Chronicorum Canonum*
EUSEBIUS	*Historia Ecclesiastica*
EUTROPIUS	*Breviarum*
FRONTINUS	*Strategemata*
FRONTINUS	*De Aquaeductibus Urbis Romae (De Aquis)*
JORDANES	*Getica*
JOSEPHUS	*Bellum Judaicum*
JOSEPHUS	*Vita*
JUVENAL	*Satires*
MARTIAL	*Epigrammata*
PHILOSTRATUS	*Vita Apollonii*
PHILOSTRATUS	*Vitae Sophistarum*
PLINY	*Epistulae*
PLINY	*Panegyricus*
PLUTARCH	*Lives: Publicola*
SILIUS ITALICUS	*Punica*
STATIUS	*Silvae*
STATIUS	*Thebaid*
SUETONIUS	*Lives of the Caesars*
TACITUS	*Agricola*
TACITUS	*Annales*
TACITUS	*Germania*
TACITUS	*Historiae*

Modern works

Alston, R. 1994, 'Roman military pay from Caesar to Diocletian', *JRS 84*, 113–23.

Anderson, J.C. 1983, 'A topographical tradition in the fourth-century chronicles: Domitian's building programme', *Historia 32*, 93–105.

Baatz, D. and Herrmann, F.-R. 1982, *Die Römer in Hessen*. Stuttgart.

Baldwin, B. 1983, *Suetonius*. Amsterdam.

Bengtson, H. 1979, *Die Flavier: Vespasian, Titus, Domitian*. Munich.

Birley, A.R. 1973, 'Petillius Cerialis and the conquest of Brigantia', *Britannia* 4, 179–90.

Birley, A.R. 1974, 'Roman frontiers and Roman frontier policy: some reflections on Roman Imperialism', *Trans. Architectural and Archaeol. Soc. of Durham and Northumberland* new series 3, 13–25.

Birley, A.R. 1975, 'Agricola, the Flavian dynasty, and Tacitus', in B. Levick (ed.) *The Ancient Historian and His Materials*. Westmead, Farnborough, Hants, 139–54.

Birley, A.R. 1981, *The Fasti of Roman Britain*. Oxford.

Blake, M.E. 1959, *Roman Construction in Italy from Tiberius through the Flavians.* Washington.

Briessman, A. 1955, *Tacitus und das Flavische Geschichtsbild.* Hermes Einzelschriften 10, Wiesbaden.

Brunt, P.A. 1961, 'Charges of provincial maladministration under the early Principate', *Historia* 10, 189–223.

Brunt, P.A. 1966, 'The fiscus and its development', *JRS* 56, 75–91.

Brunt, P.A. 1975, 'The administrators of Roman Egypt', *JRS* 65, 124–47.

Brunt, P.A. 1977, '*Lex de Imperio Vespasiani*', *JRS* 67, 95–116.

Brunt, P.A. 1983, '*Princeps and equites*', *JRS* 73, 42–75.

Buttrey, T.V. 1980, *Documentary Evidence for the Chronology of the Flavian Titulature.* Beiträge für Klassischen Philologie 112, Meisenheim.

Campbell, B. 1984, *The Emperor and the Roman Army.* Oxford.

Carradice, I. 1983, *Coinage and Finances in the Reign of Domitian.* Oxford.

Casey, J. 1986, *Understanding Ancient Coins.* London.

Castritius, H. 1969, 'Zu den Frauen der Flavier', *Historia* 18, 492–502.

Charlesworth, M.P. 1936, 'The Flavian dynasty', *CAH* XI, 1–45.

Chilver, G.E.F. 1957, 'The army in politics AD 68–70', *JRS* 47, 29–35.

Crook, J. 1951, 'Titus and Berenice', *AJPh* 72, 162–75.

Crook, J. 1955, *Consilium Principis: Imperial Councils and Counsellors from Augustus to Diocletian.* Cambridge.

Cüppers, H. et al. 1990, *Die Römer in Rheinland-Pfalz.* Stuttgart.

Devreker, J. 1977, 'La continuité dans le consilium principis sous les Flaviens', *Ancient Society* 8, 223–43.

Duff, A.M. 1958, *Freedmen in the Early Roman Empire.* Cambridge.

Eichholz, D. 1972, 'How long did Vespasian serve in Britain?', *Britannia* 3, 149–63.

Evans, J.K. 1978, 'The role of *suffragium* in Imperial political decision making: a Flavian example', *Historia* 27, 102–28.

Filtzinger, P. et al. (eds.) 1986, *Die Römer in Baden-Württemberg.* 3rd edn, Stuttgart.

Garzetti, A. 1974, *From Tiberius to the Antonines: A History of the Roman Empire 14–192.* London.

Girard, J.-L. 1981, 'Domitien et Minerve: une prédilection impériale', *ANRW* 2.17.1, 233–45.

Grant, M. 1946, *From Imperium to Auctoritas.* Cambridge.

Gsell, S. 1894, *Essai sur le Règne de L'Empereur Domitien.* Paris.

Hardie, A. 1983, *Statius and the Silvae: Poets, Patrons and Epideixis in the Graeco-Roman World.* Liverpool.

Henderson, B.W. 1927, *Five Roman Emperors.* Cambridge.

Jones, A.H.M. 1960, *Studies in Roman Government and Law.* Oxford.

Jones, B.W. 1973a, 'The dating of Domitian's war against the Chatti', *Historia* 22, 79–90.

Jones, B.W. 1973b, 'Some thoughts on Domitian's perpetual censorship', *CJ* 68, 276–7.

Jones, B.W. 1974, 'Senatorial influence in the revolt of Saturninus', *Latomus* 33, 529–35.

Jones, B.W. 1975, 'Titus and some Flavian *amici*', *Historia* 24, 454–62.

Jones, B.W. 1979, *Domitian and the Senatorial Order: a prosopographical study of Domitian's relationship with the Senate, ad 81–96*. Philadelphia.

Jones, B.W. 1984, *The Emperor Titus*. London.

Jones, B.W. 1992, *The Emperor Domitian*. London.

Kneissl, P. 1969, *Die Siegestitulatur der Römischen Kaiser. Hypomnamata* Heft 23. Göttingen.

Last, H. 1948, 'On the Flavian reliefs from the Palazzo della Cancelleria', *JRS* 38, 9–14.

Levick, B. 1976, *Tiberius the Politician*. London.

Levick, B. 1982, 'Domitian and the provinces', *Latomus* 41, 50–73.

Lewis, N. and Rheinhold, M. 1966, *Roman Civilization: Sourcebook* II: *the Empire*. New York.

McCrum, M. and Woodhead, A.G. 1966, *Select Documents of the Principates of the Flavian Emperors, including the Year of Revolution ad 68–96*. Cambridge.

MacMullen, R. 1992, *Enemies of the Roman Order* (reprint of 1966 edn). London.

Millar, F. 1963, Review of Pflaum 1961, *JRS* 53, 194–200.

Millar, F. 1967, 'Emperors at work', *JRS* 57, 9–19.

Mooney, G.W. 1930, C. *Suetoni Tranquilli de Vita Caesarum Libri VII-VII*. London.

Murison, C.L. 1985, 'The revolt of Saturninus in Upper Germany', *Echos du Monde Classique* 29, 31–49.

Nash, E. 1981, *Pictorial Dictionary of Ancient Rome*, 2 vols. New York.

Nesselhauf, H. 1952, 'Tacitus und Domitian', *Hermes* 53, 222–45.

Nicols, J. 1978, *Vespasian and the Partes Flavianae*. Historia Einzelschriften 28, Wiesbaden.

Perl, G. 1981, 'Frontin und der limes: zu *Strategemata* 1.3.10 und 2.11.7', *Klio* 63, 563–83.

Pfanner, M. 1983, *Der Titusbogen*. Mainz.

Pflaum, H.-G. 1960–1, *Les Carrières Procuratoriennes Equestres Sous le Haut Empire Romain*, I–III, Paris.

Platner, S.B. and Ashby, T. 1929, *Topographical Dictionary of Ancient Rome*. Oxford.

Pleket, H.W. 1961, 'Domitian, the Senate, and the provinces', *Mnemosyne* 14, 297–315.

Ritter, H.W. 1972, 'Zur Lebensgeschichte der Flavia Domitilla, der Frau Vespasians', *Historia* 21, 759–61.

Rogers, P.M. 1980, 'Titus, Berenice and Mucianus', *Historia* 29, 86–95.

Rogers, P.M. 1984, 'Domitian and the finances of state', *Historia* 33, 60–78.

Rudich, V. 1993, *Political Dissidence Under Nero*. London.

Saller, P. 1980, 'Promotion and personal patronage in equestrian careers', *JRS* 70, 44–59.

Saller, P. 1982, *Personal Patronage under the Empire*. Cambridge.

Schönberger, H. 1985, 'Die Römischen Truppenlager der frühen und mittleren Kaiserzeit zwischen Nordsee und Inn', *BRGK* 66, 321–497.

Scott, K. 1936, *The Imperial Cult under the Flavians*. Stuttgart/Berlin.

Sherk, R. 1988, *The Roman Empire: Augustus to Hadrian*. Cambridge.

Shotter, D. 1992, *Tiberius Caesar*. London.

Speidel, M.P. 1973, 'The pay of the auxilia', *JRS* 63, 141–7.

Strobel, K. 1986, 'Der Aufstand des L. Antonius Saturninus und der sogenannte zweite Chattenkrieg Domitians', *Tyche* 1, 203–20.

Strobel, K. 1987, 'Der Chattenkrieg Domitians: historische und politische Aspekte', *Germania* 65, 423–53.

Strobel, K. 1989, *Die Donaukriege Domitians*. Bonn.

Sutherland, C.H.V. 1935, 'The state of the Imperial treasury at the death of Domitian', *JRS* 25, 150–62.

Sutherland, C.H.V. 1974, *Roman Coins*. London.

Syme, R. 1928, 'Rhine and Danube legions under Domitian', *JRS* 18, 41–55.

Syme, R. 1930, 'The Imperial finances under Domitian, Nerva and Trajan', *JRS* 20, 55–70.

Syme, R. 1936, 'Flavian wars and frontiers', in *CAH* XI, 131–87.

Syme, R. 1939, *The Roman Revolution*. Oxford.

Syme, R. 1958, *Tacitus*, 2 vols. Oxford.

Syme, R. 1978, 'Antonius Saturninus', *JRS* 68, 12–21.

Syme, R. 1983, 'Domitian: the last years', *Chiron* 13, 121–46.

Talbert, R.J.A. 1984, *The Senate of Imperial Rome*. Princeton.

Thomasson, B. 1960, *Die Statthalter der Römischen Provinzen Nordafrikas von Augustus bis Diocletianus*, 2 vols. Lund.

Thomasson, B. 1984, *Laterculi Praesidium*, I. Göteborg.

Townend, G. 1961, 'Some Flavian connections', *JRS* 51, 54–62.

Vinson, M.P. 1989, 'Domitia Longina, Julia Titi, and the literary tradition', *Historia* 38, 431–50.

Vogel-Weidemann, U. 1982, *Die Statthalter von Africa und Asia der Jahren 14–68 n.Chr.* Bonn.

von Arnim, H. 1898, *Leben und Werke des Dio von Prusa*. Berlin.

Wallace, K.G. 1987, 'The Flavii Sabini in Tacitus', *Historia* 36, 343–58.

Walser, G. 1968, 'Der Putsch des Saturninus gegen Domitian', *Festschrift für R. Laur-Belart, Provincialia* 40, 497–507.

Walser, G. 1989, 'Kaiser Domitian in Mainz', *Chiron* 19, 449–56.

Warmington, B. 1959, *Nero: Reality and Legend*. New York.

Waters, K.H. 1964, 'The character of Domitian', *Phoenix* 18, 49–77.

Waters, K.H. 1969, '*Traianus Domitiani Continuator*', *AJPh* 90, 385–405.

Weaver, P.C. 1972, *Familia Caesaris: A Social Study of the Emperor's Freedmen and Slaves*. Cambridge.

Wellesley, K.H. 1955, 'Three historical puzzles in *Histories* 3', *CQ* new series 5, 207–14.

Wellesley, K.H. 1989, *The Long Year*. 2nd edn, Bristol.

Wilkes, J.J. 1983, 'Romans, Dacians and Sarmatians in the first and early second centuries', in B. Hartley and J. Wacher (eds) *Rome and Her Northern Provinces*. Gloucester.

Wiseman, T.P. 1978, 'Flavians on the Capitol', *AJPh* 3, 163–78.

INDEX